# Put the Law on Your Side

# PUT
# THE LAW
# ON YOUR SIDE

## Strategies for Winning
## the Legal Game

### BERTRAM HARNETT

**PERENNIAL LIBRARY**

Harper & Row, Publishers, New York
Cambridge, Philadelphia, San Francisco, Washington
London, Mexico City, São Paulo, Singapore, Sydney

A hardcover edition of this book is published by Harcourt Brace Jovanovich, Inc. It is here reprinted by arrangement with Harcourt Brace Jovanovich, Inc.

First PERENNIAL LIBRARY edition published 1986.

---

Library of Congress Cataloging-in-Publication Data

Harnett, Bertram.
   Put the law on your side.

   Includes index.
   1. Law—United States—Popular works.   I. Title.
KF387.H36   1986      349.73      86-45112
ISBN 0-06-097056-1 (pbk.)   347.3

---

89  90  MPC  10  9  8  7  6  5  4

# *Contents*

CHAPTER SIX
## LOT OF THE WORKING MAN OR WOMAN . . . AND THE BOSS 141

CHAPTER SEVEN
**GET IT IN WRITING**

Contents

# Acknowledgments

I had considerable help with this book. My wife, Ruth, ever helpful in everything I do, was generous with her comments. Marie Arana-Ward, of Harcourt Brace Jovanovich, once again my editor, continued to supply her good-humored skill, adding even more to the mounting respect I have for her. And I appreciate my brother Joel's constant encouragement. He is what I would call a real fan (and brother).

For the manuscript's production, I am grateful to that amazing artist of the word processing machine, Margaret Marusak, to John Verga for his factual research, and to Janet Trama, Janet Dowling, Beth Haroules, Maggie Fishman, and Diana Vasquez.

# Put the Law on Your Side

# Introduction

# Put the Law on Your Side

The first thing to know about the law is that it is imprecise—not always easy to recognize or apply. Spare yourself the effort of searching for a large tome with the letters *L A W* unmistakably recognizable on it. There is no such thing. Law in the United States is, instead, a process of human interaction in which lawbooks, containing statutes, administrative regulations, and reports of court cases, are only beginning points. The clearest thing about the law is that it is often unclear.

Lawyers, administrators, and judges—people all—are at the heart of the process. They draw the legal documents; they make the rules, such as they are; they decide the disputes. And these people vary greatly in their abilities and personal characteristics. That those involved in it see, read, hear, and react differently makes law unpredictable. Using the same books, looking at the same documents and papers, sitting in the same courtroom, hearing the same witnesses, people will reach different conclusions.

The lawyer you select may be not very good or very willing. The lawyer for the other side may be far superior. Either can hurt your chances at law. Poorly drawn papers or badly handled negotiations can lead to much trouble for you, and, in court, bad lawyering by your own lawyer can defeat you.

Part of the inescapable uncertainty in court comes from the differences in the way people tell their stories and in their ability to give credence to what they say. This has to do with both their personal credibility and the proof they can muster by means of documents, objects, pictures, other witnesses. Whoever is to do the judging must believe one side or the other to determine the facts necessary for decision. Judges differ, too, in intelligence, temperament, mood, character, compassion, diligence, understanding, social outlook, philosophies, prejudices, and personal preferences. A famous jurist once wrote that what a judge has for breakfast affects his decisions. To this might be added bad stock market news in the morning newspapers and matrimonial arguments after breakfast.

Much of the outcome of a case in court is just plain luck—which can help a poor case and hurt a good one. The chances of getting an inferior judge, a jury impatient to be finished, or missing witnesses are only some of the elements that should persuade people to avoid litigation if it is at all possible.

Given the risks implicit in litigation, no matter how strong a case may seem to one side or the other, all litigation must be considered gambling. The best case can be lost and the worst case can be won. You should always take this into account.

Keeping out of court starts way before. The effort begins with preventive conduct at the beginning of your transactions. This means, among other things, minimizing conduct that can get you into trouble—that is, restraining greed and taking advantage of others—and being careful of the kind of people with whom you deal. Beware of "sure thing" profits and fantastic bargains; they presage trouble. When disputes do arise, it is invariably best to try to settle them before litigation. Compromise is part of putting the law on your side. Compromise may not result in resounding victory, but it takes away the risk, expense, and emotional distress that go with litigation.

Most of the uses of the law, as it affects the average person, never get to the courthouse at all, or even to a lawyer's office. In society generally, affairs, even negotiating intricate contracts, leases, and loan papers, are conducted amicably and settled as mutually anticipated. When people do have disputes, in the vast bulk of instances they adjust or forget them before any lawyer is consulted. Even after the parties begin legal consultations, a compromise before trial is the rule, not the exception. In legal usage, a compromise that results in ending a dispute is called a "settlement." Although there are no statistics, I would guess that for every hundred private disputes that surface in a law office, only one actually reaches trial. The others are settled or dropped. In the case of criminal charges, the court stage ratio is somewhat higher.

To repeat, the best time to help yourself is before any trouble arises. Learn the basic rules affecting your rights and duties in the spheres of your activity. For instance: no agreements will be enforced in court with respect to interests in houses or leases of apartments unless they are in writing; to be effective, a will must be witnessed by at least two people who do not inherit under it and the signer must declare the document to be his* will; a person embroiled in separation or divorce problems should not move out of the home without a prior agreement; a person should never admit fault at an accident scene, never sign a release of anything important without consulting a lawyer, and never accept a first settlement offer. Compliance with such simple prescriptions as these, and many more, help put the law on your side. They improve your results; they help you get what you want. The general rules are fewer than you think. And, remember, the Golden Rule has not lessened in importance since your mother taught it to you.

Get and keep written understandings of important promises on which you rely. Bills of sale should specify what is being sold and include all the assurances of size, color, quality, style, specification, and whatever else you think you should be getting. Make sure your insurance policies specifically cover your needs—read them yourself. If contracts, wills, trusts, deeds, and leases are clearly written, including all the terms and assurances you want, there is less chance that disputes over their terms will arise later. If you want your purchase of a home to include the dishwasher, say so in writing. If you expect two coats of paint in your new apartment, your lease should say so. Attention to detail avoids misunderstanding and minimizes later disputes. It pays off both in and out of court. There is more chance that you will achieve the results you desire.

Since so many variable factors figure in the legal process, opportunities to help yourself abound. There are levers of control to touch at almost every stage of events, from before disputation arises, during the opening conduct, through to the end game in court. By knowing

---

*Throughout this book, I use "his" and "him," to simplify understanding and for ease of reading. It also means "her" and "hers" in every case, of course.

legal rules, patterns, and tactics, by saving proof, by careful written notations, by adapting yourself to the flexibility of the law and considering compromises, and by attention to persuasive devices, you help put the law on your side. Understanding that the law is pliable, not a fixed, automatic process with certain, if obscure, rules for everything, is basic to the expectations you can have of the law and of your own efforts to improve your chances. Once you understand the process, you can have a role in positioning yourself.

Throughout this book I will concentrate, not only on general explanations of basic legal rules that bear on average people, but also on the conduct and strategies that can be used in relations with others, and with purchases and sales, personal injuries, criminal misconduct, wills, family problems, leases, investments, contracts, jobs, and countless other activities, *before* any dispute arises. I will discuss what gets results and what hinders. I will discuss lawyers and other resources for help. And I will talk about pretrial settlements and about court trials. All of this must be read together—it is all part of the grander composition of what you can do to help yourself.

*Caution*: this book is not a legal encyclopedia or a text, nor is it a how-to manual on practicing law. It is a lay person's guide to recognizing common legal problems and learning tried-and-true methods of dealing with them. It tells you some ways to protect yourself. You will learn what to do before lawyers enter the scene, when those lawyers will be particularly useful, what they do, and how to work with them.

Putting the law on your side is not "getting away with murder." It is protecting your rights. It is legitimate self-assertion within the rules our society has set for itself. Indeed, it is the only sensible course in your inevitable legal encounters. Making the law work for you simply calls for a general understanding of the legal happening and the steps that can be taken to realize your benefits, to avert distress, to defend yourself, and to head off disputes, and if disputes nevertheless arise, how to see them through. In the final analysis, this understanding often requires no more than ordinary common sense.

The very genius of the U.S. legal system is its protection of the rights of the individual. Essentially, however, our legal system depends on the individual helping himself.

Although lawyers are indispensable to complicated legal affairs, they do not have the same grasp that you do of the underlying events of your legal problem, they do not always have the "feel" of things. Lawyers do not live with the consequences of their professional action. You do. Lawyers have many clients. You can work full time for yourself. I hope this book will help.

# Chapter *One*

# *Helping Yourself— with and without Lawyers*

He was tall, heavy, and craggy-faced, and spoke with a slow Texas drawl. With his white ten-gallon hat, boots, and Western-style suit, he lacked only his horse and saddle. He had found me in my New York City law office by actually sticking a pin at random in the yellow pages of the telephone book in his hotel room the evening before. Would I go with him to a meeting at a downtown law office concerning a family estate matter? Yes, but what was involved? "Not to mind," he said. "Just sit there and listen." We went. And that is just what I did—I sat through a meeting with five other people, uttering a few small pleasantries, being asked not one question, making no legal comment, and barely understanding what was going on, although my client participated vigorously. On the way back uptown in a taxicab, he thanked me and paid my fee in cash. When I asked him why he had retained me at all, since he had asked me for no advice, he replied that he considered a lawyer to be like a "shootin' iron" and he liked to have one at his side at fancy meetings even if he never had to draw. Whenever I hear about lawyers being "hired guns," I think of that incident.

My Texan was exploring his legal situation on his own, but simply felt more comfortable with an accompanying lawyer, to be used only in an emergency. He could have had a well-briefed lawyer appear for him, to negotiate without his presence; he could have appeared alone. He chose his own way of approaching his problem, unusual as it was. Most clients are less colorful.


## LAWYERS AND SELF-HELP WORKING TOGETHER

The potential of self-help in legal affairs has captured the imagination of the American people. Books for the average person purporting to explain even the minutiae of virtually every part of the law flood bookstores. They sell in great quantities both in hard cover and in paperback.

Flourishing sales, in book and stationery stores, of kits of papers with instructions for use in such relatively sophisticated affairs as forming corporations, drawing wills and leases, and getting divorces give further testimony to this new awareness. Not so long ago, there were available in office-stationery stores only short printed forms for such easy-to-use documents as powers of attorney, promissory notes, and assignment forms for stock certificates, which simply require filling in blank spaces.

People increasingly appear in court as their own representatives, without a lawyer. Indeed, there are now courts that are designed to function without lawyers; these are usually small claims, traffic, and family courts. People are encouraged to appear there for themselves. The Social Security Administration, the Internal Revenue Service, and rent-control offices are among the most prominent government agencies dealing with the public that openly encourage people to act on their own behalf.

The public has receptive ears to suggestions of self-help in legal matters for a number of reasons, the high cost of lawyers being the most apparent one. Convenience is another reason; people often need answers where they stand and do not wish to take the time and trouble for legal consultation even if they can afford to pay for it. There is, too, the suspicion that lawyers, by either design or professional conditioning, make things more complicated than they really are.

Much of what has been written about average people doing away with lawyers in their legal affairs and saving on lawyers' fees has substance. Unfortunately, those who are antilawyer and who, for their own occupational profit, rail at the legal profession distort the actuality of what the average person can do most effectively to help himself at law.

The principal legal role for lay people is prevention—right conduct forestalls or minimizes dispute. Knowledge of rules and of how to conduct yourself in early stages of disputes helps you. But once an actual legal confrontation has developed, and you are in court, in jail, or in an adversary's law office, you will need a lawyer. Your most important affairs should not be conducted on Amateur Night. Those instances when you can carry through legal affairs entirely without a lawyer are considerably fewer than the bumper crop of do-it-yourself manuals on bookstore shelves might indicate. Too many of these manuals presume knowledge and experience that you, a lay person, simply do not have, particularly when they encourage you to "sue-it-yourself."

The reality is that lawyers are indispensable to affairs where loss of liberty, considerable property, or the forfeiture of important rights (for instance, child custody) is at stake. The vast bulk of serious proceedings affecting ordinary citizens, whether they be criminal defenses, personal-injury claims, matrimonial contests, or estate administration and distribution, and of serious breaches of contract calls for lawyers. But the fact that lawyers will be involved does not preclude the role of the individual in helping himself. In fact, working effectively with your lawyer is an important form of self-help.

If you do have a lawyer, you must communicate frankly, and without reservation, to him all of the facts of your case, you must tell him your feelings, and you must exert yourself to see that he has every scrap of proof available to you. Do not be lazy, stubborn, or withdrawn about this.

The point to remember is that lawyers and self-help are not mutually exclusive. Lawyer or no, you can do things to help yourself. You are not only in your lawyer's hands; you are in your own as well.


## ACTING WITHOUT A LAWYER

An infinite variety of structured opportunities, which do not involve your having a personal lawyer, awaits you in investigating your legal rights, getting licenses, receiving payments or whatever else you require. Much of this has to do with governments.


## Government Offices

Oftentimes the action you seek falls within the functioning of a government agency and you can go there without a lawyer.

You may, for instance, have trouble reconciling a Medicare partial payment, or you may be an insurance broker seeking a change in your license, or you may have trouble filling out your tax return or require civil service employment information. Perhaps you want to know about travel visas, veterans' rights, government financial guarantees, or conditions in a city or state in which you are contemplating starting a new business. In such instances, a visit to the government office concerned will often give you the knowledge you need to proceed effectively and with confidence. An explanation by an official of what his agency expects of you may be all you need.

The more important government agencies distribute standard information and forms, and often give advice in personal interviews on how to complete and file returns, forms, or reports. Consumer complaint offices are customarily available, too.

Government law-enforcement officials are sometimes available to help in cases of sales fraud, swindling, and other white-collar crime. They will not, however, serve as collection agencies. Federal prosecutors of the office of the United States Attorney (part of the Department of Justice) are located in regional offices in cities throughout the country to handle tax, mail, and interstate fraud, as well as drug trafficking, bank robberies, and the range of federal crimes. They also represent the federal government in civil (noncriminal) legal work, which includes government-contract violations and personal-injury claims when the government is a defendant.

The commonly denominated state official who deals with both criminal and civil violations is the attorney general or state's attorney. He usually concerns himself with consumer fraud, public corruption, election-law violations, public-land acquisition, taxes, and advice to state agencies.

At the county level, for criminal-law activity, the district attorney or county attorney looks after homicide, stealing, rape, and the bulk of nonfederal crimes. Municipal attorneys may prosecute violations of local ordinances, such as building-code violations and traffic offenses. On the civil side, the local legal officials are the corporation counsel, for cities, and the county, town, or village attorney, according to the government entity involved. They handle the laws of, and the claims for and against, their entities. They write contracts and advise their associated agencies.

Do not be naïve. Government officers will not tell you how to get around legal obstacles. They will tell you how to comply. If you seek advice on how to shave the rules, or how to apply complicated or ambiguous requirements to your particular situation, your own lawyer is the one to ask.

In dealing with a government agency, always find out, and save for future reference, the name and title of the person with whom you speak. Asking for these gets you more respect and attention. The official no longer has the luxury of anonymity, and usually becomes more careful. This helps your claim, if the need arises, that you acted in reliance on the advice of an official. A specific name beats a vague "somebody on the telephone" every day of the week.

### Private Organizations

The American Civil Liberties Union (ACLU) and the Legal Defense and Educational Fund of the National Association for the Advancement of Colored People (NAACP) can assist in legal problems that fall within their missions of civil rights and racial equality. Trade unions are good sources for their members of job-related advice and legal referral in general, as are the American Legion and other organized veterans' groups for veterans' benefits. Various trade associations and fraternal and environmental groups offer counseling to their members. Legislators may guide you to the government offices suitable for your inquiry. If you put your mind to your particular affiliations, assistance may be but a telephone call away.

Useful advice can be obtained from professional people other than lawyers, often at lower cost. Accountants prepare tax returns and advise on ordinary tax affairs. Bank officers may draw simple wills. Title-insurance companies execute real estate sales when local law permits. Insurance agents may give advice on general estate planning. Social workers advise on Social Security, social assistance, Medicare and Medicaid. With the exception of social workers, these people are at constant odds with local bar associations, which may claim that they are practicing law illegally. The lawyers, it seems, do not need or want the social workers' legal trade.

## Kits and Forms

Do-it-yourself divorce kits for uncontested divorces are satisfactory if there are no children of the marriage or if no meaningful money or property is wanted or demanded by either side. Court personnel are usually helpful in the completion and filing of the forms, and in giving instructions about when court appearance will be required.

Simple, straightforward wills for small estates with uncomplicated assets and straightforward dispositions to beneficiaries (but not trusts) can be made using forms if the witnessing instructions are faithfully observed. Apartment leases and even the formation of simple corporations can be accomplished by using forms generally available at legal or large stationers. But if any tailoring of significance is required, a lawyer should be consulted.

## Pro Se, *Anyone?*

The most dramatic form of self-help in the law is to appear in court for yourself, as your own lawyer. The Latin *pro se* (for self) is the classic phrase used to describe self-representation in court. *Pro se* representations are encouraged in some courts, but actively discouraged in most.

### Traffic, Family, and Small Claims Courts

Unless a jail sentence or a driving-license forfeiture is a realistic possibility, traffic offenses do not require representation by a lawyer in court; not enough sentencing improvement is promised by a costly legal presence. Similarly, in family court appearances to adjust family disputations—if child abuse, juvenile delinquency, or crime is not the subject—a lawyer is often not expected and may be useless. You will not need a lawyer in small claims court, although, in most states, corporations, even small ones, are required by law to be represented by a lawyer.

*Courts of Record*

The higher courts are generally known as "courts of record." This is because all testimony is stenographically or mechanically transcribed and kept for appellate (appeals) purposes. Personal-injury, breach-of-contract, and matrimonial suits take place in these courts, as do prosecutions for felonies and misdemeanors. Do not appear *pro se*, as your own lawyer, in any court of record.

*Pro se* representations are frowned on by the trial courts, particularly by those that hold jury trials. Lay persons tend to be disruptive. Not only are they ignorant of rules of trial practice and evidence, but also their emotions are likely to get out of hand in face-to-face confrontation with their foes. Lay persons tend to fall into argument with hostile witnesses and with opposing lawyers, and so become distracted from any strategy they might have planned. Lay advocates are chronically unable to cope with objections raised by opposing lawyers to the form or substance of questions. Often a lay questioner becomes frustrated and loses his head, and his case right along with it. Representation by a competent lawyer aids your chances in a trial and helps to put the law on your side.

If a prospective litigant arrives in court without counsel, the proceedings will normally be deferred by the judge, for days or weeks, until counsel is obtained. If he cannot afford a private lawyer, the judge may refer him to the local legal-aid society or public defender, a law-school clinic, or the local bar association. The judge may assign a lawyer, who may or may not be paid, at some reduced scale of charges or according to the client's means.

Books that encourage people to represent themselves in trial court do them a disservice. The court you pick must be the right one for your case, and your suit must be made within certain time limits, known as "statutes of limitation." One book, for instance, suggests that a litigant rely on court clerks for the applicable time limits for bringing his suit. This is bad advice. It is unusual for court clerks to know the ramifications of the statutes of limitation. The rules of time limits within which to sue are customarily subject to variation and exceptions, which vary from case to case.

Even professional lawyers should not represent themselves in court. A lawyer representing himself is said to have a fool for a client. Unhappily, the lay person who chooses self-representation often has a fool for a lawyer as well.

# LEARNING HOW TO CONDUCT YOURSELF

There are ways to conduct yourself in putting the law on your side. It pays to know them.

### *Learning the Basic Legal Rules*

Lawyers spend years of hard study getting their legal education, and then constantly hone their skills through experience in the daily practice of law. An average untrained person cannot bring himself to the degree of legal competence of a trained lawyer in a short period, and should not expect to do so.

However, there are basic patterns in every legal subject and ways of conduct that can serve a serious person well. Throughout this book I will touch on them. You can educate yourself here, in a library, and in your lawyer's office, if it becomes necessary, in the legal generality of your situation. You can learn the governing rules. This knowledge can help you in both the formative stage of a transaction and, later on, with your case.

Do not look for specific legal advice here. No one book—no library, for that matter—can lay out the entire law. State and federal laws vary in too many ways. For an effective legal response, you must not only look to the law of your own particular place, but also examine carefully all the facts and circumstances of your case, even those that may appear unimportant at first. Lawyers are trained in the inevitable ifs, ands, and buts of applying the law to your actual case. You are not.

### *Need for Preparation*

Always prepare in advance for any legal encounter or any interview, argument, or meeting.

The need to prepare for *pro se* appearance in court is reasonably obvious. But the desirability of prior preparation does not stop there. Meetings and interviews, even informal discussions, which are meant to get results should be approached with deliberation.

Perhaps you feel that meetings (with adversaries, partners, civic groups, government officials, and the like) should be spontaneous, that you can just go with the flow. If you do, you are wrong. In fact, if you are intent on getting your own way, you must learn that meetings are volatile; they tend to take on lives of their own. The truly professional lawyer goes to every meeting knowing what he wants to say. Directions and goals should be kept firmly in mind. Because the course of meetings is unpredictable, it is best to prepare for all contingencies.

Rehearse in your mind what you want to say and how you will say it. Organize your thoughts into a positive presentation. Write an outline of points, to remind and direct you; and keep it in front of you. Agendas are useful.

In the course of discussion, note points you forgot to raise and raise them when appropriate. Notes can also help you organize any rebuttal you care to make. Unless you jot down your points, they may get lost in the heat of discussion.

Harvard Law School is famous for preparing lawyers, but do not make the mistake of one student there. His friend noted his glumness after an examination and asked what was wrong. Their dialogue went this way:

*Student:* I studied for this exam for three weeks, day and night.
*Friend:* So why so glum?
*Student:* I made a six-page outline condensing the whole course.
*Friend:* Terrific.
*Student:* Then I boiled the outline down to three pages, then to two pages, and finally to one page.
*Friend:* I think that's wonderful.
*Student:* I even squeezed the page to one paragraph. Mind you, the whole course in one paragraph.
*Friend:* Even better.
*Student:* Then I thought and thought and got the whole course down to one sentence, and then . . . then . . . to *one word*.
*Friend:* But that's utterly fantastic. Why so glum then?
*Student:* When I got in the exam room, I forgot the word.

## Be Conciliatory

Claims are best pursued and disputes best settled in a calm atmosphere. *Keep your cool.*

Litigation is stressful at any time, and within a family is bound to be particularly emotional, whether it be a divorce, dividing an estate, or breaking up a partnership. When battles of the sexes, the generations, or the siblings get going, rationality flees.

Good demeanor is not restricted to court claims. In daily dealings, a lot of trouble can be averted by proper conduct. With store managers, real estate agents, traffic police, for instance, and the myriad of strangers with whom you might have some dispute, it is important to appear credible, pleasant, not too shrewd, and not to introduce the element of contest, of trying to beat out the other person. Do not be abrasive. Try to achieve an accommodation of goals. If you feel you are getting your own way, never rub it in. Both parties should feel that they have walked away with something. Try to win disputes, not arguments.

When the yelling begins and the personal charges fly, it is time to recess. School is out!


## Tear Up Your Angry Letter

People love writing letters when angry or feeling put upon. Faced with a dispute with a neighbor over his dog, a builder over extra costs, a partner over improper expenses, a store offering faulty merchandise, they reach for their pens and dip them in vitriol. The result usually is lengthy, digressive letters full of recriminations and irrelevancies. Such letters do more harm than good, since they can be used against the writer. In writing such a letter, you may err in some of the minor things you say, or offer gratuitous facts, about which you can be tripped up. You may seem to be unsociable, cantankerous, or overwrought.

Where letters are necessary to raise a claim, they should be respectful, concise, and to the point.

If a harangue is something you cannot resist, sit down and write a first draft, then revise it into a biting second draft. If necessary, go on to an even more clever third draft. When you are satisfied with it, tear it up and file it in the wastebasket. You will feel a lot better and you will have risked nothing.


## Getting a Lawyer's Letter

You will receive letters, too. Do not panic over a pointed letter from a lawyer. Threatening language is a lawyer's specialty, and is meant to scare you. No harm comes to you simply from a lawyer's letter. Unless some clear error is involved, such as the attempt to collect for a bill you have already paid, an error you can clear up with a phone call or a straightforward letter and a photocopy of both sides of your canceled check, turn the letter over to your own lawyer.

If you feel you are being harassed by a collection lawyer or the representative of a seller, you may want to take the letter to your local consumer complaint office, a regional office of the Federal Trade Commission, or any other agency with jurisdiction; they may provide some help.

### Read the Document

People can resolve themselves questions they bring to lawyers, if they simply read with care a document which troubles them. Letters, notices from a stockbroker, a form from a corporation in which you have an investment, a simple lease, a sales slip, all can be studied for their meaning by a reasonably intelligent adult. It simply requires care, patience, and confidence in yourself.

In part, confidence is what lawyers sell. They may tell you what you can read for yourself if you will persist. It could be that, as a legal colleague of long ago told me, "the answer lurketh in the text."

### Never Surrender Original Documents

Original documents are the actual ones you receive in a transaction, not their copies. They may be signed contracts, bills of sale, deeds, or licenses. Always keep them. Even if your own lawyer asks for them, try to get him to accept photocopies instead. Never, never, surrender an original document to the other side in a dispute, unless a court order directs you to.

That original document helps you prove your claim. Sometimes, as in the case of a bill of sale, it is the entire basis of your claim. Also, if you hold the original document, the other side cannot alter it or lose it.

### The Need to Enforce Contractual Rights

A contract does not automatically guarantee that you get what you bargained for. Too many people take the moral leap that what is promised to be done will be done without more ado. I wonder how many times I have heard people say, "He has to pay me. I have a contract."

A contract does not punish the one who breaches it. A judge must do that. It is the judge who enforces the contract. If someone breaks his promise to you and will not make good on it, your only alternative to forgetting about it is to go to court. That may cost you money, time, and upset, but that is the way it is. Unscrupulous people know this, too, and they may take advantage of it. They may refuse to act, counting on your unwillingness to sue and their hopes to settle for less than they originally promised to do.

Though there will be more on contracts later, the short lesson is: Deal with trustworthy parties.

## Possession Is Nine Points of the Law

How many times have you heard that one? It just might be true.

The law generally favors possession, and, however it may be phrased, there is an unspoken tendency for the law to maintain the state of things as it is—unless it can be proved that there is a need for change. Other things being equal, the parent with custody has a better chance to retain it; so does the person in possession of a coat, a place in line, a bundle of cash, or a disputed bicycle.

When the right to money is at issue, the holder of the money has an advantage. The one seeking to get it has to go to some trouble. If you have it, the other party cannot spend it. You can. Accordingly, in every argument or negotiation, try to keep the money or the object in question in your possession. Make the other side come to you. Put the burden or risk and inconvenience on the other side. It is better that you owe the money while the dispute is being resolved.

An obvious illustration is the holding back of some money from a building contractor renovating your home. If, for instance, the final twenty percent of the contract price is not to be paid until the job is totally finished, the contractor's attention to your desires is assured. If he does not satisfy you, he does not get the balance of his money unless he wants to undertake the costly measure of legal action against you—which he may lose if you are right.

## Secured Creditor

When property is mortgaged or pledged by a debtor (the one who owes money), the creditor (the one owed the money) has legal rights in it. It is the creditor who is "secured" and has "collateral." That security (collateral) may be a home, stock, a car, a bank account—anything.

An "unsecured" creditor has only the debtor's promise to pay. A contract to do something (like repaying money), remember, is not self-enforcing; it takes a lawsuit to force payment. The secured creditor is obviously better off than the unsecured creditor, who must go through a full-blown lawsuit, with possible defenses raised by the debtor, to collect his debt. The secured creditor has something that is more or less self-enforcing. He can, normally, turn his collateral into money quite easily—that is, can foreclose—if the debtor defaults. Foreclosure may or may not require a court proceeding (usually in véry summary fashion), depending on the particular documentation of the security. With good collateral, a debtor's good will or character becomes less important, although a crook is capable of posting worthless or forged collateral.

Holding collateral is the best way for a creditor to ensure the collection of sums owed to him. An insurance company guaranty, called a "bond," is usually good security, but it is not collateral, in the strict sense.

On the other hand, if you are the debtor, your lot is easier if you have not posted collateral. Since the creditor cannot directly foreclose on your property and faces a costly lawsuit to collect from you, he is likely to be more tractable in agreeing to payment in installments, or even to a compromise on a lesser sum.

## Quit While You Are Ahead

A good principle in argumentation generally, and also specifically, is to stop talking when you get what you want. Lawyers and judges call this "Quit when you are ahead." If you convince someone to do what you want, do not keep explaining or arguing. If a store gives you your refund, stop complaining. If the other party says he will sign your paper, stop giving him more reasons to sign.

It is also good practice, unless there is a social obligation to do otherwise, to get off the scene as soon as you have your own way in a dispute. Do not wait around for the other side to change its mind. A hugely successful insurance executive who is a close friend of mine told me that when he was a young salesman for a national insurance company, his instructions were that, after making a sale, he leave the buyer's office right away. He was not to wait for the elevator on the buyer's floor, but, instead, he was to walk down one floor and there press the elevator button to go down.

### Loose Talk Costs Rights

Many people delight in impressing others with tales of themselves. Do not brag about your transgressions, your power, your wealth, or anything else. Whether this is ego nourishing or compulsive, it is never helpful. It can rouse envy or resentment in others, which may lead to a communication to the government, your spouse, your partner, or your competitor. It may rupture a relationship.

The Internal Revenue Service pays a reward to informers. Litigants send investigators to the most unlikely places and sources.

Beware of betraying secrets in a crowded elevator or any other public place.

### Take Your Time

If you are not sure about what you are doing, do not be afraid to take your time to think it over.

The bromide of acting in haste and repenting at leisure applies whether you act alone or with a lawyer. Resist if your lawyer or anyone else tries to hurry you into something you do not understand or about which you have reservations. If you do not, you may have to do something you do not like or do it earlier than you would like.

Be especially careful with real estate or insurance salesmen, who may try, for instance, to hustle you into a legal transaction and advise you not to bother with a lawyer. Tell them it is no bother. Salespeople often feel that lawyers complicate deals, and that their negativeness kills them. This is often true—many a salesperson has lost his sale because a lawyer was consulted—but just as often this is for good reason, so make sure you have a lawyer anyway.

## *Be Assertive*

Stand up for yourself; stand your ground and say what you think.

Politeness is a virtue to a point. But if someone is abusing you or your property, speak out. Silence is often taken as acquiescence.

Suppose your new neighbor regrades his property and causes flowing rain water to accumulate on your property. What should you do? If you hold off for fear of offending, he may later argue that you knew about and therefore agreed to his action. Your waiting gives credence to that; it may suggest, too, that the condition at issue is not all that bad.

Often the other side misjudges you. He thinks you are agreeable to his suggestion and acts accordingly, whereas you do not agree but are reluctant to say so. Here are the seeds for later trouble. If you feel the garment does not meet your specifications, say so right away. Do not wait until after the store alters it.

## *Do Not Admit to Being in the Wrong*

This is a tough rule for many people to follow. How many times have you spontaneously apologized when bumping into someone when it was really his fault?

Never admitting your fault at an accident scene, for instance, is good legal advice generally. The other side's lawyer has enough ability to get to you without your help.

It is never useful to you, legally, to make a voluntary admission of wrongdoing, particularly in writing. If you were late in taking an action, do not apologize if there is any chance you will want to, or have to, protect yourself at law. Be wary of written apologies, even for small things, such as a slight color variation or specification difference in goods you sold. Your candor and good nature can be used against you. Bite back your impulse to be agreeable.

Never admit any crime—that, say, you were drunk, or you knowingly lifted an item from a shop counter. Under the criminal law, you have the absolute right to put the prosecution to its proof. Do not incriminate yourself because you are remorseful.

The advice to refrain from admission of wrongdoing applies most particularly to early proceedings—at a criminal or accident scene, in exchanges of letters before a claim of breach of contract, in arguing that a purchase was unsatisfactory.

Although a time may arise when you want to plead guilty to shoplifting, or give up your defense to a contract, or compromise generously, give yourself time to take stock of your situation, to talk to your lawyer, and to assess the reasonableness of the actions contemplated by the other side. Wait until you know what the full impact of the situation will be on you.

## IS THERE A LAWYER IN THE HOUSE?

### When Lawyers Are Essential

If you are accused of a crime, you clearly need a lawyer. Any claim against you with serious effects, such as heavy fines, loss of child custody, loss of inheritance rights, eviction from your home or repossession by a creditor of your property, suspension of your business, or loss of a driver's license, calls for the assistance of a lawyer.

Sometimes the need for hiring a lawyer relates to the nature of the transaction and not to the amount of money involved. If you buy a suite of furniture for $2,500, you will not need a lawyer, but if you buy a vacant lot for $2,500 you will. This is because straight purchases of furniture, as a rule, have no initial legal complexities beyond a bill of sale, but land purchase may involve deeds, surveys, and title searches. The signing of a simple note at a bank is not a transaction that requires a lawyer, but a loan that requires a pledge of all the assets of your business *is* work for a lawyer. This is because the papers of a customary secured bank loan limit your business conduct, and call for the filing in the office of the county clerk of liens and security interests.

As a general rule, you should use a lawyer in any transaction involving important continuing relations, such as matrimonial arrangements, partnership contracts, and agreements dealing with significant sums of money, including copyright and trademark and patent rights. This rule should cover all manner of actions that require a contract, including setting up a business, leasing machinery, or agreeing not to compete.

If you are confronted by a lawyer for the other side, get your own. The same lawyer should not represent both sides in a transaction.

Sometimes you have no real choice in what you sign; your prospective employer tells you to sign his form of contract or you have no job. Even if you have no negotiating room, take the contract to a lawyer, who can explain to you what you are getting into.

### Finding a Good Lawyer

How do you find a lawyer? The best way is through the recommendation of a respected friend, business associate, or anyone else whom you trust and believe to be well informed. Your minister, doctor, teacher, or accountant may do. At least one of these is bound to have a lawyer to recommend. An employer is a good source if the legal action you have in mind does not affect your workplace. Unions, fraternal organizations, and various associations will also refer you to lawyers.

Law firms that are known by public reputation may be good, although they tend to be costly. Many lawyers now advertise low-cost legal services by means of public signs, posters, and billboards; on radio and television; in newspapers and the telephone book. These are generally acceptable if your matter is not complex, and if you can interview and be satisfied with the lawyer who will actually do your work.

Legal directories are a popular reference source. The *Martindale-Hubbell Law Directory* is the standard one for the legal profession. Arranged geographically, it gives information on lawyers in every sizable community in the country and sometimes includes professional résumés and listings of specialties. *Martindale-Hubbell* is available in all good law libraries and most well-stocked public and university libraries. Among other directories are the *Lawyers' Register by Specialties and Fields of Law*, published in Solon, Ohio, and the regional directories published by Legal Directories Publishing Co. of Los Angeles. Directories are best used to assemble background information. Nothing replaces interviewing the lawyer in person.

If you cannot afford to hire a lawyer, go to the Legal Aid Society or the local bar association. Find these in your telephone book. The American Bar Association publishes a useful directory of free or low cost legal referral sources throughout the country.

### Is the Lawyer Good?

The best way to test for a "good" lawyer is to meet him. Experienced lawyers can usually gain rapport with other lawyers by telephone, especially if they have a résumé in hand, but lay persons do not have the necessary background for this.

The first indication of a good lawyer for you is your instinctive confidence, your feeling of comfort in the way he talks to you. You must be able to communicate with each other. Has he dealt with the exact kind of matters you are now asking him to deal with? Ask about his education, honors, experience, special training, written articles, speeches, lectures, bar association work. Does he seem knowledgeable? Has he held public office? What kind of support help does he have? Does he have time for you? *Who* will actually do your work and who will talk with you? Is there a law library readily available? It may take a little nerve to ask all these questions of a white-haired, pipe-smoking gentleman in a three-piece suit—but try. It is your life, your case.

### Cost and Quality

These are relative terms, for there are different lawyering worlds in this country. There are lawyers with elaborate support staffs and facilities who service large business enterprises and wealthy individuals for high fees. The country is replete, however, with capable and diligent lawyers who can serve people in most economic ranges. Good representation is as critical to the success of a case as the quality of a surgeon is to the success of an operation. Seek out a capable lawyer whose fee you can manage. That legal fee may not be a pleasant prospect, but it may well be worthwhile and, indeed, necessary.

There are cost efficiencies in picking lawyers. Your case may not warrant the expense of the "best." If you are engaging a lawyer for a minor business transaction, routine debt collection, consumer complaint, or run-of-the-mill landlord-tenant problem, the legal meter of a specialized lawyer, good as he may be, can read more than the ride is worth. Generalists with small offices and practices, often younger lawyers, can do the job for your price.

Specialized lawyers are best for negligence, criminal, trial, tax, labor, pension, immigration, copyright, securities, bankruptcy, patent, or admiralty (marine law) work. Where large funds or sophisticated transactions are concerned—say, in affairs of real estate, corporate securities, and trusts and estates—special expertise is also indicated.

Quality law firms, as opposed to individual practitioners, can provide a good mixture of generalists and specialists.

### Prior Fee Understanding

Talk frankly to your prospective lawyer about his prospective charges. Do not be embarrassed or feel that this is bad form or undignified. The rules of the American Bar Association specifically urge lawyers to have prior and specific written fee understandings.

Make sure this rule is followed—that the question of fee is settled, in writing, in advance. This is usually done in a letter. A lawyer who will not be specific about his charges is probably a bad legal and economic risk.

Do not expect guarantees of success in the legal representation. If you get one, be assured you are in the wrong place.

### Have a Lawyer on Hand

It is good to look ahead, to have your lawyer available even before a problem arises. A person who moves into a new community often locates a family doctor right away for possible emergencies later on; so should you locate a family lawyer for legal emergencies. With a reassuring relationship in place, it will be easy to call for quick inquiry and to move with confidence when full lawyering is necessary.

You will be surprised how much free or inexpensive advice is forthcoming from lawyers who consider you a regular client. Your easier questions will be carried against the day when you have a personal-injury action, or buy a home, or die with an estate to probate and administer. Most lawyers must cultivate their sources of income. A regular customer in any business gets the edge; so does a regular legal client.

When you do go to a lawyer, organize your thoughts in advance in writing, so you know what you want to say. Leave nothing out. Bring all your documents on the subject to the first meeting, and let the lawyer judge the relevancy of what you have.

Important legal matters go better with lawyers. They help put the law on your side. Do not be misled by the massive availability of practical guides, for once legal action is afoot in earnest, there is usually comparatively little you can or should do for yourself without your lawyer. The popular cry to dispense with lawyers may sell books and help out on the lecture circuit, but it is out of tune with hard reality.

# Chapter *Two*

# *Claims for Personal and Property Injuries*

## SOME DEFINITIONS

One of the country's leading enterprises is the collecting of money for injuries to person or property caused by the negligence of others. The foremost example is the automobile accident. A full fifty percent of the civil business of the New York Supreme Court in Nassau County, where I sat as a trial judge for almost nine years, dealt only with accidents that involved an automobile. Negligence actions are not, however, limited to automobile cases; they include injuries from tripping on sidewalks or steps, from defective goods or machinery, from malpractice of doctors or dentists (which is really professional negligence), and from other sorts of accidents on land, at sea, and in the air. Negligence actions for automobile and all other injuries account for two-thirds of the litigated civil cases in the country. If all negligence cases of every kind were suddenly removed from our civil courts, they would be close to a wasteland.

Recognizing and asserting a genuine injury claim is part of putting the law on your side. Unfortunately, there are so many inflated, even artificial, claims for money that many people have become cynical about the whole negligence-law process. Undeniable abuses aside, however, there is no question that it is legitimate to enforce your rights when you are genuinely injured through the negligence of another.

An injury to a person's body, usually physical, but also mental on certain occasions, is referred to either as "personal injury (P.I.)" or as "bodily injury (B.I.)." Injury to property, such as a car, a tree, or the side of a house, is usually known as "property damage (P.D.)." Lawyers dealing in accident cases talk freely of P.I. and P.D., and insurers use the same terminology. Since most personal-injury cases arise from negligent harm, the field of personal-injury recovery is usually referred to as "negligence," and its lawyers form the "negligence bar."

Actually, the broad legal term for the rights and duties of people in personal- or property-injury claims is "tort." This is strictly a legal word, otherwise obsolete in ordinary speech. In essence, a tort is a civil wrong done by one party to another, which is neither a breach of contract nor of trust, for which money damages or an injunction may be had.

While negligence—careless conduct that unintentionally injures another person—is the principal tort and has many subdivisions, deliberate action with intent to harm another is also a variety of tort. Intentional torts, those not involving negligence, include assault, battery, trespassing, false imprisonment, taking the property of others (called "conversion"), and defamation. New torts, such as poisoning the air or water—the so-called toxic torts—are continually being developed by legislatures and courts to keep pace with the realities of modern life.

Many torts, such as taking the property of others (stealing) and attacking with weapons (assault), are also crimes. While the underlying conduct may be the same, the legal consequences are different. Designation of conduct as a "crime" reflects public concern and can lead to imprisonment and to fines that are paid to the government. Conduct that is called a "tort" involves only the private relationship between people and companies that may lead to the private payment of damages by the wrongdoer to the victim. Someone who assaults another may be held liable both criminally and civilly. The assaulter may both go to jail *and* be required to pay damages to his victim.

All tort cases have two elements in common: there must be some act or omission by the accused wrongdoer for which he is legally liable, and the victim must have suffered some damage that entitles him to some relief under the law, usually money.

# SHOULD YOU PURSUE YOUR CLAIM?

Many wrongs are minor in effect and are simply part of the great body of annoyances with which we have to contend in society. Jostling in a crowd may technically involve a touching, and therefore the tort of "battery," but what is the damage? Offensive language spoken into your ear by a passer-by on a public street, even if obscene and even if provable, involves no damage and cannot be considered a tort. The temporary headache caused by a jackhammer in the street, by the honking of car horns, or by the exhaust fumes from a bus, and the taxi that frightens you by stopping suddenly at your feet come under the heading of irritations that must be borne.

A moving automobile may simply brush against your flapping coat, causing a physical touching but no damage. Suppose, instead, that the car runs over the edge of your shoe, the driver takes off, and you get his license-plate number. You are not hurt, but your fifty-dollar shoes are ruined. This is damage; but is it worth the bother and expense of finding the driver and suing him?

If your tailor burns your trousers and offers to pay you what they cost on the spot, take it. If he scratches you inconsequentially with a pin, take his offer of free service in recompense. Similarly, if you find half a bug in your soup, and the restaurateur wishes to make amends by giving you two free meals, accept them, if you are not feeling sick. You should not go to court about such trifles.

Yet do not agree to withhold the filing of an accident report required under your local law, regardless of whether you or another person intends to file a claim. Instead, be sure that you do file a report. The person who pleads that he does not want his boss or his wife to know, or that his insurance rate will go up, is the very person who will turn around and sue you for personal injury, claiming that you stopped short in front of him or whatever.

## *Never Sign a Release without Consulting a Lawyer*

Never sign any release for anyone at any time for any personal injury done to you without consulting a lawyer. A release is a document in any form that says you forgive the other side for any liability. If a driver lightly bumps your standing car, apologizes, estimates he has done seventy-five dollars' damage to your fender, and offers to pay you in cash on the spot, take it if the damage is indeed slight, but do not sign a release.

Now assume that the elevator operator in your building negligently closes the door on your thumb, which remains bruised and sore for a week. You do not go to a doctor, but you report it to the building superintendent. An adjuster from an insurance company for the building owner arrives a month later with a check for $350, to be delivered to you if you will release the elevator operator and the owner of the building from liability. Should you take it or go to a lawyer? My advice is to go to a lawyer any time an insurer for someone who injured you approaches you with a check. Insurance companies are almost invariably prepared to pay more money than they offer at first. It might be beneficial to hire a lawyer to pursue a claim. Offer him a fee that is based on a percentage of what is recovered over the $350 initially offered to you.

### Early Need for a Negligence Specialist

Many factors, of which the severity of your injury is only one, enter into the worth of a case. There are the questions of legal liability, of the ability of the wrongdoer to pay a money judgment—known as "being good for the money" or "having a deep pocket"—and of whether the wrongdoer can technically be sued under the circumstances.

Because of the expertise needed in dealing with personal-injury cases, the first and best move in putting the law on your side when you are the victim of a tort is to engage a lawyer who has had actual experience in trying tort cases. The lawyers that insurers respect—those who can and will fight effectively in court—are the same lawyers who will arrive at the best settlements, thus short-cutting delays in payment of damages that result from drawn-out trials, and hedging against the risk of losing your case. Insurers wait out lawyers they perceive as ineffective.

Do not delay. Whereas in usual civil legal matters, such as business contracts or landlord-tenant disputes, there may be time to act and react, tort cases require investigating the circumstances quickly, obtaining statements from witnesses, and preserving evidence, such as a damaged car. Photographs of the scene of an accident or of injuries that will have healed by the time you appear in court may be needed.

If because of an accident you are injured in any significant way, or are obliged to seek medical treatment, or are made to lose time from work, by all means go to a lawyer without hesitation. Let him tell you whether you have a case. This is, of course, where the injuries are not caused by your own carelessness. If you stick a pencil in your own eye while writing alone in your room, expect no more than sympathy from anyone.

Tort liability is not customarily an intricate legal field, important though it may be. The primary focus is on marshaling the facts, on advocacy, which is the way of presenting the case orally and in writing, and on tactics, such as which parts of the case to stress, when to settle, and when to sue to the end. Certain types of tort cases, however, do require greater expertise. Injury or death as a result of an airplane crash, for example, may require a lawyer versed in technical aspects of meteorology, flight regulations, and aircraft design and construction. Similarly, the proof of medical malpractice in a back operation for a ruptured spinal disk may require special expertise in understanding and developing medical testimony.

Personal-injury lawyers for plaintiffs work on a contingent-fee basis. They receive a percentage of the damages paid, usually thirty-three and one-third percent. If you have a case with very large damages, you can negotiate a lower fee. In recoveries of less than $5,000, however, the fee may be forty or fifty percent. All disbursements involved in your case, such as court fees and payments to investigators and expert witnesses, are subtracted from the recovery *before* figuring the contingent fee. They do not come from your share alone.

## IF YOU ARE CHARGED WITH INJURING SOMEONE

You may not only be the victim of a tort; you may commit one. If you do, you may be sued, in which case your choices are to pay or to resist the suit. You should have insurance to take care of these choices.

### Do You Carry Adequate Insurance?

Automobile liability insurance is essential to anyone who owns a car, and it is required, one way or another, in most states. The amount of coverage you carry should be determined by your economic status, not by the statutory minimum. The added premium for higher coverage is relatively small, almost negligible in relation to the sense of security it can bring to you. Automobile accidents can happen to any driver, and in these United States there are few bashful suers left.

Every tenant and homeowner should carry adequate insurance, not only against fire and theft, but also against liability to people who trip on rugs, walk through glass doors, fall down stairs, or slip on the ice of a just-shoveled sidewalk. For anyone with any means at all, insurance against all other kinds of legal liability is highly desirable. When someone is trying to put the law on their side and against you, an insurance policy is really your sleeping money. Indeed, there are now catastrophe or umbrella types of liability coverage that can be superimposed on your existing coverages and protect you for astronomical sums, at very low cost, against almost all legal liability, including legal expenses, for accidents.

### Prompt Written Notice to Your Insurer of Claims Against You

When you receive a letter of claim or are sued for legal liability and you are insured, it is essential to notify your insurer in writing at once.

Better, if you ever become aware of an accident for which you may be charged, you should report it to your insurer in writing, immediately, even if a claim has not yet been made. Do not hesitate in fear that your premiums may be increased even though no claim eventually arises. The claim will probably come. Most insurers, in deciding whether to cancel policies, take only actual and paid claims into account. There are exceptions, but there may also be prejudice in delay. All liability-insurance policies contain various kinds of provisions that require prompt notice of claims covered under the policy. Some policies specifically require reports of incidents as well as of actual claims.

Do not rely on insurance agents to forward claim notices just because they say they will. Write directly to the insurer. Describe the accident briefly, the parties involved, and cite your insurance policy number. If you do not have the name and address of your insurer, get it from the agent from whom you bought the insurance. Send your letter to your insurer by certified mail or deliver it in person and obtain a receipt. Enclose any claim letter or summons you have received. Keep copies of everything you send out.

One great advantage of liability-insurance coverage is that the insurer hires and pays the lawyer to take over the full defense of your case. The insurer pays, if you lose, not only the amount of money sought against you, but also the costs of the case, such as lawyers' fees, which may be considerable. The insurer, typically, makes all decisions, including any settlement, which it also pays. Strictly, however, your permission is necessary for any settlement by your insurer. Unless the case goes to court, and relatively few do, you may never be troubled by it again after you have notified your insurer, except for statements you may have to give to the lawyers for both sides, or for legal papers.


## Claims against You in Excess of Your Insurance Coverage

It sometimes happens that a claim against you exceeds your insurance coverage. Suppose, for instance, that a claim is made against you for $375,000, and your insurance coverage for that claim is only $50,000. Further suppose that the claimant is willing to settle his case against you for the $50,000. This settlement would leave you safe. But your insurer insists it will not pay more than $10,000. The case goes to trial, and the jury awards a $200,000 verdict to the plaintiff. Your insurer must pay $50,000, for which you are covered, and you have now no choice but to pay the remaining $150,000 (unless, of course, you win on an appeal). Your insurer's unwillingness to pay your $50,000 coverage before trial has cost you dearly.

This highlights an increasingly common happening in insurance practice. An insurer is liable only up to the limits of liability stated in its policy. In the example above, the insurer is liable for only $50,000. By refusing to settle a case within its policy limits, it can expose you to personal liability in a subsequent trial for all damages found in excess of its $50,000 policy limit. Here, the insurer takes for you an unnecessary trial risk. Insurance companies will often try to pay less than policy limits; this is called ''saving something'' on its policy. If, however, the insurer is unreasonable in its grounds for failing to pay out its full coverage and thereby exposes you to great personal liability for a case that could have been settled within the policy limit, the insurer has acted in bad faith. The legal rule is that insurers must act in good faith to settle and extinguish claims in excess of their policy limits.

If you can establish that your insurer acted in bad faith, you can often recover your loss from the insurer, and sometimes punitive damages as well. Punitive damages are arbitrary court awards to punish the miscreant and to dissuade others from similar conduct. Insurers are wary of exposing themselves to claims of bad faith in failing to settle claims within their policy limits. You should press your insurer to settle within the policy limits. A letter emphasizing your request is often helpful.

Keep in touch with the lawyer supplied by your insurance company. Insist that he communicate with you, so you will know when you may have to make a move. This is particularly important when your coverage is low in relation to a reasonably expected damage award. If you have reason to believe you face damages over and above your policy limit, or if you have enough assets to encourage a claimant, it is a good idea to hire your own personal lawyer to sit in with the lawyer the insurance company furnishes.

To be sure, many claims are for "pie-in-the-sky" figures. It is not unusual in metropolitan areas for an unemployed claimant with a simple neck sprain to sue for $250,000, in a situation where the insurance coverage is an ample $100,000. The realistic anticipated award in such a case might be $3,500. The insurer does have a right to protect itself. It need not pay an absurd amount to cut off your theoretical exposure. At a minimum, consult your own lawyer to learn whether the damages claimed are realistically framed; ask where he believes the pie is—it may just be you.

Sometimes, when realistically high damages in excess of your policy coverage are threatened, the insurer may ask you to contribute your own funds toward a settlement of the case. You may want to do this to eliminate the risk of being found personally liable in court for a greater sum of money.

Bear in mind, always, that when the claim exceeds the coverage, your personal interests necessarily conflict with those of your insurer. The insurer may gamble on a trial (as opposed to a settlement) to save something on its policy, so long as it feels the record demonstrates that it is acting in good faith. It is, however, always to your interest, as the insured, to settle within your policy limit. When a claim against you is settled within your policy limit, effectively you have put the law on your side. You pay nothing for the discharge of your liability.

### Not Insured?

If you are not insured against a claim because, for instance, you let your policy lapse, engage a lawyer immediately. Your need is the same as that of the one suing you.

If you have an insurance policy and you believe you have coverage, but your insurer refuses to cover you ("denies coverage"), write to the insurer insisting that it defend your case. Although the insurer may not wish to admit that its policy covered the particular happening, as a precaution it may agree to defend you by furnishing a lawyer and paying the litigation costs, and leave the question of its liability, if any, to you for later determination by a court or by mutual agreement. The insurer's written advice to you that it is following this course is known as its "reservation of rights."

If your insurer refuses to defend you, go to your own lawyer. Your lawyer may be able to persuade the insurer to defend you. If not, your lawyer can either defend you in court or bring an action to compel the insurer to defend you. After a case in which your insurer refuses to pay, you may want to sue the insurer for its policy coverage, if liability was found, and for your legal fees in any event.

Denial of insurance coverage is serious business; do not accept it and simply hope for the best.

## RULES OF NEGLIGENCE LAW

Since negligence cases are by far the most common of torts, it is important to know the rules of legal liability in them. Is the other person liable to you? Are you liable to him?

Negligence is your breach of the standard of care the law considers you owe to another. Classic cases include the duty of care that a person driving a car owes to everyone on the road and on the sidewalk, and the responsibility of a landowner for all those who come onto his property and of a tenant for the people who come into his apartment or shop. The tort of negligence is determined by three criteria: the standard of care, or what a reasonable person would have done under the circumstances; "proximate cause," or the relation of the conduct to the injury; and the actual damages.

Damages typically include medical and hospital expenses and lost income. However, the bread-and-butter of negligence practice is "pain and suffering." That phrase covers the intangible injuries, the discomfort and disruption of the victim's life. The large personal-injury verdicts usually result from the finding of considerable sums for pain and suffering.

## Kinds of Negligence

There are as many kinds of negligence as there are opportunities for human conduct. Although misuse of an automobile is the single most frequently encountered example, it is but one among many.

The owner of a building, for instance, may be negligent in failing to repair broken steps or in leaving a stairwell unlit. A landowner may be liable for maintaining an "attractive nuisance"—an unguarded high pile of bricks or an unprotected swimming pool, which entices children and puts them in danger of physical injury. A landowner has different duties for different people who enter his property—in esoteric legal categories, trespasser, invitee, and licensee.

Medical malpractice is the negligence of a doctor or dentist in failing to use his professional skill according to the accepted professional practices of the community. There may be successive acts of negligence, making allocation of liability difficult. Suppose a woman tenant falls down broken stairs in a poorly lit apartment house, is injured, and is taken to a hospital, where her injuries are made worse by a malpracticing doctor. Who is liable to her, and for which injuries? The general rule is that all of them—the owner of the stairs, the hospital, and the doctor—are fully liable to the woman, but that the total liability may be divided among them, in shares a jury decides.

## Defenses

A common defense in negligence cases is that the complained-of conduct was not negligent and that it was acceptable behavior under the circumstances. It may also be argued that the negligence did not cause the injury, or that no injury resulted.

A classic defense against a negligence charge is "contributory negligence," applicable in thirty-four states. Under this defense, even though the defendant was negligent, if the plaintiff was also negligent and his own negligence contributed to his injury, there is no liability due him. Failure to wear a seat belt is an example of contributory negligence in an automobile accident. Even if the defendant's negligence is far greater than that of the plaintiff, under strict contributory-negligence theory the plaintiff still loses. The unfairness of such an outcome has led sixteen states to adopt the doctrine of "comparative negligence," according to which the relative proportion of fault between the parties is determined by the court, and the defendant is liable for only his share. Where contributory negligence is the rule, many juries will simply ignore minimal negligence on the part of the plaintiff in the face of serious misconduct by the defendant, no matter what the judge tells them. The difficulties encountered in making all these determinations, not to mention the calculation of the elusive phrase "pain and suffering," mean that the differences of opinion and the sympathies of juries and the skills of lawyers figure prominently in the outcome of negligence cases.

"Assumption of the risk" is a defense that, in effect, excuses the plaintiff because the defendant knew of the hazard and chose voluntarily to take his risk. Under the legal doctrine of "last clear chance," the defendant may be wholly liable if in the end he could reasonably have been expected to avoid the accident after becoming aware of the plaintiff's contributory negligence.


## Defective Goods or Machines

In earlier times, *caveat emptor*—let the buyer beware—was the rule. Today, the shoes are on the other feet; it is the manufacturers and sellers who must beware. They can be sued for injury from defective goods or machines, or products whose labels or instructions fail to apprise consumers of the likely hazards of improper use. Manufacturers and sellers can be liable for negligence, for breach of implied warranty, or under the modern theory of strict liability, which basically means that a consumer has a right not to be hurt by using a product in its normally intended manner and according to instructions.

Manufacturers will, typically, defend their products by claiming that they have been used improperly, that they have been altered, or that they are not unreasonably dangerous. But the trend in this area of the law is in favor of consumers. Because of heavy public-relations burdens that arise from charges that products are defective, and because of growing interest on the part of government in unsafe products, many manufacturers have become "settlement prone." Hidden defects in cars, even old ones, have recently attracted much litigative attention, for example. Thus, many automobiles are recalled by their manufacturers simply because of growing fear of legal liability.

The best course of action for a person injured by a product is to sue everyone connected with the product in any significant way—the designer, the manufacturer, the seller, the installer. This helps ensure that no party who may have caused or contributed to the injury has been left out, and, in the event that settlement is reached, provides additional pockets, usually those of insurers, from which to draw. Recent changes in laws governing product liability have manufacturers, suppliers, and sellers running scared, but they have improved the lot of consumers.

## LIABILITY WITHOUT FAULT

There are areas where there is legal liability for personal injury without regard to technical definitions of fault, responsibility, or negligence. For instance, people who keep wild animals, such as snakes or lion cubs, are generally strictly liable for injuries done by their pets, though there is no fault on their part except that they have them. There is no liability for injuries caused by domestic pets, such as dogs and cats, unless their owners have prior knowledge of their "dangerous proclivity." The ageless reference here is that "every dog is entitled to one bite."

Certain activities are unusually hazardous. The builder who uses dynamite to demolish an old building, for example, will usually be liable for any damage caused to the adjoining property, and carriers of explosives or poison gases have the same liability. The very existence or use of hazardous substances or conduct causes danger and gives rise to absolute liability without resort to traditional notions of negligence.

Historically, two favorite objects of negligence suits have been automobile drivers and employers; requirements of fault or negligence as a basis for collecting damages from them are significantly treated by special statutes on a "no-fault" basis.

Claims by victims against those who injure them by negligence but who carry liability insurance are traditionally known as "third-party" liability claims, since the negligent party's insurer pays directly to the victim in honoring its policy commitment. If an insured person makes a claim against his own insurer, that is known as "first-party" liability. The classic examples of first-party coverage are fire insurance, under which the insurer pays the insured for fire damage, and health insurance, under which the insurer pays policy benefits directly to the insured. This distinction between first- and third-party liability is significant.

## *No-Fault Automobile Liability*

No-fault statutes, with varying provisions in twenty-two states, leave limited opportunities for negligence suits to arise from automobile accidents. These statutes provide that victims injured in automobile accidents, often an innocent driver involved, are to be reimbursed by their own insurer for medical expenses and lost income resulting from their injuries, regardless of anyone's fault or negligence—but they are not reimbursed by their own insurers for pain and suffering. Thus, the insurance becomes first-party coverage. Because these statutes do not take into account whose fault caused the accident, they are called "no-fault" statutes.

One consequence of the no-fault system is that, unless you qualify, you cannot sue anybody for your pain and suffering. You lose that right. The circumstances under which you can still sue, through a regular negligence suit, for pain and suffering resulting from an automobile accident are when there are serious injuries (such as loss or fracture of a limb) or medical expenses of a specified dollar minimum, known as the "threshold." Because of the significance of the amount of the medical expenses incurred, it is doubly important that you save your bills for required treatment.

When negligence suits are permitted, they are the same as actions taken generally by victims against negligent parties, and damages are paid by the negligent party's liability insurer. They are typical third-party liability situations.

Because of this two-tier system of responsibility for injury by automobiles, insurance policies covering automobile related personal injury are customarily divided into two parts. The first provides coverage for an automobile policyholder should he suffer personal injury in an automobile accident. The second part is standard liability coverage for personal injuries the policyholder may cause to other people, who may sue him under the specified threshold conditions.

The general premise of the no-fault scheme is that everyone has some automobile insurance, stemming from his or her family's automobile ownership. Since this is not universally true—passengers and pedestrians may have no automobile insurance policy personally or through their families—there are special provisions extending the coverage of the car owner's policy to his passengers and to any pedestrian the car may strike. Therefore, negligence on the part of the operator of the car is not required, nor is the passenger or pedestrian blocked from statutory coverage for medical expenses and loss of income by any contributory or comparative negligence of his own.

There are also special latitudes for victims to sue reckless drivers and those impaired by alcohol or drugs.

Because no-fault statutes usually do not permit negligence suits unless some threshold has been crossed, they have reduced the number of lawsuits for minor injuries, particularly soft-tissue injuries, which do not show on X-rays, as well as stiff necks presumably caused by whiplash, and aching backs.


## Workers' Compensation

Negligence as a basis for finding an employer liable to an employee in a work-related accident has been curtailed or cut back by workers' compensation statutes in all states. Therefore, the worker no longer needs to show, except in obvious cases, that the employer was at fault, negligent, or responsible for his injury. But workers' compensation coverage is limited to medical expenses, loss of income, and some recompense for disfigurement.

The consequence has been that in a work-related accident the thrust is to find a third party—not the employer or employee, but a supplier, a builder, or an independent contractor—on whom to pin a third-party lawsuit for pain and suffering. If a ladder breaks, its manufacturer will do; if a wall buckles, its builder is susceptible to the lawsuit. In short, in work-related accidents, where your rights to recovery for your pain and suffering are blocked by workers' compensation, look for a builder or supplier or serviceman who may be separately liable under regular common-law negligence principles. This provides you with a chance for recovery for pain and suffering, notwithstanding workers' compensation laws.

# INTENTIONAL TORTS

The term "intentional torts" covers a wide variety of conduct—trespass, conversion, fraud, false arrest, assault, battery, and many other acts. If you are the victim of an intentional tort, you must prove, generally, that the wrongful act was done with malicious intent if you are to recover damages.

From the plaintiff's point of view, a positive factor in suits for intentional torts is the possibility of recovering "punitive" damages, about which more will be said later. A negative factor in suing privately for intentional torts, many of which are crimes for which the offender may be prosecuted by the government, is the usual lack of insurance coverage to assure payment if a favorable verdict is received. Liability-insurance policies typically exclude coverage for intentional torts or punitive damages. The one against whom the suit is brought must be someone who has sufficient personal resources to pay, unless only a symbolic victory is sought. Few lawyers will represent the plaintiff in intentional tort cases on the basis of contingency fees.

## *Common Intentional Torts*
### *Trespass*
One of the more usual intentional torts is trespass, although technically trespass can be unintentional as well. The tort of trespass ranges from someone's walking physically onto your property, to building

on it, through causing various odors, to damage caused by flowing water and sewage and pollution. Sometimes the offensive action is called "private nuisance."

### Conversion

Conversion occurs frequently, and means taking someone else's property, altering it, or misusing it.

### Fraud

Fraud is another frequent intentional tort. Most fraud is trickery or swindling by misrepresentation.

### False Arrest / Imprisonment

"False arrest" is maliciously causing someone to be unlawfully arrested. "False imprisonment" is unlawful restraint. It arises not only when someone is illegally put in jail, but also when a department-store guard suspects you of shoplifting, for instance, and detains you in a locked room. Typically, these cases are brought against government, hotels, and department stores, as well as against the police, private security guards, and store or hotel detectives.

### Assault and Battery

Contrary to what most lay persons think, assault, as a tort, need be only a threat of physical harm, without any touching. Assault damages may be recoverable for fright or mental distress. Battery, as a tort, is actual touching.

Customary incidents of these are brawls or unprovoked acts by one person upon another. Doctors who do unauthorized operations or who touch their patients unnecessarily may also be liable for battery.

In modern practice, many courts are willing to expand tort liability to include the deliberate infliction of fear or mental suffering, even when no physical threat or touching has occurred. They also include abusive tactics by collection agencies. The imposition of liability for mental distress without physical harm or its threat is still pioneer territory and differs greatly from courthouse to courthouse.

### Malicious Prosecution

Malicious-prosecution actions usually arise after a lawsuit has been brought and lost. The defendant who won the case then claims that the suit against him was frivolous and not bona fide. Do not assume, however, that, merely because you won the earlier lawsuit, you can recover more by this prosecution. In many states, such an action can be brought only if the earlier action was a criminal proceeding or if your property had been improperly attached. "Abuse of legal process" is an allied tort; it complains of the use of the ordinary processes of the courts, such as summonses and orders of attachment, in order to harass or to inflict harm. Harassment is the key to both torts.

The general policy of the law favors people having their day in court. Under governing rules, suits for malicious prosecution and abuse of legal process are rarely won by their plaintiffs.

## Defamation

Defamation is a classic tort, better known to the public as "slander," its oral form, and "libel," its written form, which includes television and radio transmission. They are false utterances that hold the subject up to ridicule or contempt and cause him injury.

Sometimes punitive damages may be awarded in a particularly unfair or reprehensible defamation.

### Essence

Defamation depends not only upon an offensive message that derogates a person, but also upon "publication" of it, which means communication of it to others. A one-to-one exchange of words cannot be slander, nor can writing be libel, unless the author says or displays it to a third person. This requirement often makes it difficult to prove libel or slander, for witnesses have a habit of melting away or becoming confused in their recollections in these highly personal situations.

### Obstacles to Suing

Although occasionally a big defamation award is given to a celebrity who has been luridly described in a magazine, newspaper, radio, or television account as a crook, a plagiarizer, or a quack of a doctor; to a businessman who has been maligned as financially unsound or as a liar; or to a woman who has been called promiscuous, defamation cases are rarely won for large sums by most people. The constitutional right of free speech is a deterrent, as is the difficulty of proving concrete damages.

There are fine lines between honest, if pungent, expressions of opinion, on the one hand, and defamation on the other. "I think Jones is no good," for example, is not defamation. Specific harmful allegations, such as "Jones stole my watch and robbed the store," must have been made.

Some successful defamation cases, however, have arisen out of malicious comments by former employers concerning terminated employees to prospective employers seeking references.

The plaintiff has the burden of proof, which he may not be able to carry. The ardor to sue for defamation dims with the realization by the wronged party that, to the public, loss of a defamation case is tantamount to proof of the defamatory charge, no matter what the legal nicety that caused the suit to be lost. The whole story is aired publicly, and the defamation receives more attention than it did originally. Moreover, many defamation cases wind up with, at best, nominal damages or an apology, small solace for the harsh reality of an emotional trial and huge legal expenses.

### Defenses

TRUTH. Truth is an absolute defense in a lawsuit for civil libel or slander, which is a contest between private people or companies for the payment of damages to private reputation. Truth is not a defense in a criminal libel case, the trial of a crime for which the one uttering the libel may go to jail. Truth is not material to criminal libel because the essence of that charge is saying or writing things with the idea of stirring up public disorder.

PRIVILEGE. Some people are privileged to say things that would be actionable defamation in the mouths of others.

Public officials, including judges and legislators, have "absolute privilege" in what they say or write in the course of their duties, and business associates have "qualified privilege" for statements made in the course of their business dealings, provided, in both cases, there is absence of malice.

The press also has qualified privilege to make "fair comment" on matters of public interest, in addition to protection under the First Amendment. Newspapers can generally print what they like about people in the public eye if what is printed does not reflect actual malice, which includes reckless disregard of the truth or knowledge that what they are publishing is false.

## Some New Torts

Action for invasion of rights of privacy is now recognized and allowed. Briefly, this tort is appropriation of your name or likeness for commercial advantage, such as for advertising someone else's product; intrusion upon your physical solitude or seclusion; public disclosure of true, but private, facts about you; and placing you in a false light in the public eye. For the most part, where permissible, these torts proceed on the assumption that the wrongdoer's acts are truthful but that society must seek to preserve the privacy of those who want to remain private.

In addition, but without exhausting the list of torts that may affect your life, the courts recognize that there is damaging conduct, for which it should be possible to recover damages, even though the conduct does not fall within any classic definitions of tort. Courts have also developed new torts, sometimes called "prima facie torts," which, in essence, recognize that unjust conduct that causes harm should be recompensed, even when that conduct does not fall within the strict definitions of torts already recognized. An example might be someone hiring away your employees simply to hurt your business. The imaginative use of prima facie torts, where applicable, is a good way of protecting your rights and putting the law on your side.

## Punitive Damages

Punitive damages, also called "exemplary damages," may be awarded in cases of torts that harm the public. They are meant to punish the wrongdoer and deter others from the same conduct, not necessarily to recompense the victim for actual damages, although the award goes into the pocket of the victim.

This means that the award exceeds the expense of any actually proven damages. Fraud, defamation, and some prima facie torts are the most likely common-law cases in which punitive damages may be awarded. In cases involving statutory torts, such as antitrust activity, civil-rights violations, and environmental-damage actions, punitive damages are authorized by statute.

## SPECIAL PROBLEMS IN BRINGING SUIT

It should now be clear that the law entitles you to recover damages in many situations and is expanding to allow damage suits in new areas. Be alert to any situation in which you, your property, your reputation, or even your feelings are substantially injured. Do not simply accept injury as "one of those things," as an "act of God," or as the hand of fate. Consult a competent lawyer to review the situation; if he tells you that you have no case, make him explain why.

But just as the law endeavors to give you remedies for wrongs, it creates balancing factors to weed out, or prevent, lawsuits—sometimes even in apparently meritorious cases. To help put the law on your side, you should be aware of some of those factors.

### Time Limitations

A common obstacle to bringing a tort case, otherwise valid in every way, is the statute of limitations. This is a statute that defines the period after which legal actions, including torts, become irretrievably stale and suit cannot be brought. In other words, a case can be lost simply by the passage of time. You must sue on time.

These statutes, for torts, vary from one to six years from the time of the wrong to the time suit is actually brought, depending on the state and the tort. But, since statutes of limitations sometimes bar claims that might otherwise be valid or that cannot be discovered in time to bring suit, various rules have been developed to soften their strict measure. These special rules apply to certain torts that are not immediately noticeable: the sewing of a pair of scissors into a surgical patient, say, or fraud that has been concealed by further fraudulent activities.

The time within which a minor must bring suit is usually suspended—called "tolled" in the law—until he reaches adulthood. It is also tolled for such matters as the time needed to appoint an executor when the plaintiff has died or delay caused by bankruptcy.

Governments are subject to suit only if they permit it. Most do, but with certain qualifications—particularly, short time limits in which notice of claims can be filed and suit can be brought. For instance, notice of a claim against a municipality for injury caused by a break in a pavement may have to be filed within sixty days of the incident.

When suing a unit of government, be alert to a short time limitation for notifying it of the accident and for filing your suit.

## *Immunity of Defendant from Suit*

Another balancing factor is that some parties are simply not suable. Employers are ordinarily not, for work-related negligence, by virtue of workers' compensation. Spouses generally cannot sue each other for tort, nor can children below the age of reason—sometimes ten, sometimes twelve—be sued for torts they may have committed. Parents are not usually liable for their children's torts unless they participate in them or have prior knowledge of a child's propensity to harm.

Government officials are generally immune from personal tort liability, except by statute, for conduct in the course of their official duties. Failure to enforce safety codes, overzealous use of force by firemen, and wild accusations by legislators are but some examples of actions covered by this immunity. Although the courts tend to be protective of government officials, there are a growing number of statutory exceptions to official immunity for those who are malicious or act recklessly. This is illustrated by trends to discourage police brutality by making the offending officer personally liable. State and local government officials, for another instance, are by federal statute forbidden to deprive people of their civil rights, and may be held liable for damages if they do.

Governments have sovereign immunity from suit, and may be sued only in strict conformity with statutes that permit it. Suing a government is generally burdensome; forms may have to be filed and procedural requirements strictly met. Since permission to sue is subject to sovereign grace, and the government is a big juicy target, it is understandable that its exposure to liability is limited.

The principle of sovereign immunity is reflected in the fact that municipalities, for instance, are not liable for accidents caused by holes in the streets unless they have had notice of the condition and a reasonable opportunity to repair the holes. In New York City, a broad-based committee of lawyers was formed, the "Pothole Committee," solely to report to the city potholes in the streets, thus putting the city on notice of the condition. This is an apt illustration of lawyers' putting the law on their side, since each correctly identified pothole, and possible accident source, could be analogized to a gusher of legal fees.

## Class Actions

You usually know when you have been injured and whether you have brought a lawsuit to recover for an injury—but not always. A type of lawsuit known as a "class action" has evolved in which one person may bring a suit on behalf of himself and many other unnamed persons in a similar situation, which could include you. Class actions are used when many people have been injured by the same conduct but their individual injuries are so slight that they would not bring suit on their own, or when the injuries to all are substantial but so many people have been injured that a single suit is preferable. Examples include suits against factories that emit fumes throughout a community, and against drug companies that market drugs later found to be dangerous. The law permits one injured person to bring the suit, but any recovery or settlement is made to all injured persons.

You may actually be a party to a suit and bound by any decision in or settlement of it, even if you never knew about it or wanted it, or even if you would have preferred asserting your own rights on your own behalf. In fact, by being "bound" to the results of a class action, you may be prevented from bringing your own suit, even though the amounts you could recover on your own would be substantially greater than those obtained on your behalf in the class action. Watch for a "notice." The law requires that notice of a class suit be given to the unnamed members of the class, usually in a newspaper. Should you learn of such a class action in which you may be bound, you should call it to your lawyer's attention. Your particular injuries interests, or circumstances may be such that you may not be bound by the suit brought on your behalf by some strangers. You might prefer bringing your own suit, even after the class action has been filed.

# CALCULATION OF DAMAGES IN NEGLIGENCE CASES

The object of most legal action is to collect money. In tort cases, particularly negligence, the presence of actual damages is a prerequisite of the case. Damages usually come in two broad categories: special and general. The latter is essentially "pain and suffering"; the former consists of special items of medical-related costs or income lost as a result of the accident.

## Special Damages
### Medical Expenses

Reasonable and necessary medical expenses, which include the fees of doctors, dentists, nurses, therapists, and other health-care professionals, hospital charges, and the costs of X-rays, prosthetic devices, and medicines, are recoverable in negligence cases under the heading of special damages. The costs of psychiatric care to minimize the effects of the injury are also recoverable, as are the costs of transportation to and from the place of treatment.

In order to prove special damages, it is essential to save all bills and canceled checks. Future medical expenses—those that may be incurred after the trial—may be included within special damages and are usually determined by submitting to the judge and jury expert testimony as to the likelihood that such expenses will be incurred.

Medical expenses such as the costs of diagnostic procedures and X-rays made in preparation for the trial, as opposed to treatment and health care, are not recoverable as special damages. They are disbursements of the case, which should be subtracted from the recovery before applying the percentage of the legal fee.

Defendants' lawyers will often challenge medical procedures as unnecessary, strongly hinting that they were undertaken to build up the case or that the charges were unreasonably high. If proven, both allegations serve to reduce the special damages awarded. The necessity for medical treatment and the reasonableness of its cost are for juries to decide.

### Loss of Income

Loss of income is simply what the term implies—wages lost due to absence from work or income lost through inability to conduct a trade or profession.

In the case of wages, the damage is simply mathematical; multiply the normal wage by the number of days of work lost. Extra income lost might include income from a second job and even customary overtime, if its regularity can be proven. Lost tips are in the same category. Disability–income-insurance proceeds paid to a victim do not reduce his recovery in negligence actions.

Self-employed people must prove their lost earnings by records of past earnings and by demonstration of opportunities lost during the period of disability.

Determination of future loss of income, that anticipated to be lost for all time after the case is over, is governed by complicated rules. In general, the amount of net income that would have been earned throughout the claimant's expected working life is determined, then discounted by an actuarial formula to reach the present value of that sum. Determinations are much more difficult to make if the claimants are in business for themselves. It is common practice for juries simply to estimate lump-sum awards for the future on some "gut" basis and not to consider using formulas to figure out the subsequent financial loss.

### General Damages

General damages in negligence actions are, to repeat, "pain and suffering." Sometimes "mental anguish" is added.

This is the most difficult and subjective of measures, for tolerance of pain differs greatly between one person and another, and well-adjusted people fare better than those who are unstable or maladjusted. People happy in their work return to it more readily than those who are discontented.

People who are articulate, even dramatic, tend to present more compelling pictures of suffering than those who are taciturn or shy but have the same injuries. There are those who so habitually reject illness and discomfort in their daily life that they tend to destroy their own cases for pain and suffering by their very stoicism.

Depression, anxiety, and neurosis brought on by injuries are indexes of pain and suffering. Scars and the removal of limbs will cause future mental anguish beyond any experienced earlier, and are thus subjects for compensation. Interference with the daily routine of life, loss of consortium with a spouse, side effects from medicine, and continuous pain also come under the heading of pain and suffering.

Intensification of disabilities from which a person already suffers is grounds for damage. A man who cannot hear, for example, is that much more disabled by the loss of his sight. A person with a bad back before an accident may be in a still worse state after it. A nervous person may be made more nervous. It is said in the law that the wrongdoer takes his victim as he finds him.

Lawyers learn the attitudes toward general damages that prevail in their communities and settle their cases on the basis of these expectations. It is surprising how the common feeling of the community about the money value to be assigned to injury reaches general consensus and repeats itself. This practice accords with the theory that the jury award works the communal will.

Sometimes, for purposes of a settlement, general damages are computed by lawyers as artificial multiples of special damages. The amount of money proper for pain and suffering, for example, might be computed at five or ten times the amount of expenses or special damages. The evident theory is that the more extensive the medical treatment, the greater will be the pain and suffering. There is no rule of law, however, to this effect. The multiplication is only a rule of thumb for lawyers and insurance adjusters who must deal with carloads of cases.

Legal advocacy, a sympathetic plaintiff, an unpopular defendant, preferably a wealthy one, and the extent of injury and its lingering consequences are the elements that add up to high awards for pain and suffering.

Punitive damages are almost nonexistent in common-law negligence cases. They are more common in intentional torts, and increasingly common in cases of product liability.

### Subrogation

Subrogation, which means succeeding to the rights of another by virtue of paying for his loss, is an important principle in negligence law, although it turns up in all manner of legal situations. It is popularly referred to as "standing in the shoes of another." For example, assume that a plaintiff collected his medical expenses from Blue Cross for treatment of injuries sustained in an ordinary accident case. Blue Cross might, in the event of a judgment or settlement that includes recompense for medical expenses, step in and claim from the wrongdoer the amount of the medical expenses it had already paid to the plaintiff victim.

Workers' compensation agencies commonly seek to recover, through the doctrine of subrogation, payments they have made to accident victims who subsequently benefit from jury verdicts. Since workers' compensation payments typically cover only medical expenses and loss of income, not pain and suffering, well-informed attorneys for plaintiffs try to have verdict or settlement proceeds explicitly allocated to pain and suffering (not to medical expenses or loss of income), so that the proceeds cannot be reached by the workers' compensation insurer through subrogation. The allocation is not material to wrongdoers, for they must pay someone in any event. The significance of the allocation is only to the victim, who nets more money, and the workers' compensation insurer, who might otherwise have subrogation rights in the proceeds. Shrewd lawyers often attempt to persuade insurers with subrogation rights in the proceeds of the case (subrogees) to waive part of their actual rights simply to facilitate an overall case settlement. Subrogees in these cases reason that without the lawyer and a case settlement they would receive nothing at all. In reality, the subrogees are contributing to those settlements.

Subrogation reduces what the plaintiff actually pockets from a suit. Negligence lawyers are customarily given a third of the proceeds of a recovery. Amounts paid to a subrogee should not be considered as recovered or paid to the client for fee purposes. Insist on that. To illustrate, assume a negligence verdict of $9,000, of which $3,000 is for medical expenses. If a health insurer has subrogation rights in the $3,000 (by virtue of having paid that much to the victim at an earlier time), the legal-fee percentage should be measured only on the $6,000 pain-and-suffering component of the verdict, in which no one has subrogation rights. At one-third of $6,000, the lawyer's fee is only $2,000, not one-third of $9,000, or $3,000. Some lawyers, in fact, arrange to collect a fee from the subrogee out of what the subrogee collects. Your lawyer should tell you of any such arrangement. In no event should your lawyer be allowed to collect twice for the same recovery.

Another frequent subrogation occasion arises when a plaintiff in an automobile-accident case sues for both personal injury and car damage, and collects $6,500 for personal injuries and $450 for property damages. Assume that he has collision insurance with a $50 deductible and that his own carrier has already paid $400 to him of the $450 in damages. The insurance company carrying the collision insurance appeared in the case because it is entitled to collect, by subrogation, its $400 share of the property-damage recovery in the lawsuit. The only real interest of the plaintiff in the property damage is the $50 deductible that he paid and is entitled to recover.

# HELPING YOURSELF TO A BETTER NEGLIGENCE AWARD

The negligence case is part of American folklore; it is also, unfortunately, often a money-making enterprise rather than an excursion into justice. Historically, the field has been riddled by scandals of fake injuries, falsified medical reports, switched identities, staged accidents, exaggerated claims, and all manner of perjury. Much of this doubtless still goes on, in varying degrees, as it does in all fields of human endeavor. My effort here is to help you put negligence law on your side by means that are lawful and moral.

## *At the Scene of the Accident*
Your conduct at the scene of an accident is regulated by how badly you are hurt. Obviously, if you are rendered immediately unconscious and wake up in a hospital, you have no chance to observe the postaccident scene. Similarly, if you are in shock, bleeding profusely, in great pain, or trembling with nervous upset, you are unlikely to be able to assemble your wits in your normal manner.

To protect your legal rights, never admit you were wrong and never say you acted improperly at the scene of an accident. Do not apologize for anything. If you feel guilty because you acted badly, were completely in the wrong, and have so much insurance that you feel absolutely compelled to concede wrongdoing, go ahead. Moral choices are uniquely appropriate; but remember, concessions hurt your chances with the law.

The problem with admissions and apologies at the scene of an accident is that you may be making them under the influence of shock or lack of knowledge. You may not have appreciated what really happened. Moreover, what you see as involvement in a trivial automobile accident may later be blown up immorally by the other party into a big case against you. Be quiet until you find out the dimensions of the situation you are in. There is always time later for your apologies.

Do not be stubborn about receiving medical help at the scene of the accident. If there is any doubt, wait for an ambulance. If you were rendered unconscious, even momentarily, go to the hospital. If the impact was severe, or if you have any visible distress, at the least go to your family doctor directly from the scene of the accident. When an automobile accident happens at night, for instance, a whiplash injury to the neck will usually not appear until the next morning, and interim relaxants may help. Besides being good for your health, this advice helps your case, too. Belated discovery of injury or undertaking of medical care militates against your recovery of rightful damages. Get medical advice immediately after any apparent injury in an accident.

If you are sufficiently alert immediately after an automobile accident, exchange driver's license, registration, and license plate information with the other driver. In many states, motor-vehicle accident report forms must be filed promptly after accidents. Note the accident scene carefully; take notes on it if you can. It is very important to take down the names, addresses, and telephone numbers of any witnesses. Some people may volunteer to serve as witnesses; try to strike up a personal relationship with them. Take any card offered you, whether it be from the operator of a tow truck, a doctor, a lawyer, a photographer, or anyone else. Many people materialize quickly when accidents have occurred because they cruise the highways and follow the regular police radio calls that report accidents and their locations. Do not employ, on the spot, anyone from the crowd, but the cards may be helpful later in recalling who was at the postaccident scene.

### Later On

Later on, move quickly to engage a competent negligence trial lawyer, so that he can start the investigation right away, get statements, and marshal facts while everything is fresh and likely to be available. He can consult police records and interview officers while their memories are fresh, and can also be in touch with your doctors for information that they must supply. As indicated earlier, it may be that important legal notices must be given within a very short time. If you were injured in a public bus accident, for example, or through the negligence of some other city or state agency, many statutes require formal notices of claim to be filed within a period as short as one or two months. Parenthetically, in such situations, prompt notice of claim may make the defendant's claims representative more willing to assume the legitimacy of your claim and more inclined to settle it.

Help your lawyer by keeping notes of everything that is relevant, so you can give a full story. Hold nothing back from your lawyer; do not let any awful truths surface for the first time in the open courtroom. Tell your lawyer of any vulnerable spots you may have.

Ask your lawyer's advice on how to proceed when the insurance investigator for the wrongdoer visits you. Do not discuss the accident with any stranger without first clearing it with your lawyer. Do not discuss anything personal or accident-related with purported pollsters or survey gatherers by telephone or personal interview. (This is good advice in general.) Be alert to surveillance by the insurance company. Tell your relatives, friends, and associates that they may be questioned about you, and ask them to let you know if they are approached. Insurance investigators can be devious. They can tell your friends that you are looking for a job and gave them as a reference, or that you are being considered for promotion—intimations that usually bring optimistic responses. They may imply that they are government officials. Keep notes of any such occurrences reported to you.

Follow your doctor's advice. Don't be a hero, or a heroine. Not only is your health at stake, but also your pain-and-suffering award may well be related to the extent of your medical treatment. Similarly, do not be heroic about returning to work too soon, even to light duty. By extending yourself, you may limit your recovery both in health and in damages awarded.

Do not permit the insurance company's doctor to examine you without giving your lawyer the opportunity to be present. Do not volunteer information or exaggerate, but do not minimize any pain you may feel in the sites affected by the accident. Resist the normal temptation to tell this doctor about all your other aches and pains; that doctor is not there to help you, but to bury you.

You might want to return to the scene of the accident soon after the event to refresh your recollection of it. Again, take notes of the locations of the parties and the movements of any vehicles. Fix the occurrence in your mind.

## VALUING YOUR CASE

You must value your case realistically in order to set your goals. If your expectations are exorbitant, you will neither settle your case nor realize your expectations in court. If your sights are too low, you can settle too soon and deprive yourself of what is rightfully yours.

Negligence cases, like most other cases, are better settled than tried to a verdict. For one thing, settlement removes the gambling element—the possibility of losing all. Settlement means certain money in hand, not uncertain money later. Trials are stressful; they take time away from other affairs and are generally to be avoided.

But this choice assumes a settlement that is favorable to you. Rely heavily on your lawyer's advice in a projected settlement. He should be your expert in valuing your case. If you do not trust your lawyer, get another. Listen to, but do not automatically accept, any lawyer's advice. If you want to "go for broke," and you do not require the assurance of a settled sum, by all means go for it. But if gambling is your game, remember that your lawyer is the odds maker, it is you who are throwing the dice, and it is your chips on the table.

Keep in mind that reports of huge verdicts in the newspapers are lightning strokes. All the right symbols must line up on the litigation slot machine—persuasive legal liability, grave injuries, desperate consequences, a sympathetic plaintiff, a generous jury, excellent case presentation, an unsympathetic defendant who has large monetary resources (usually insurance), and good luck. If your case has less than all these, face reality, and carefully weigh the facts at your disposal against the facts of life.

Fractures bring greater compensation than sprains; major fractures are worth more than minor ones; when occupational disability is at issue, a broken finger may bring higher damages than a broken toe; a scar on your face is worse than one on your back; a facial scar is worse to a young girl than to an old man; mental difficulties are hard to prove. This litany could go on endlessly.

Some plaintiffs are personally appealing; you may not be one of those. Widows, children, veterans, and well-spoken professionals tend to attract sympathy; unfortunately, foreigners and members of racial, religious, or ethnic minorities often do not. Some defendants are good targets. These include insurance companies, utilities, transportation companies, and large corporations. Governments are ambiguous. In metropolitan urban areas, juries tend to hit them; in rural areas or smaller cities, jurors think of themselves as the taxpayers who will eventually foot the bill, and they are more protective of the government.

A subtle but real difference lies in the degree of injury. Normally, death brings a lower verdict than does the expectation of a long life of painful total disability. The element of pain and suffering obviously differs.

Insurance is a critical factor. Where defendants are not target defendants, the possibilities for recovery are pragmatically limited. Although insurance coverage is not supposed to be mentioned to juries, most people are aware of automobile insurance and home insurance. They just do not know how much there is. Although occasionally defendant's counsel tries to withhold information about coverage, this information is usually shared by the lawyers somewhere along the line in discussion of a settlement, perhaps even late in the trial, when it is necessary to break a deadlock.

Always, the utter lack of insurance is loudly trumpeted between lawyers. When there are multiple defendants, such as the drivers of both cars in an automobile accident, an injured passenger in one car may have two insurers to draw from. If that passenger is subsequently the subject of malpractice in the hospital to which he was taken, he may have three or more insurers for the damages pool.

A substantial verdict against an uninsured defendant of limited means may not be worth a great deal. You cannot get blood from a stone. Moreover, personal defendants in this position may secrete their assets or file for bankruptcy. They may even flee. Many plaintiffs are reluctant to foreclose on the home of a defendant, especially if the defendant is sympathetic and the result of the accident not horrible. As a practical matter, in common negligence torts, damage is limited to insurance proceeds.

One of the traditional negligence stories concerns a man who fell on the street in front of a small shop several doors away from Highly Famous, a rich department store of national reputation. His lawyer listened carefully to his whole story of injury and pain. When the man finished, the lawyer's first question was, "Why didn't you drag yourself in front of Highly Famous?"

# Chapter **Three**

# *Divorce, Annulment, Separation, and Child Custody*

Home may be where the heart is, but a hotly contested marital litigation is heartless. When the playwright observed that hell has no fury like a woman scorned, he might have added that men do not take to it much either. Because matrimonial disputes are so personal and emotional, and tread on old ties, many people become reluctant in them to act to put the law on their side. But once the marriage is dead, they should not be.

Disputes between a husband and a wife, seeking to change their marital relationship, are known as "matrimonial" cases—"matrimonials" for short. These include actions for divorce, annulment, and separation. Demands for alimony for the spouse, usually the wife, and custody and support for the children of the marriage may accompany any of these actions.

Fortunately, not all matrimonial matters are hotly contested. Indeed, most of them are not contested in court at all; these are known as "uncontested matrimonials." In 1983, in New York, 63,129 matrimonial cases were brought in the Supreme Court, of which 53,119, or eighty-four percent, were uncontested.

Uncontested (also called "undefended") matrimonials are normally granted in court on the initiative of one spouse alone; the other spouse either defaults by failing to appear in court, or acquiesces, either in person or through a lawyer. Disputes over arrangements are resolved in lawyers' offices before the court date. Although uncontested matrimonials are usually granted on an understanding between the parties (although sometimes the defaulting spouse simply disappears), one of them remains the formal petitioner in court. The relief requested is technically granted at the request of that party. Whether contested or uncontested, if proper procedures are followed, there is no difference in legal effect.

## TYPES OF MATRIMONIAL ACTION

When matrimonial cases are contested in court, they become regular pieces of litigation, subject to regular rules, except that they tend to be bitterer than commercial cases. The need for putting the law on your side in a matrimonial action persists just as surely as it would if the suit were for personal injuries, breach of contract, or a criminal prosecution. It is an error to feel that the usual cautions can be relaxed simply because of the family context. The parties may argue about grounds, and they may expose personal and family irritations, but the dominant issue in court is usually money. Even in this enlightened era of sexual equality, the mother is conceded child custody in the great bulk of cases, although issues of visiting and the upbringing of children are plentiful.

### Divorce

A divorce is a dissolution of a marriage. It is the breakup of what is conceded to be a marriage validly contracted.

Divorce is exclusively a state affair; the federal government has no jurisdiction over matrimonial or child-custody cases in any of the fifty states. Since the state laws are diverse, it is the rules for procedure and grounds for action in the petitioning spouse's state of residence that must be consulted for particular application.

The grounds for divorce vary not only from state to state, but also from time to time. The usual grounds are adultery, cruel treatment (which may be physical or mental and which is usually interpreted loosely), refusal or inability to cohabit, desertion, abandonment, nonsupport, insanity, and imprisonment for a stated period. Refusal to have sexual intercourse may be treated in one place as abandonment, in another as 'cruelty. More than half of the states permit some kind of "no-fault" divorce, the grounds for which are usually framed as "irreconcilable differences." Living apart for a year or two under a judicial separation decree or under a valid written separation agreement, with which the party seeking the divorce has substantially complied, may also be sufficient grounds for divorce in some jurisdictions, as in New York, for example.

The petitioning party has the burden of proving the grounds for divorce, which is important only in contested cases. In uncontested matrimonials, the petitioner simply alleges the grounds, and these allegations are sufficient, since no one contests them.

A period of residence in a state is normally required before a party can get a divorce there. Historically, Nevada, with a six-week waiting period (and a virtual automatic dispenser of decrees), used to be the national divorce capital. Indeed, "going to Reno" was, at one time, synonymous with getting a divorce. Today, however, most states have considerably relaxed their residency requirements and the grounds for divorce that they recognize have widely diffused the divorce trade. Waiting periods are typically three months, six months, or a year.

Divorce decrees terminate the marriage, make provisions for alimony and property division, fix child custody and support, and permit the wife to resume her prior name.


### Annulment

An annulment is a marriage made void. In loose terms, the marriage is erased as if it had never taken place, although alimony and child-support obligations may be attached to an annulment decree. There are many special rules to protect the legitimacy of children of annulled marriages and the rights of these children to inherit.

Customary grounds for annulment are failure or inability to consummate a marriage, fraud in inducing the marriage (which may include hidden lack of desire to have children or homosexuality), certain degrees of blood relationship, use of force or threat of harm in inducing consent to marry, bigamy, marriage under the legal age, and lack of mental capacity to understand the marital relationship.

In some states there are limitations to bringing annulment actions beyond specified lengths of time after discovery of the grounds. Procedurally, annulment actions normally follow the rules of divorce actions, except that the burden of proof may be greater, particularly in the need of corroborating evidence beyond that given by the parties themselves.

Corroboration of grounds for annulment tend to the farcical. A favorite ground, particularly in uncontested cases, is fraud in the matter of desiring children. Somehow or other in most annulment proceedings that I heard from the bench of New York divorce courts, the story was this: the couple, before the wedding, sat at dinner with the family of the wife-to-be. The happy husband-to-be (it was usually he) loudly proclaimed his desire for children. But the daughter turned to tears when, at a similar dinner shortly after the wedding, the new husband said he did not want to have children. If you had any doubt, the disappointed wife's mother or father was there in court to tell you the truth—as a corroborating witness.

## Separation

Separation is an in-between status; it is one in which the marriage continues, but the husband and wife live apart, with a consensus on child custody. Separation may be by court decree, the parties may have a formal separation agreement, customarily in writing, or the parties may simply live apart and have a tacit or informal understanding about their relationship.

When a separation decree is sought from a court, the procedures and grounds usually resemble those of divorce in the state involved. Separation agreed to voluntarily by the parties (often by formal written agreement) requires no grounds at all. Separation decrees and agreements typically make provision for alimony and for children.

Formal separations seem to be waning, since once a couple has decided to separate, divorce is usually indicated. Informal separations—simply living apart—offer the best hope of later reconciliation. They are trial periods.

## CUSTODY OF CHILDREN

In families with children under twenty-one (sometimes under eighteen), or with older children who are in college and are economically dependent on a parent, provision must be made for their custody and support whether the parents simply separate or seek divorce or annulment.

While the legal and sociological pundits proclaim that the custodial arrangements must be in the best interests of the child, the child's best interests are rarely the subject of any penetrating investigation. The child has no lawyer, and any disposition that is based on true concern for his best interests, if he is consulted at all, is a matter of his good fortune. At the threshold, fundamental discord between parents is not in the best interests of the child. Children of broken homes are under a handicap. Putting the law on the side of the child is a pious mouthing, since in practice younger children are treated as chattels; they have minimal legal rights of their own and there is little mechanism for enforcing what rights they have.

### *Judicial Discretion in Child Custody*

In the overwhelming number of instances, one parent or the other is awarded custody of the children, and the other receives visiting rights (called "visitation"). A vast range of discretion is exercised here by trial judges. Typically, if the parents can agree on a visitation schedule, the court will go along. Usually this means that the visiting parent will take the child one or two days a week, possibly every two weeks, in addition to either the Christmas or the Easter recess, and for some part of the summer vacation. There are usually provisions for joint consultation on medical treatment and, in wealthier families, for making decisions about camps and private schools. The initial award of visitation rights, but, much more often, its subsequent enforcement, may lead to separate litigation over custody, in which case the court is obliged to review its original custody and visitation orders for renewal or revision.

Whether the parties agree on custody and visitation or force the judge to resolve matters, the issues become more troublesome if one or both of the parents become obstructive. Around Christmastime and before the summer vacation period begins, floods of visitation and custody issues come to court by way of *habeas corpus* writs or whatever process may be appropriate in the jurisdiction. Even during an ordinary week, court business on custodial issues is never less than brisk.

The cardinal rule is that if a judge is not satisfied with the conduct of the custodial parent or the visiting parent, he can change his prior order or that of another judge of equal rank and can even override an earlier agreement between the parents themselves. He can change custody. The law does not afford absolute custody or visitation rights to any parent, and the discretion allowed the judge is greater than all the lawbooks could possibly articulate.

Dreadful custodial sequences involve the withholding of visitation rights because one parent, usually the father, is in presumed default on child-support payments, or, on the other hand, is withholding child-support payments because the other parent, usually the mother, is in default in permitting visitation. These replays of the old wars are common in courthouses.

The effects on the children of matrimonial bitterness are monstrous. "He will not pay for your new dress, but his new wife's daughter gets everything she wants"; "she spends the money I give her for you on herself"—these words, and many like them, are sprinkled liberally over the matrimonial records in courthouses across the country. While it is easy to criticize either of these offensives, it must be borne in mind that withholding the children or the money is a quick and logical defensive reaction. Initiating court proceedings is long and costly. While withholding tactics may force the other side to a court initiative, judges recognize this and often assess legal expenses in such a way as to punish the apparent offender. Willingness to use children as pawns is a factor many judges take into account in changing custody decisions.

Judges vary in exercising their discretion as to whether a child should testify on the witness stand in a matrimonial dispute. The rule of thumb for hearing young witnesses is their ability to understand and relate. Generally speaking, the permissible testimonial age for custodial purposes is about eight or nine years.

Many judges will take children into their chambers for interviews, either alone or, preferably, with a member of the court staff present, and sometimes with the opposing lawyers. If a child is younger than six or seven, most judges will not speak with him even in chambers, concluding that he is too young for useful discourse. Some judges will speak—in varying degrees of sensitivity, to be sure—to younger children if they seem to be unusually mature, as I did, or perhaps out of an intuitive judicial sense.

Judges will generally consult a child as to parental preference if that child is more than twelve years old. When an older child is involved, judges give weight, according to age and apparent understanding, to the preferences of the child, particularly when he prefers the parent of the same sex. It is an unusual judge who will not award a child of more than twelve to the custody of a willing and able parent of the child's determined choice.

## Judicial Preference for Mother

Modern law states that the claims of the parents to custody are equal. To the despair of many fathers, however, mothers benefit in practice from the strong preference of judges for awarding custody to them, particularly when the children are young. Through customary judicial rationalizations, the prospect of custody by the mother emerges under the banner of "the best interests of the child."

In times gone by, denial of custody to the mother was rare unless indiscreet adultery or demonstrable parental unfitness was shown. Notwithstanding sociological changes, the mother is still heavily the preferential choice of judges. With the increasing number of workingwomen, including those whose vocational training and work time is at least equal to that of their husbands, fathers seeking custody are becoming somewhat more successful in their efforts. Part of that progress, however, is the result of greater willingness on the part of mothers to give up custody of their children in favor of more interesting careers and less restrictive life styles.

Adultery by a mother is no longer the potent custody disqualifier it once was, although decisions here vary greatly with judicial attitude, the circumstances of the adultery, and the demonstrable maternal qualities of the mother seeking custody.

In one matrimonial case over which I presided, custody of a nine-year-old boy was the only real issue. The mother conceded that she and the boy lived in a small apartment with a male co-worker of hers. The father, now residing with his parents, sought a divorce on the grounds of adultery; the mother neither contested it nor sought alimony (to which she was not entitled anyway because of the conceded adultery), but she did ask for custody of the child and payments for his support. The husband vigorously contested her custody claim. The mother appeared to be an excellent caring parent, and the bond of devotion between mother and son was most apparent. From the testimony it appeared that the lover was a reasonable adult, and he and the boy got along well. The father's lawyer was plainly incensed at the situation. He produced as an expert witness a psychiatrist to testify on the father's behalf. But he started off on the wrong foot when, after describing the facts, he said to his own witness, "Now I ask you, Doctor, is this right?" The psychiatrist frowned and asked, "Right?" Exasperated, the lawyer urged, "I mean, is this normal?" Replied the witness, "Well, it depends on what you mean by 'normal'!" Before the lawyer could untangle himself, he had caused his own expert witness to establish that the boy needed a male role model (and he felt the lover was a suitable one) and that the boy's interests would be better served if he lived with the mother and her lover than if he lived with the mother alone. Custody of the boy and modest child support were awarded to the mother. Visitation rights in that case, often sticky in live-in-lover cases, were resolved by having the mother deliver the boy to the father at places other than the boy's residence.

## Custodial Gains for Father

The father who seeks custody of his child, over the objection of the mother, must understand that his is a hard road. The citation by the father of his frustration with "women's lib," and its resemblance to a one-way street in his case, is of small legal avail.

However, there is some willingness on the part of more and more judges to grant paternal custody. It is not a general trend; so do not count on it. A father's chances of being awarded custody are better if the child is male. The father must feel very strongly about custody and must have good economic prospects, flexible work time, and the willingness to subordinate his personal activities to those of his child.

A father may have a better chance of switching custody away from the mother than of gaining it in the first place. This may be because the mother, now having had a clear chance at custody, presumably unharried by matrimonial discord, has a recent record of separate custody that can be examined. The court has a starting point with her, and this subtly becomes her second time under attack. If the mother's conduct toward the child is open to criticism, and she has been unsuccessful in coping with her own problems, the court will give greater credence to a father who gives evidence of good parental prospects himself.

## Joint Custody

Joint custodial arrangements are gaining some popularity, although whether they are really in the best interests of the child remains uncertain. Strictly interpreted, this means that both parents have custody, so custodial time is divided and decisions are made jointly. It works best for infants, who can be given half the time to the mother and the other half to the father. As the child gets older and wants to be with his friends and to be involved in continuous activities in his local school, clubs, or neighborhood, cracks begin to appear in the joint arrangement. Some parents approach this problem with surprising ingenuity. I recall one case in which the child stayed put in the family home and the parents took turns in residence. A more usual joint arrangement is for the parent leaving the hearth to take up residence nearby, thus allowing the child to function within a continuous cycle of school, friends, clubs, and religious affiliations.

The prime difficulty with joint arrangements, apart from the willingness of the parents to arrange their lives around their children's living requirements and apart from their willingness to get along with each other, is in the quality of the child's upbringing. The division between what is essentially two households tends to confuse a child, deprives him of family stability (although he does keep both his natural parents), and weakens the sense of family and disciplined continuity that seems essential to successful child rearing. Experience with joint custodial arrangements, where the child's physical custody is significantly divided, is still limited, so generalizations tend to be subjective. The arrangement itself is relatively rare, for it is not easy, and it takes two exceptional parents to make it work. Such exceptional parents usually stay married.

## Manipulative Children

A fact of child-custody disputes generally is the extent to which children can manipulate their separated parents. Too many parents continue their matrimonial war into their relations with their children, and the children sense this. The parent who has custody is the disciplinary parent, who brings up the child, makes him eat properly, go to bed early, attend to his studies, and behave properly. This is the parent who may even spank the child now and then. The weekend parent, on the other hand, is "Good-Time Charley." The child is forever going to the movies, ball games, and fast-food restaurants, and stays in front of the television set until the wee weekend hours. The child returned to the disciplinary parent on Sunday in time for an evening bellyache is familiar on the divorce scene. It is small wonder that many children favor the weekend parent of the good times.

While some weekend parents seek to seize on the child's apparent preference for them, judges are alert to this, and slow in switching custody. Judges tend to look more to the total objective circumstances of the custodial home. It is harder to fool a matrimonial judge than is widely believed. Judges see and hear a great deal, since matrimonial-related business is booming in court.

## MONEY AS THE ROOT

Matrimonial disputes are almost invariably about money. While genuine issues of child custody sometimes arise, the father, in the typical instance, is more often playing on the mother's fears of losing her children, hoping to make her submissive to easier financial terms in the bargaining. Even if one party, usually the husband, resists the divorce and argues that he wishes to maintain the marriage intact, he may be secretly creating a bargaining chip for financial relief.

## Alimony and Child Support

Two types of payment, alimony and child support, are traditionally associated with matrimonial cases. They may be decreed by a court or they may be determined by a separation agreement (sometimes called a "marital agreement").

Alimony (also called "maintenance") is payment for support of a spouse, almost always the wife. Interestingly enough, less than fifteen percent of divorced women are actually receiving alimony payments. The emergence of women as money earners outside the home has had its effect in reducing alimony awards and, to a lesser extent, child support.

Technically, alimony may be of two types. The first, temporary alimony (alimony *pendente lite*), is often awarded by a court on the wife's motion at the very beginning of a matrimonial action so that she may have support while the case proceeds. Temporary alimony is tentative, and is estimated by the judge from comparative financial statements of the parties, which court rules require. Tax returns are useful devices to screen income and expenses. Often, the husband (the one with most of the family means) will be required, under a temporary alimony order, to pay an advance against the wife's legal fees. Where the matrimonial situation is acrimonious and there are small children involved, courts will also usually order the husband to move out of the family home.

The second type of alimony—the one more popularly known—is that fixed by final court order. Alimony computations vary so widely that generalization about them is difficult. Courts take into account years of marriage, number and ages of children, standards of living, relative means and earning abilities of the spouses, their ages, and the state of their health. In most states, a wealthy wife, at fault in the marital proceedings, may conceivably be required to support her poor husband, particularly if he is disabled by age or physical infirmity or if the disparities in their economic means are great. It is unconstitutional for a state to deny alimony to a man. All this having been said, however, alimony payments to men are rare.

The measure most often used for the aggregate alimony and child support in most metropolitan areas, under ordinary circumstances, is about thirty-three and one-third percent of the husband's income before taxes; in other places, from twenty-five to forty percent of net income. Child-support payments are stated separately from alimony, but are usually calculated informally within the percentage measure. Child support is always stated in terms of specific weekly or monthly support sums, and usually continues until the child is of age or until his schooling has been completed. If a wife is awarded possession of the marital home, it is generally expected that the taxes, mortgage, and maintenance expense will be included in the percentage measure. Extra provisions for medical, dental, and educational expenses of the child are customary.

Alimony and child-support payments are treated differently for legal and for tax purposes, so it is important to state them separately. Alimony fixed by a court ceases at the death of the husband or the wife, or on the wife's remarriage, although by marital agreement payment of alimony may be continued after the wife's remarriage or may continue as an obligation of the husband's estate after his death. Alimony that is to be paid for at least ten years is usually tax deductible by the husband and is treated as taxable income of the wife.

Sometimes, however, a wife may desire her alimony to be paid in one lump sum, rather than in periodic installments. It is usual then to provide that the husband get the divorce, based on the wife's fault. This procedure serves as a precautionary measure for the husband, since the wife cannot then come back and claim further support payments under a decree granted because of her fault.


## *Financial Terms in Marital Agreements*

A specific strategy in matrimonial litigation is to negotiate before divorce, legal separation, or annulment, a marital agreement in which all the economic, custodial, and inheritance incidents of the marital parting are spelled out. Such agreements are sometimes so detailed as to provide for the division of libraries book by book or of china and tableware piece by piece. Quite often, items of family gift or inheritance are sorted out. Each party keeps his or her own personal effects. But whose hi-fi set is it, anyway?

It is customary for courts to incorporate in their official decrees the marital agreement of the parties, thus giving that agreement the extra force of a court judgment. Technically, if the court makes the parties' agreement part of its decree, and fails to specify that the marital agreement continues to have separate validity, that agreement loses its separate identity as an enforceable contract, and its terms exist only as a part of the decree. Thereafter, the terms can be changed by the court. If the agreement and the court decree expressly provide that the agreement should survive the decree, however, the agreement remains an enforceable contract between the parties and may be continuously enforced by either of them, but, more important, can be amended only by both of them. In other words, the judge can change alimony provided by court decree, but he may not change the alimony provided in an enforceable surviving marital agreement.

Marital agreements cover not only alimony and child-support expenses, but also possession and maintenance of the family home, deprival of inheritance on death, and sometimes they provide for life-insurance or health-insurance payments. Life insurance is a good feature for a wife to negotiate, since alimony ceases on the husband's death in the absence of agreement to the contrary. The general rule is still that the husband is to pay the legal fees of the wife's lawyer, although if the wife has adequate means this may be relieved.

The "extras" that the parties can stipulate between themselves are marked benefits of voluntary agreements. These accomplish things that courts will not do, such as providing the life insurance or pegging alimony payments in the future to a percentage of the husband's later income.

Always seek to have a favorable marital or separation agreement survive any court decree.

## Equitable Distribution, Community Property, Dower and Curtesy

Alimony as a historic concept has been unsatisfactory for women. Traditionally, alimony is a replacement of income and is geared to how much the husband can afford to pay from his income. There was no right in the wife to have any capital at all. This was a throwback to the romantic common-law notion that the husband and wife were one, and the husband was the one.

As a matter of practice, many husbands have settled capital or property on their wives as part of a divorce arrangement. This is based in part on a sense of fairness and in part to induce agreement to the divorce. Very often the marital home has been given to the wife, even though it was in the husband's name and she could not have gotten full title to it in court.

This unfairness of economic division is partially redressed in sixteen states by rights of one spouse in real estate of the other. The wife's rights are called "dower," the husband's "curtesy." In those places where these rights in real estate still exist, they cannot be cut off without consent.

In the community property states—Arizona, California, Nevada, New Mexico, and Texas (which follow the Spanish tradition), Louisiana (which follows the French tradition), and Idaho and Washington—earnings and capital accumulated during marriage become part of a communal pool in which both spouses share equally as a matter of right.

If there are no provisions for community property or no dower or curtesy rights in real estate, each spouse usually keeps what is in his or her own name upon divorce or annulment. Alimony continues to be only a form of income that continues after a marital breakup, and in theory is reckoned without capital being taken into account. The inequity, after a long marriage, of depriving a homemaking wife of a share of the family capital, which is usually in the husband's name, has led in New York to the breakthrough doctrine of "equitable distribution," by which a judge is empowered to divide the capital acquired during marriage between husband and wife. Experience has not yet established legal patterns for how these distributions are to be made, although spouses of long duration tend to have greater rights, and the greater the family pie, the greater the slices. To eliminate court risks in determining "equitable distribution" of property, marital agreements are marked by increased attention to property division. Plainly, wandering away after pretty young things has become much riskier in New York. Equitable distribution has also spurred premarital agreements, which are legally enforceable, spelling out the mutual rights in event of divorce.

## Palimony

Notwithstanding the boisterous publicity given to movie stars, palimony is not alimony. If a couple live together without being married to one another, one member may be able to collect some money from the other upon the dissolution of their relationship, but only on the basis of an express or implied contract. One must have promised something, and the other must prove it. This is a tough row to hoe. If you seek economic reward from a live-in relationship, see your lawyer and get your promises in writing; better still, arrange a present transfer of assets, outright or in trust.

## MATRIMONIAL LEGAL TACTICS

### Get the Right Kind of Lawyer

Matrimonial law is largely a matter of tactics, most important of which is to engage a strong lawyer early. Practical experience is especially important in matrimonial work, because of its relatively small technical legal component and its many strategic nuances.

The mutual friendship of a lawyer with both parties can sometimes provide a bridge for reconciliation or settlement, but more often, once the couple has locked horns, the personal stresses of matrimonial litigation seem to call for a professional warrior on each side, unencumbered by the emotional baggage of friendship.

Lawyers are taught, and tend to repeat by rote, that their first obligation in a matrimonial case is to attempt to reconcile the parties. This, of course, is almost universally a lost cause for lawyers who are essentially strangers to the couple, and who in any event are untrained in marital counseling and are constrained by tactical considerations to avoid giving ground too early and too easily. Most lawyers do not have their hearts in the attempt, and few actually give it any real concern. Do not count on a lawyer to save your marriage.

The hard-nosed lawyer, savvy and quick, whether he is quiet or flamboyant, is the advocate to have. Beware of bombast and abrasiveness—they are not synonymous with toughness. But do not look for someone who will minimize the unpleasantness; in the words of a professional baseball manager some years ago, "Nice guys finish last." Divorce is inherently unpleasant. Look for the tough lawyer who can settle your case satisfactorily and will fight if necessary. Settling the dispute out of the court is by far the best disposition.

An increasingly favored tactic for a husband, particularly in a case involving children, is to hire a woman lawyer. There is then no longer a solid male phalanx against the wife, and a feminine point of view creeps subtly into the husband's appeals through his lawyer.

### Evidence

Evidence and preparation are the keys to financial success in court. If a marital case is contested, proof must be shown, as in all other litigation. Bills and receipts should be saved to document expenses and support. Letters and notes may be useful in showing grounds for divorce and may indicate poor character. Many an errant husband has been stabbed by his Diners Club card or hit on the head with his business diary.

Tape recordings abound in matrimonials because of the ease of planting the recorders. I recall one case over which I presided as trial judge that involved a wealthy young couple; the wife's domestic servant was really her private detective, and the husband's "old friend" who stayed with them for a month was his private detective. Quite a household, with his and her detectives! The husband called as a witness the plumber who had supposedly observed scenes of unmotherly conduct toward the son. When that same plumber (who was our family's plumber, as well) later came to my home to fix my shower, he told me I had blown the case by awarding custody of the boy to his mother.

Handwritten diaries are useful matrimonial trial devices, both to aid memory and to provide contemporaneous notes to help guard against impeachment on cross-examination. It is not a nice thing to do under normal circumstances, but useful evidence is often turned up by going through the effects of the other spouse when he or she is away.

Many parents try to use their children as witnesses against each other. This practice backfires more often than it works, since children are privy to more of what goes on than their parents realize. They can tell a lot about both sides. Just because their heads are not at adult eye level does not mean they cannot hear and understand. Most parental invocation of the testimony of their children, particularly young ones, in the horribly conflicting circumstance of parent versus parent is despicable, and some judges take it as an index in itself of parental unfitness.

Mutual friends seem to be good witnesses, for they often know what went on, but often they do not like to become involved. Indeed, many friendships have foundered over testimony given or refused in matrimonial cases. Be wary of relying on the testimony of mutual friends; they are often not forthcoming when they are needed to testify.

Avoid the temptation to discuss your case with your friends. Many people take a colossal morbid interest in other people's marital problems. You will become hopelessly confused by all sorts of well-meant and poor advice, you will lose faith in your own tactics, and, most important, you will paint yourself into an emotional corner from which you will have trouble escaping when it comes time to compromise. Losing face before your friends then becomes a real but totally unnecessary factor in your decisions.

### Stay in the House

When living together becomes intolerable, one spouse or the other may leave the home or the apartment. In matrimonial battle it is important legally not to leave the residence in the absence of a written agreement or court order and not to lock out a spouse who has left. Unilateral leaving or locking out may become proof of abandonment or disregard of marital obligation. This is applicable in all matrimonial contests—divorce, separation, and annulment.

### Resist Provocation

Husbands particularly, but wives also, should take specific care to avoid being provoked by the other. Many a kitchen knife raised in anger has cut its wielder in court.

Striking a wife goes down poorly in court. Once more, remember that judges are people. If you are seen by them as a bad person, you tend to be treated badly. Although assault has nothing legally to do with the determination of alimony, a brutal husband may just be hit by the judge in the alimony department.

### Spending during Litigation

It is a good idea for both the poor-mouthing and the expense-ridden spouses to avoid extravagant spending during matrimonial litigation. In many instances, parties suppress their true income levels to mislead alimony expectations.

### Delinquency in Payment

A prime tactic for the wife, when the husband is consistently delinquent in alimony or child-support payments, is to apply to have the payments made directly to the court.

In most states there are provisions for sending alimony and support checks to the court, which forwards them to the party entitled to them. Among other things, this procedure puts an end to the interminable disputes over whether and when checks were sent and received. Matrimonial disputants are often great liars on this subject.

### Remarriage—or Maybe Not

Alimony must generally be paid until a wife remarries. Unless the marital agreement provides that alimony continue past remarriage, it is cut off. In today's moral climate, remarriage is not the imperative it once was. Many women live with men but do not marry them for fear of losing their alimony from their former husbands. (The same thing goes on in the Sun Belt, where many elderly people live together without marriage for fear of compromising their separate Social Security benefits.) Unlicensed cohabitation becomes particularly irritating when the lover lives in the old matrimonial house with the children, and the divorced husband is paying both alimony and child support and, by inference, the rent of his replacement in the bedroom.

State laws vary, but in New York, for instance, the wife's alimony is safe so long as she and her lover do not represent themselves as husband and wife. Signing hotel registers as married couples or making purchases and receiving mail as Mr. and Mrs. are taken as representing oneself as married. One man was so pleased when his former wife remarried that he sent the loving couple a handsome color television set as a wedding present. In other instances, husbands have offered cash sums to induce their wives to remarry and cut off the alimony.

Technically, the same rules apply to husbands receiving alimony, but they are rare birds indeed.

### Get Thee to the Bank on Time

If the parties are civil to each other and will keep their assets intact, there is no need to safeguard them. But with matrimonial lawyers on the scene, this much civility is frequently too much to expect. Once a lawyer has entered the proceedings, one party or the other will probably go to the bank, withdraw joint funds entirely, and deposit them, in his or her own separate name, somewhere else. Similarly,

safe-deposit boxes will be emptied and their contents placed elsewhere.

There may be cash in that safe-deposit box that no one will admit
to owning, for it may be proceeds of some illegal enterprise, including tax cheating. If that happens, the one holding the cash is likely
going to keep it without any accounting. Remember the saying that
possession is nine points of the law. Careful records should be kept
of what is removed from the box, possibly with witnesses present,
minimizing later accusations, against the party who removed them,
of holding out.

Unfortunately, it is often necessary for the more impecunious spouse,
usually the wife, to reach for family bank accounts if she is to support herself and her children while the divorce is being sorted out.
Husbands are great for putting on the economic pressure in the divorce mill.

The tactics of lawyers vary greatly in this matter. The so-called
bombers go for everything as soon and as hard as possible. Other
lawyers stress maintaining whatever vestiges of civility can be mus-
tered and advise simply taking half the assets. Individual situations
vary, but experience tends to favor more aggression, rather than less,
as the preferred legal tactic.

During this period of economic realignment, the parties should be
mindful of necessary changes in wills, insurance policies, bank signatures, and all manner of charging privileges.


## The "Right" Judge

More than in any other field of law, the subjectivity of the judge comes
to the fore in divorce proceedings. The happily married judge may be
affronted by the wife beater or child beater to a greater degree than
the judge with a troubled family life of his own. The stresses of a
judge's own family life affect his analysis of what he hears.

Some judges who earn $50,000 a year bridle at the thought of
awarding a wife $75,000 a year. Some judges are more adept at
piercing complex financial affairs than others. Obviously, the judge's
view of the proper roles of men and women in society is generally
significant. And there are judges who oppose divorce as a matter of
conscience.

Local lawyers know their judges. In this most personal of legal trials, lawyers try hard in the frowned-upon, but flourishing, practice of forum shopping—maneuvering their cases toward or away from certain judges whose tendencies are known to them.

## CIVILIZATION?

It is a mistake in a matrimonial contest to think of the parties as the charming civilized couple they once were. Now they are enemies, and one usually wants to hurt the other. The couples themselves must change their thinking. For wives, particularly, docile acceptance means disaster. And husbands ridden by guilt at leaving wives of long standing should not be careless. Offering too much too early is very costly in marital combat, which may go on for months or even years. When the economic pendulum swings and the husband's resources dwindle, he is unlikely to find an understanding ex-wife willing to accept reduced alimony. Among life's ironies, it is the decent wife and the decent husband, initially inclined to largesse, who are hurt in the long run by economic rolls and reverses.

People put a lot of stock in friendly, or at least civilized, divorces. Many do preserve a veneer of civility, if only for the sake of the children. In nine years in the courthouse, however, I never saw a truly civilized divorce trial; they may be there, but they do not stand out on the contested calendars. Doubtless there are less hostile affairs on the uncontested calendars, which include the agreed-upon cases. That is cut-and-dried judicial enterprise, in which decrees are awarded in bulk, impersonally. But once a fight spills out onto the floor of the courtroom, civility blows away. The "civilized" people settle out of court more readily; the courthouse is at the edge of the jungle.

The rules of the settlement game, described later, apply fully to matrimonial litigation. The parties must remember that their arrangements may be for a long time; to accept too little or give too much may be to make oneself an unwilling hostage to fortune later. Times and fortunes change, and allowance for change must be made. Matrimonial settlements require hardheaded judgments, as do the business transactions they are not.

## DO-IT-YOURSELF DIVORCE

Do-it-yourself kits have proliferated in the divorce field. Part of the reason lies in the avalanche of divorce actions, but part also in the great legal expense of sometimes minor formalities.

There is no harm in using these kits without the aid of lawyers if only a divorce is sought, the other spouse does not oppose it, there are no children, there is no property to divide, *and* there is to be no written agreement. If you want nothing, expect nothing, have nothing to lose, and, especially, have been married a short time, these lawyerless proceedings, with the help of court personnel, are not harmful. They get the job done.

## ANTENUPTIAL AGREEMENTS

Antenuptial agreements are agreements entered into before marriage, usually for the purpose of providing limited inheritance rights for one spouse if the other dies first. In some states, the parties can by contract also fix alimony payments in advance in the event of divorce. In modern marriages, even the sharing of anticipated living expenses may be established in advance by contract.

Antenuptial agreements are common in second marriages, when either or both spouses may have significant means. Adult children are often hostile or suspicious of late-in-life remarriage of their parents. They see "gold diggers" and "fortune hunters" very quickly. The desire to protect the children of prior marriages, as well as to keep assets in family succession, underlies most antenuptial agreements.

The key to the enforceability of all these agreements is full and fair disclosure of economic worth by both parties and the making of provisions that are reasonable under the circumstances.

Negotiation of these agreements is delicate in the extreme. Negotiate them with care—they are matrimonial dynamite. Many marriages have failed to come about in the wake of the revelations and distrust that come to the surface in formation of these arrangements. They emphasize separateness and militate against the harmony of a shared life. Greed, stinginess, and the desire to dominate may manifest themselves too plainly to be ignored. Many lawyers, negotiating at the insistence of their clients, bear the scars of prematrimonial dispute and come to be regarded with suspicion by the blissful couple, who later arrive at the conclusion that lawyers are an awful nuisance.

# Chapter *Four*

# *Afoul of the Criminal Law*

In criminal arrest and prosecution, there are no smashing victories; the best you can do is break even, get away, be free from jail. Running afoul of the criminal law is nothing but trouble.

Plainly the stakes are high in criminal arrest, trial, and punishment, so the knowledge of your rights and how to conduct yourself is supremely important. There is much ground for maneuver and much to be done to see that your rights are protected—that the law is on your side, and stays there.

## LAW AND PRACTICALITY

### Criminal Law

Crimes are serious acts, such as stealing, hurting people, damaging their property, and other doings harmful to society as well as to individual victims. Unlike torts, which are limited to private harm, crimes are public wrongs, although both the tort and the crime may involve essentially the same conduct. For instance, attacking someone with a club may be a tort, for which the wrongdoer may have to pay personal-injury damages to the victim, and also may be a crime, for which the wrongdoer can go to jail.

The United States Constitution remains the ultimate compass in the navigation of criminal-law enforcement. Criminal statutes must not be vague, and guilt must be established beyond a reasonable doubt. The accused criminal is presumed innocent until proven guilty.

People are entitled to due process of law and equal protection of the laws under the Constitution. They also have constitutional rights to bail and to freedom of speech and assembly. They cannot be compelled to incriminate themselves.

By constitutional design, the obligation of the government—federal, state, and local—as prosecutor, to honor these rights makes it harder to convict people. Although many people associate constitutional rights with softness on crime, the Constitution remains the law of the land.


## Practicality

If you are accused of criminal misconduct, you also face practical factors that sometimes work to your disadvantage but more often work to your advantage. The sheer bulk of crime in present-day society and the overall failure of the mechanisms of criminal justice to keep pace hamper the enforcement of criminal law. Much that is done with criminal intent remains undetected or unresolved. Most of those arrested by state authorities avoid prosecution. Many who are prosecuted are not convicted. In the chaos of criminal justice in large urban areas, there is, inevitably, constitutionally imperfect work by police and prosecutors, and inability of prosecutors to prove to judges and juries guilt beyond reasonable doubt. This is all sad social commentary, but the points mentioned are the facts of life in criminal prosecution.

The prosecution is often hard-pressed to prove the criminal case it brings. Hampering factors include limited facilities, constitutional limitations on search and seizure of evidence, obtaining of confessions, and identifying suspects. These tend to reduce the number of trials carried through to conviction. Therefore, the temptation for prosecutors to drop or reduce charges runs high, and criminal lawyers, knowing this well, take full advantage of it. They try to persuade prosecutors to drop charges, to reduce the severity of the charges, or to plea-bargain. Accordingly, criminal justice absolutely mandates the use of an experienced criminal lawyer, one who not only knows the legal rules well, but also is pragmatic enough to turn the system to his client's benefit.

Federal prosecuting policy differs from that of the states in criminal-law enforcement. When a federal arrest is made, prosecution almost always follows, unless the charge or the punishment is reduced by plea bargaining. Federal crimes are not normally street crimes, and they represent only a small fraction of the total prosecutions in the country. They are often white-collar crime or serious drug-abuse cases, preparation of which is intensive. In 1983, there were less than 40,000 major crime arrests by federal authorities, while there were 2,400,000 state arrests for major crimes. To lend some further perspective, there were 9,300,000 state arrests for lesser crimes, of which 2,000,000 alone were for driving while impaired by alcohol or drugs.

## LEVELS OF CRIME

The federal, state, and local governments all have criminal jurisdiction, but there are differences in criminal procedure and even in the definitions of criminal behavior among the jurisdictions.

### Felonies, Misdemeanors, and Violations

States classify criminal misconduct in three levels: felonies, misdemeanors, and violations (also called "offenses"). The vocabulary may vary from place to place. Only felonies and misdemeanors are crimes, creating criminal records. Violations, or offenses, are lesser kinds of misconduct and do not create a criminal record. The federal government calls its third and most minor criminal category "petty offenses." In contrast to the practice of the states, acts at this level are, under federal law, crimes for the record.

Felonies are the most serious crimes and are usually punishable by more than a year's imprisonment. Murder, manslaughter, kidnapping, robbery, burglary, larceny, rape, arson, and heavy drug trafficking are the most common state felonies. Misdemeanors are less serious, sometimes lesser versions of, felonious acts. They include petty thievery, usually money or property valued at less than $1,000; minor assault; and often varieties of what is known as "victimless crime," such as gambling and prostitution. They also include lesser drug-related misconduct, including possession of illegal drugs. Such crimes as mail fraud and transporting stolen property across state lines are usually classified as federal felonies, even though some states may classify that same physical activity as misdemeanors.

Crimes punishable by more than six months' imprisonment carry the right to trial by jury. Violations, such as traffic infractions, loitering, intoxication, marching without a parade permit, and departures from building codes, are transgressions that carry the lightest punishments; they usually involve only fines.

### Accessories

Criminal liability attaches not only to those who physically commit crimes but also to those who assist them in doing it. These helpers are known in criminal law as "accessories" or "accomplices." An "accessory before the fact" is one who cooperates in the planning and preparation of the crime; "accessories after the fact" are those who help criminals escape or cover up their crimes. All are subject to punishment. Even if the principal criminal is a relative or a friend, an accomplice or an accessory becomes a criminal under the law. While a spouse or a parent who facilitates an escape might be forgiven, mercy is a social bonus, not something to be counted on.

In many statutes, accomplice status and accessory status are merged under the general heading "conspiracy," which is an agreement or common purpose among persons to commit a crime that precedes an overt act by one of the conspirators in furtherance of the crime. Depending on local law, all the conspirators may be equally guilty of the crime that is committed, regardless of the extent to which they actually participate in it.

## ACTS THAT ARE CRIMES

Most people are familiar with the commonly known crimes. They may not understand, however, that each general crime is graded according to its severity, and the strictness of punishment follows that grading. Felonies are usually graded by degree, such as murder in the first degree. Misdemeanors may be graded by letters, such as a Class B misdemeanor.

Crimes are usually divided into categories: those against persons physically and those against their property. There are also crimes directly challenging the governing order. The principal crimes which follow are by no means an exhaustive list:

## Crimes against Persons
Diverse killings, the homicides of murder and manslaughter, and offensive touchings of the body.

### Murder in the First Degree
Premeditated, malicious killing—the ultimate crime against a person.

### Murder in the Lesser Degree
In the second or third degree, or more—generally characterized by lack of premeditation.

### Felony Murder
Murder committed in the course of committing another felony, such as burglary.

### Manslaughter
Killing without the malice of murder. Voluntary manslaughter is a calculated killing in response to a provocation. Involuntary manslaughter is where the action was calculated but death was not anticipated as a consequence. Negligent operation of a car or machinery, for instance, may also constitute some degree of manslaughter.

### Assault and Battery
Physical attack.

### Mayhem
Maiming or disfiguring someone.

### Kidnapping
Abducting and holding a person against his will.

### Carrying Concealed Weapons
Such as guns or knives.

### Bigamy
Marriage to more than one spouse at a time.

### Rape
Forcible intercourse, either actual or presumed, according to the age of the victim.

### Sodomy
Various "unnatural" sex acts, usually those committed against a person's will.

### Incest
Sexual relations with close relatives.


## Crimes against Property
Takings and destructions of property.

### Burglary
Breaking into a building or an enclosure (such as a truck) to steal.

### Arson
Setting a fire.

### Larceny
Stealing personal property. There are many degrees and kinds of larceny. Grand larceny is theft of things the value of which is greater than a minimum, perhaps $1,000, established by each state. It is usually a felony. Petty, or petit, larceny is theft of things of lesser value and is usually a misdemeanor.

### Swindling
Taking property by trickery or fraud.

### Robbery
Stealing by force.

### Embezzlement
Stealing money or property initially coming into your hands legally.

*Forced Entry*
Breaking into a home or office or private place.

*Vandalism*
Malicious destruction of property of another.

*Forgery*
Falsely signing or altering a check or one, or more, of a whole range of documents.

*Extortion and Blackmail*
Obtaining money through threats.

## Crimes against the Governing Order

Other crimes have elements of direct offense against society or authority, which I call the "governing order." The failure to observe countless regulatory provisions of government at all levels finds its way into the criminal courts regularly.

*Treason*
Selling military secrets, spying, or giving comfort to the enemy (such as harboring a treasonous person).

*Sedition*
Working to overthrow the government.

*Contempt*
Refusing to obey a valid court, legislative, or administrative order.

*Perjury*
Lying under oath.

*Bribery*
Giving money or property to influence public officials.

*Corruption*
Exercising undue influence over public officials or doing official favors for private gain.

*Vagrancy*
Disreputable conduct by someone without visible means of support.

*Obstruction of Justice*
Hindering arrests or prosecution.

*Disturbing the Peace or Riot*
Boisterous, violent, or destructive public conduct.

*Counterfeiting*
Manufacturing currency without authority.

# Double Jeopardy

Double jeopardy is a constitutional rule that bars prosecution of a crime
for which a defendant has already been tried. The prosecution does
not get two bites at the apple; you cannot be tried twice for the same
crime. Because of the concurrent jurisdiction of state and federal governments, however, it is permissible to be tried in both jurisdictions
for essentially the same act. A state court might acquit you of larceny
charges, for example, but the federal authorities can convict you on
charges of mail fraud for essentially the same stock-swindling conduct.

# DEFENSES

When charged with a crime, you may simply plead guilty, thus admitting that you did the charged act, and punishment will be fixed by
a judge. If, however, you wish to contest the accusation, you plead
"not guilty" and rely upon any defenses that may be available to you.

# Failure of Proof of Guilt

The classic defense to criminal accusation is the inability of the prosecution to prove guilt. It is critical to understand that the burden of
proof is on the prosecution. The accused may remain silent. The
prosecution may fail, all by itself, to prove a case, as an affirmative

matter. Or the accused may help establish his innocence by means of an "alibi"—by proving, for instance, that he was somewhere else at the time the crime was committed.

### Self-Defense

Self-defense is a classic defense to charges of murder, manslaughter, or assault. This sometimes raises the question of whether your resisting force was excessive.

### Mistake

Proof that an action was done by mistake negates the element of criminal intent that underlies many crimes, particularly the taking of other people's property. If you pick up and take away a valuable package through an honest mistake, you should not be convicted of stealing that package.

### Insanity

Insanity, as a defense, may be either pathological or temporary. The gist is whether the accused knows right from wrong and can understand the quality of his actions.

### Under the Influence

Drug use and drunkenness are sometimes used to show that there was no intent to commit a crime, because the accused did not know what he was doing—hence the phrase "not knowing the wrongfulness of one's action."

The defenses of insanity and being under the influence of drugs or alcohol are used primarily in crimes involving personal violence, and are controversial, particularly temporary insanity and alteration of the mind by drugs or drink. Witness the public indignation when an unsympathetic killer escapes punishment because of temporary insanity. On the other hand, a confessed killer the jury finds sympathetic might be forgiven on the grounds of temporary insanity, which is another way of saying that the killer's actions were understandable to the jury and therefore justifiable as a matter of human relations if not strictly a legal justification.

Defenses may not bring acquittal—a finding of not guilty—but they sometimes have the effect of lightening the sentence.

# ARREST

Let me walk you through the mechanics of criminal arrest and prosecution. The exercise is hypothetical, but someday you may want to know this, for yourself, or a relative.

## *Try to Avoid Arrest*
You can probably help yourself the most at the arrest stage. The process of criminal law begins with the police. You probably know that most criminal cases begin with arrests. You may not know that most arrests are for crimes that are not very serious or are petty offenses, and the arrests are often avoidable.

### *Be Calm and Credible*
The police simply cannot and do not arrest all the offenders they encounter. There is necessarily wide latitude in police discretion to make arrests, particularly when the harm is not serious. How much noise or profanity, for example, requires arrest for the offense of disorderly conduct? When does a street quarrel rise to the level of a criminal assault? The police are often called upon to make these and, indeed, more difficult judgments.

Although the police are given guidelines, the very nature of their work requires that they be afforded sufficient leeway in deciding whether to make an arrest or whether to attempt to resolve a situation without an arrest. Police work is tempered by human nature. To be sure, many police officers seek to make arrests because of a desire to "produce," to obtain commendation and even to secure pay benefits—commonly called "collars for dollars." However, there are many disincentives to making arrests, not the least of which are the paperwork, the necessity of securing evidence and cooperative witnesses, and the time that must be spent in the courts.

Usually, a police officer arrives on the scene after the crime has been committed and is called upon to assess the situation quickly. Are the persons on the scene credible? Has a crime been committed? Who can be charged? The decision to arrest is highly judgmental and, like all human endeavors, is subject to error. Should the officer err in his judgment, it behooves you to do your best to see that he errs in your favor, for once the decision to arrest has been made, it sets in motion a chain of events that will take on irreversible momentum, entailing prosecutors, courts, and, in short, a lot of your time and money.

In any encounter with a police officer, bear in mind that ordinarily he will not know who you are. His observations of your demeanor and conduct affect his assessment of your credibility—an important factor in his decision whether to arrest you. The quickest way to assure your arrest is to act belligerent or hostile toward the police officer. Even though the police are trained to deal with difficult situations, they are also human, and by negative interaction you can tip the scales against yourself. Further, by unnecessarily aggravating the situation you may give the officer no recourse but to place you under arrest. It may be easier for him to let the courts resolve the situation. In any interaction with the police, it is always in your interest to remain calm, civil, and courteous and to avoid the escalation of hostilities.

*Do Not Turn Abusive*

Avoid self-serving remarks, such as "I know my rights" and "You can't do this to me." They will get you nowhere, except perhaps to jail. Police officers are only too well aware of your rights, and of their own as well.

The police have the general right to stop you for questioning and to ask for an explanation of your conduct. The police also have the right to request that you produce identification. Most important, they have the right to make an arrest and search your person if there is "reasonable cause." Simply stated, reasonable cause exists when there is reason to believe that a crime has been committed, either in a police officer's presence or elsewhere, and that you committed it. The police need not have conclusive proof of your guilt "beyond a reasonable doubt," which is the standard necessary to convict you in court. Reasonable cause comes easy.

Another way to assure your arrest is to accuse a police officer of bias or misconduct or otherwise to impugn his integrity. By calling into question the propriety of his conduct, you may force his hand. The only way he can vindicate himself is to make an arrest and let the judge decide who is correct. Although you might prove to be right in the end, you will not find the trip through the system pleasant, and the victory will hardly be worth the price.

Do not attempt to purchase your freedom, either before or after arrest. Bribery itself is a serious crime. Do not put your faith in unsubtle displays of money. You have heard of many people—although you cannot recall them specifically—who have supposedly done this successfully, but perhaps you have not heard of those who got deeper into trouble by trying it.

The rewards of civility and dignity in your encounters with the police can be immediate—the avoidance of arrest and consequent embarrassment, upset, and expense. Even if your arrest should prove unavoidable, you will find that not alienating the arresting officer may serve your interests in the end. Police officers are the eyes and ears of the prosecutors. District attorneys often rely upon their assessment of you to determine what type of person they will be prosecuting. And the impression you make on the police will invariably be conveyed to the district attorney, who will make judgments as to what offenses to charge you with, the position to be taken on bail, and his later plea-bargaining position. It is also not unusual for a police officer to intercede on behalf of someone he has arrested and say positive things in court.

### Avoid Drunken Driving

The best defense against charges of drunken driving is abstinence or waiting until you are sober before driving. Be advised that all over the country the police are making more and more arrests for drunken driving. Many authorities are now resorting to spot checks on highways. When you are detained on a charge of drunken driving, you will be faced with the dilemma of whether to take a Breathalyzer test. In most states, failure to take the test will jeopardize retention of your driving license, yet the test may be the only way for the government to make its case against you. Experienced criminal lawyers advise that you never take the test if you have had more than two drinks; failing a Breathalyzer test is easy and almost certainly leads to conviction.

The rule of thumb is that one standard 1.5-ounce drink of liquor equals 5 ounces of wine or 12 ounces of beer. It takes an hour or two for the effects of liquor to subside in normal situations.

Speaking of automobiles, be careful what you keep in them. Many people are in the habit of keeping in their cars emergency supplies and certain items, such as guns, knives, liquor bottles, and unlabeled bottles containing prescription drugs (and worse), that they do not want in their homes. These can be misinterpreted during a police search. In certain situations, any of these can incriminate you.

## What to Do Once You Have Been Arrested

If, despite your good efforts, you are indeed arrested, stay calm. Being placed under arrest is frightening. The sudden sense of the loss of freedom and dignity can be quite a shock. You can make it even more unpleasant simply by causing the situation to get out of hand.

### Do Not Resist Arrest or Flee

Do not, under any circumstances, resist arrest. You only invite the imposition of force by someone who is specially trained in its use. By the same token, suspicious or furtive movements can easily be misinterpreted and invoke an unnecessary reaction, sometimes a display of force, by the police officer. Apart from the obvious danger to your own body, resisting arrest is itself a crime, and it may be more serious than the offense for which you are being arrested. The prosecuting attorney could find that there is insufficient evidence for the original charges brought against you and be willing to drop the case, but he might feel obliged to prosecute you on the charge of resisting arrest.

Similarly, should it become apparent that you will be arrested, do not attempt to flee. Flight can be interpreted as evidence of guilt and can be used effectively later by the prosecutor in arguing the case before a jury. After all, the saying might go: Innocent men need not run when they have nothing to fear. Flight may also weigh heavily in the mind of the judge who will have to fix your bail.

### Avoid Making Statements

Once you have been placed under arrest, protestations of innocence will ordinarily be unavailing; the police officer is no longer at liberty to release you, but must now comply with standard booking procedures. This entails transporting you to the police station and filling out an arrest report charging you with an offense. In some instances it is possible for a supervising officer to intercede; he may investigate the situation, hear you out, and overrule the arresting officer by voiding the arrest and releasing you from custody at the station house. Do not count on any such good fortune, however; this occurs only infrequently.

As a general rule, once you have been placed under arrest, avoid making statements to the police in any way relating to the crime charged. To the extent that you choose to talk, measure your words carefully. Bear in mind that from the very moment of your arrest, the police officer's primary responsibility is to establish and accumulate evidence that can be used to convict you at your trial. Police officers know the importance in establishing proof of guilt of statements or admissions made by arrestees. Since it is unlikely that you will be able to talk your way out of an arrest once it has been made, there is little to be gained by speaking to the police. If you do, the result can be devastating. You may end up providing the police with the very evidence that will convict you. As a general rule, one that cannot be emphasized enough, once you have been placed under arrest, do not speak to the police, except for bare civility and for personal necessity, until you have had an opportunity to talk with your lawyer.

Do not volunteer information; it may incriminate others or yourself. If you have information that you believe would interest the police, do not be too eager to provide it. In the first place, it is doubtful that your cooperation will bring about your release from custody or enable you to avoid prosecution. Second, since it is the district attorney, and not the police, who will decide what charges are to be brought against you, the time to trade information or even confession for leniency is after the district attorney has become involved. The police generally do not have the authority to make deals that will bind district attorneys. Your lawyer, whether privately retained or supplied by a public legal-assistance office, will know better than you how and when to use your cooperation to maximize its benefits.

Under any circumstances, it is important that you provide the police with accurate descriptive information about yourself. Supplying inaccurate information or attempting to conceal something, when discovered, will ordinarily be brought to the court's attention when it decides the question of bail. The court will be less inclined to release you on your own recognizance (without bail) or to grant reasonably low bail if you have been less than forthright with the authorities or have otherwise attempted to deceive them. A history of lying and deception can also be used effectively by prosecutors at your trial to impair your credibility.

### Giving You Your "Rights"

At some point in the arrest or the booking process, you will be told what are commonly referred to as your "rights"—the so-called Miranda warning. You may know these from television and the movies. The words may vary, but the music remains the same:

You have the right to remain silent and refuse to answer any questions.

Anything you say can be used against you in court.

You have the right to consult a lawyer now, and have a lawyer present during any questioning.

If you do not have a lawyer or cannot afford a lawyer, a lawyer will be provided for you free of charge.

These rights are important; exercise them. They are designed to assure that any statements made by you are made voluntarily and knowingly and are not the product of police coercion. Do not be timid or obsequious. Do not answer any questions about the events surrounding or leading to your arrest without your lawyer present. You cannot and will not be your best advocate and can only damage your case.

Immediately upon being arrested, you should exclaim, "I wish to speak to my lawyer." Once you have said this, all questioning by the police must stop immediately. Bear in mind that your rights protect you against the police, not against yourself. The Constitution does not prevent the police from using any statements that you make, whether in response to questions posed by them or not. Do not volunteer any statements or information to the police. Avoid making any statements to anybody about your arrest or the events leading up to it. These statements can be used against you in court. It is not uncommon for the police to listen through the crack of a partially closed door. You must also assume that anyone, other than your lawyer and perhaps your spouse, can and will be compelled to testify about any statement made by you, even if you made the statement "in strictest confidence."

# BOOKING

Following your arrest, you will be taken through the booking process, which is the entry of your arrest in the official police records.
This means that you will be fingerprinted and photographed (your "mug
shot").

## *Opportunity to Telephone*

At some point in the booking process, you will be allowed to make
phone calls, though you may be permitted only one. It is essential
that you use this opportunity to make contact with the person who is
in the best position to assist you. In most instances, this will be your
lawyer. If you do not have a lawyer, or cannot reach him, call a
member of your family. Ordinarily, it should be the member of your
family who will have the most interest in your well-being and be in
the best position to secure legal assistance.

You should advise your contact that you are under arrest and tell
him in which precinct or booking facility you are being held and the
name of the arresting officer. Obtain this information before you make
your call. This will enable your lawyer to reach you quickly and to
notify the police not to question you when he is not present.

You should avoid discussing the particulars of your arrest or the
circumstances surrounding it, but report the bare charges if you know
them. Try to learn them (but do not argue about them) before your
call. This information will also be helpful to your lawyer. The most
important information to convey, however, is your location.

## *Your Lawyer*

Remember, it is best to call on a lawyer who specializes in criminal
matters when subjected to a charge of misdemeanor or felony. You
should remember that if you are unable to afford a lawyer, the court
will assign one to you, without cost. Insist on a criminal lawyer. Do
not save money you can afford to spend by economizing on your
criminal lawyer. Good ones are expensive; marginally qualified or indifferent ones in private practice are dangerous. Assigned attorneys,
whether they are legal-aid attorneys, public defenders, or appointed
members of the bar, usually specialize in the practice of criminal law.

Although as a group they may not have the talent or experience of the lawyers on the very top rung of the professional ladder in criminal-defense work, they could be on the second rung.

Criminal lawyers usually ask for their full fee in advance. Costs vary greatly by geographic area, nature of the crime, and your apparent ability to pay. Qualified criminal lawyers in private practice in metropolitan areas charge at least $500 to $750 for such one-day appearances as, for instance, drunken-driving charges customarily entail, all the way to six figures for a lengthy trial and appeal in a fraud case.

The selection of the right attorney is always subjective, and, to repeat, in the case of criminal accusation, when personal liberty is threatened, it is a critical one. Do not trust your fate to a lawyer who specializes in commercial matters, divorces, or other aspects of the law. You need a lawyer who knows his way through criminal law and around the courthouse. The best guide is your own instinct. Is he sincere, does he listen to you, does he appear well informed, concerned, and interested in your predicament? Is he believable? Since he will serve as your advocate and mouthpiece, particularly before a jury, his credibility will invariably be related to your own. Be wary of criminal lawyers who promise you quick results or profess connections; such blustering is usually unfounded.

## Release

In most jurisdictions, the police are authorized to issue some limited kind of release document that will secure your release from custody but command you to appear in court at a future date. In many jurisdictions, particularly urban areas, this release document can prevent your being held in custody for an extended period.

This releasing authority generally exists only in the case of lesser crimes, such as violations or misdemeanors, and then only pursuant to certain guidelines that are designed to assure your later appearance. These guidelines hinge upon whether you can establish that you have roots in the community—residence, ownership of property, employment, and family—that make it unlikely you will try to flee to avoid prosecution. Cooperate with the police, therefore, by providing them with correct information as to your residence, employment, and personal situation. In other words, be sure to give the police your correct pedigree; establish who you are.

The benefits of early release are manifold. Besides sparing you a stay in jail or a detention room, it diminishes the likelihood that you will be required to post bail after you do appear for arraignment, since there is now a record for the court that indicates it is unlikely you will flee to escape prosecution. Since you now possess some official credential for reliability, the likelihood of the imposition of a jail sentence upon conviction may be reduced.

## ARRAIGNMENT, CHARGING INSTRUMENTS

After you have been booked, the police are obliged to bring you before the court without undue delay to be arraigned. Arraignment is the first court notification of the charges against you. It is your first court appearance. In most places, you are arraigned twice, once in a receiving court right after your arrest, for charges to be lodged against you and bail fixed, and then, within weeks, in the court in which you will be tried. At the second arraignment your formal plea of guilty or not guilty will be entered in the court records. There are many local procedural variations of the arrest and arraignment sequences.

By the time of your initial arraignment, the arresting officer will have met with the prosecuting attorney, who will determine the appropriate charges to be brought against you. These charges will be set forth in a charging (accusatory) instrument. Its filing with the court formally begins the prosecution against you and vests the court with jurisdiction over your person and the case. Upon the filing of the charging instrument, you are known as the "defendant."

Charging instruments fall into one of three categories: complaint, indictment, or information.

### Complaint

A complaint is a sworn allegation by a person, called the "complainant," charging you with committing one or more crimes. In state courts, these are used to prosecute lesser offenses, such as misdemeanors. In federal practice, complaints are used to inform you of charges against you after your arrest has been made, but also may be used to provide the basis for an arrest warrant.

### Indictment

An indictment is a charging instrument returned by a grand jury charging you with the commission of one or more serious offenses, such as felonies.

A grand jury is convened to review criminal cases and to determine whether there is sufficient evidence to indict an accused person and require him to appear in a trial court. Grand juries vary in size, but they are larger than the normal trial jury complement of twelve.

Indictment need not be by unanimous grand jury vote; the proportion required to indict is fixed by local law. In many jurisdictions the grand jury process is the only means of prosecuting someone for a felony. In state practice, a person is usually placed under arrest before a grand jury hears evidence. In federal practice, it is customary to arrest only after the grand jury indictment, except in street crimes involving drugs or gun transactions. Occasionally, state grand juries will indict before an arrest, especially for white-collar crime or official corruption.

### Information

As an alternative to the grand jury process, a defendant may waive a hearing by the grand jury and bring his case directly to court through an information. This is a charging instrument, like an indictment, but it is filed directly by the district attorney. In state courts, this is usually done when the prosecutor and the defense lawyer agree that the defendant will plead guilty at the arraignment. In federal practice, an information is a device typically used to bring misdemeanor charges to adjudication.

# IMMUNITY

Of the three accusatory instruments, the grand jury indictment procedure is the only one that involves the taking of testimony. You may find yourself summoned—by a piece of paper called a "subpoena"—to appear before a grand jury. You will first want to know whether you are to be there simply as a witness or whether you are indeed the target of the investigation. Ask! The policy of the U.S. Department of Justice and of a number of states is to advise you if you are the target. Once you know you are the prosecution's candidate for defendant, you had better be doubly careful.

When you testify, your testimony can be turned against you. For instance, if you admit you are a robber, you can then be indicted for robbery. However, if the prosecution gives you immunity, you will be protected against the consequences of your testimony. If you are a target, it is unwise to testify before a grand jury without being granted immunity from prosecution. Adherence to this rule is not always feasible if you are a public official or someone who has something to lose by appearing to be evasive, despite the fact that by not testifying you are only standing on your constitutional rights.

## Types

Immunity is of two types: transactional and use.

If you have transactional immunity, you cannot be prosecuted for any conduct related to the transaction about which you testify. For instance, if you testify about a drug sale, you cannot be prosecuted for any participation in that sale. The transaction is the drug sale and the circumstances surrounding it.

If you are granted use immunity, it means only that the government cannot use the testimony given in that particular instance against you. Accordingly, if you testify about a drug sale, the prosecution can indict you for participation in that sale, but cannot use your own particular testimony against you.

## State Rules

At the state level, the general rule is that you receive transactional immunity to the subjects of your testimony simply by testifying before a grand jury. Where you have immunity, you cannot incriminate yourself by testifying. Treat any waiver-of-immunity papers put before you as you would a live snake. State prosecutors will not call you if they harbor thoughts of prosecuting you, so do not sign any of their proffered waivers of immunity. Do not give up your rights.

A state prosecutor can compel you to testify, but if you have not signed a waiver of immunity, you have automatically gained immunity. If you refuse to testify after you have received immunity, fearing perhaps that you will incriminate an associate, you can be cited and jailed for contempt.

### Federal Rules
In federal criminal practice, testifying before a grand jury does not in and of itself give you immunity as it does in state criminal practice. When you are in the clutches of the federal authorities, do not testify without receiving immunity, which will be slow in coming if you are the target. Consult a lawyer about your rights here. If the federal prosecutor wants your testimony badly enough, he will grant you use or transactional immunity. Once that immunity has been offered to you unconditionally, you must testify before the grand jury or face charges of contempt.

### Value of Immunity
Voluntary testimony before a grand jury, without immunity, is chancey. The grand jury is essentially a creature of the prosecutor. He alone is entitled to question witnesses as a lawyer, although, depending on local rules, a grand juror may ask questions. The prosecutor asks direct questions and cross-examines you without opposition from any lawyer of yours. In some states, but not in federal jurisdictions, if you are a target, your lawyer can be in the room with you, although he is not permitted to question you or speak in any way before the grand jury. He may only counsel you privately.

Unless you are a high public official or someone else who has something to lose by appearing to be evasive, the only time it may make sense for you as a target to testify without immunity is when you believe your testimony will evoke such sympathy or present such mitigating circumstances that the grand jury is likely either to decline to indict you or to reduce the charge sought by the prosecutor. For instance, you may establish that the government entrapped you in a matter of selling stolen goods. Your testimony before a grand jury when you know you are a target is a melodramatic effort to nip the prosecution in the bud. The odds are against it. Many criminal lawyers, given their way, will not countenance it at all. An interesting modern device for evoking sympathy is to hold a press conference and tell your story through the media. This works only for celebrities or in those areas in which grand jury doings are big news.

Defense lawyers often dicker with the prosecutor to gain immunity for a client as part of a bargain under which the client agrees to testify fully, thereby, the government hopes, incriminating others.

## PLEADING

At your first arraignment, you are formally advised of the offenses for which you are being charged. You and your lawyer are provided with copies of the charging (accusatory) instrument in which the charges are set forth. After the reading of the charges, you are called upon to enter a plea, either "guilty" or "not guilty."

A plea of guilty, which is an admission of the truth of the charges, often follows a plea agreement, reached by the defense lawyer and the prosecuting attorney and acceptable to the judge. This often occurs before arraignment, but may be done later on. In federal courts, defendants also have the option of pleading *nolo contendere*, a plea made famous by former Vice President Spiro Agnew in his federal income-tax-evasion case. It means that the defendant does not wish to contest the charges and is prepared to submit to the power of the court to impose punishment without an admission or a finding of guilt. This is common in tax-evasion cases.

## PLEA BARGAINING

### Meaning
The great majority of criminal cases are disposed of by plea bargaining. This is the process by which an agreement is reached between

the prosecuting attorney and the defense lawyer under which the defendant enters a plea of guilty to an agreed-upon charge, ordinarily a lesser charge than the original one, and in many cases receives an agreed-upon reduced sentence. In some instances, the plea bargain is limited to an agreement on the charge to be made, the prosecutor and the defense lawyer leaving the question of a sentence entirely to the judge's discretion.

Plea bargains avoid the necessity of trial and protect innocent victims of the crime from the trauma of cross-examination and the publicity attendant upon a public trial. Essentially, plea bargaining is a compromise. As its label implies, it is a bargain; it is actually the counterpart in criminal law of a settlement by parties to a civil case.

Much plea bargaining, particularly in less serious cases, takes place at the arraignment stages, to facilitate their quick resolution. Prosecuting attorneys and judges see this as an opportunity to concentrate their limited resources upon the more serious cases. In many of the congested urban courts, judges are encouraged to seek early disposition of less serious cases, and they take an active part in the plea-bargaining process. For this reason, many defense lawyers feel that the best bargain can be struck early, at the arraignment level, since it imposes less work on the prosecutor and the judge and relieves congested court calendars.

The extent to which judges actively participate in and encourage plea bargaining varies greatly from judge to judge and from state to state. Some judges will agree in advance to a definite sentence. Others will not agree, but will allow the plea of guilty to be withdrawn if the defendant is dissatisfied with the sentence imposed. Others will give no sentencing assurance whatsoever on a plea of guilty to a reduced charge. In federal court, judges are barred from actively engaging in the plea-bargaining process.

The plea-bargaining process rests on the belief that well-informed defense lawyers and prosecutors are able to predict the eventual outcome of a given case accurately. Defense lawyers obviously seek the dispositions that will favor their clients the most, and they hope that pleas to lesser charges will bring lesser penalties (reduced jail sentences or no jail at all or the dismissal of other charges). Prosecutors, on the other hand, try to avoid the risk of losing at trial by securing an immediate conviction, at the same time conserving their limited resources for the prosecution of cases deemed more serious.

Much criticism has been leveled at the plea-bargaining process. Civil-rights advocates claim that such bargains result from prosecution and court delays, with the time and expense involved, which cause inno-cent parties to plead guilty to get it over with. Supporters of "law and order," on the other hand, believe that plea bargaining enables a culprit to take advantage of the problems of the criminal-justice sys-tem and get off with a lesser sentence. They are both right. But plea bargaining is the lesser of two evils. The congested court calendars and the limited prosecuting and judicial resources of today make it desirable to avoid the necessity of trying every case to a conclusion. Administratively, the system of criminal justice has come to depend upon bargained pleas of guilty. If all criminal cases were fully tried to a conclusion, the system would collapse entirely.

Compromise is built into our way of living. People are wary of great risks, so that plea bargaining comes naturally. I have seen civil libertarians and law-and-order enthusiasts alike reach for the plea-bar-gain pill for themselves.

## Seriousness

Remember that a plea of guilty is serious, since it has the same effect as a conviction after trial. Make no mistake about this. Be sure you understand the consequences of your plea. It may end your pain, and eliminate your risk of imprisonment, but it may also restrict your later job opportunities and have many other undesirable social effects. A plea of guilty must be made knowingly and voluntarily.

By pleading guilty you waive your right to a trial, to cross-examine witnesses and confront the evidence brought against you, to compel the attendance of witnesses on your behalf, and to take the stand on your own behalf, all of which you will have to affirm in open court. Also, you must be prepared to admit the facts of the charge before the judge who will accept your plea of guilty. Whether you should accept a plea of guilty depends upon the circumstances of the case, your attorney's assessment of the prosecutor's evidence, and the like-lihood that you will be convicted if the case goes to trial.

## Assurances on the Record

In plea bargaining make certain that all promises made to you are placed on the court record. Do not rely on an informal assurance that someone will "put in a good word" for you sometime or somewhere. Everything left out of the record is left out at your risk.


# BAIL

After you enter your plea to a charge, the court takes up the question of bail—an important strategic consideration. The primary purpose of bail is to secure, under the penalty of money forfeiture, a defendant's appearance in court when required. It is not to keep a dangerous person out of contact with society. That is called "preventive detention" and is frowned upon in a democratic society, since the accused has not yet been convicted of the crime for which he is detained.

A defendant who is unable to make, or produce, bail, and thus must remain in custody during the long wait for a trial, may be inclined to plead guilty and take a definite jail term. Otherwise, the total time spent in jail might be greater than the duration of imprisonment required by sentence. If it is unlikely that a defendant will receive a jail sentence on conviction, but will remain in custody if he pleads not guilty, the incentive to plead guilty and escape the rigors of jail is obvious. Most important, a defendant free on bail is less likely to plead guilty, and most likely to plead not guilty, if he believes the court will jail him upon conviction.

A judge fixes bail by stipulating that if a specified sum of money is posted in court to secure his attendance, the defendant will be permitted to remain at liberty while the criminal proceeding unfolds. A judge may, instead, authorize the posting of a bail bond, which is a kind of insurance policy. In the event that the defendant fails to appear in court, the person or company posting the bond must pay the amount designated in the court order fixing bail. The bail of a defendant who fails to appear is forfeited. It is, therefore, a money penalty for not appearing, making it more likely the defendant *will* appear.


### Release on Own Recognizance

As an alternative to bail, a judge may release a defendant on his own recognizance, or that of his lawyer. This means that the defendant may remain at liberty without bail on the condition that he will appear in court whenever his attendance is required. Here, it is only moral force that is expected to compel attendance.

### Setting Bail

Under the Constitution, bail must not be excessive. Bail is determined at the judge's discretion, although all courthouses have rules of thumb according to the nature of the charge and the record of the accused.

In determining bail, judges consider many facts about the defendant: character, reputation, habits, and mental condition; employment and financial resources; family ties and the length of residence in the community; any criminal record; previous record of appearing in court when required; and, finally, the weight of the evidence in the pending criminal action and any other fact that may indicate the probability of conviction.

Since your family ties will be considered, it is helpful to have your family present in court when your bail is being fixed. A show of concern and support by your family may help convince the judge that it is unlikely you will flee and that you should be released on your own recognizance or that minimum bail should be set. Similarly, it would help to have your employer present, if possible.

Cash deposits to ensure appearance are refunded when all appearance requirements have been satisfied. Bail-bond premiums are paid to private insurers and are not refundable.

Since its effect on the poor is much greater than on the rich, and since bail is easily posted by people in organized crime, the fairness of the entire bail procedure has become debatable.

## PROCEDURES BEFORE CRIMINAL TRIAL

Subject to local conditions, trials follow final arraignment by from six months to one year. There are, however, pretrial safeguards to protect the rights of criminal defendants. The prosecution is not supposed to take unfair advantage of the defendant.

## Pretrial Discovery

Discovery motions are the means by which a defense lawyer learns what the prosecution's case is all about, usually by demanding that the prosecution disclose certain pieces of evidence, any statements made to the police by the defendant, a transcript of the defendant's testimony before the grand jury, any document concerning the defendant's physical or mental condition, any scientific proceeding, such as ballistic tests or fingerprint reports, and any photographs, drawings, or recordings made by the police. The defense lawyer may also call for the approximate date, time, and place of the offense charged. The particulars of the charges set out in the charging instrument are usually phrased in general terms, only sufficient to bring the activity within the coverage of the criminal statute alleged to have been violated.

The prosecution is under a constitutional mandate to disclose any and all information, demanded or not, that is exculpatory—that is, information that implies, directly or indirectly, the defendant's innocence.

Discovery procedure in criminal cases, however, is quite limited. For instance, neither the parties nor the witnesses can be compelled to be examined as to what their testimony will be at the trial. Indeed, because of the desire to protect innocent victims and to encourage the citizenry to be cooperative, criminal defendants are not ordinarily given a chance to learn the names and addresses of the prosecutor's witnesses so as to be able to interview them before trial. Under such a handicap, a defendant may never be able to ascertain the strength and nature of the evidence that will be used against him. This uncertainty invariably affects his decision whether to gamble by going to trial or to accept a plea bargain. For this reason, among others, the criminal defendant must be candid with his own lawyer. If you deceive your own lawyer, you deceive yourself.

## Motions to Dismiss an Indictment

Before a criminal case goes to trial, a defense lawyer may move to dismiss an indictment on the grounds that the evidence presented to the grand jury is legally insufficient to sustain the charges. After inspecting minutes of the grand jury, the judge determines whether the evidence is legally sufficient. Should the judge find the evidence to be insufficient, he will not ordinarily dismiss the charges outright but will give the prosecutor time to present the matter to the grand jury again in an effort to secure a new indictment. If the prosecution fails to obtain this new indictment, or the judge, upon a second motion to dismiss, finds the evidence again insufficient, the charges are usually dismissed and further prosecution is then barred.

These motions to dismiss are sharply curtailed under federal practice. There, the right to inspect grand jury minutes is limited to the time of trial.

## *Motions to Suppress Evidence*

In criminal defense, it is important to consider motions to suppress the production of certain evidence. These motions are essentially requests that the judge prevent the prosecution from introducing certain evidence at the trial because it has been obtained illegally under constitutional standards. Suppose, for example, that a defendant confessed a crime to the police. Obviously, a prosecutor would want to use that confession at the trial as evidence of the defendant's guilt. But suppose that the confession was made by the defendant before he had been advised of his constitutional rights. Under such circumstances, a judge would rule that the defendant's confession could not be used by the prosecutor. For another example, suppose that a complaining witness has been requested to identify his assailant from a police line-up. One person in the line-up, the defendant, fits the general description given by the witness to the police. None of the other persons even remotely resembles this description. The witness naturally picks the defendant. In such a situation, a judge might conclude that the witness's identification of the defendant was tainted, and therefore inadmissible at the trial. In either example, the effect of granting the motion to suppress might be to remove crucial evidence of a defendant's guilt, thereby rendering the prosecutor's case insufficient to obtain a conviction. Suppression of evidence illegally obtained often cuts the ground out from under the prosecution.

Because motions to suppress may affect the prosecution's case significantly, defendants are often best advised to forgo plea bargaining until any motions to suppress that may have been made have been decided.

## Habeas Corpus

*Habeas corpus* is a court order directing a person holding another person in custody to appear with the detainee in court to justify the detention. Writs (petitions) of *habeas corpus* are commonly submitted by or on behalf of prisoners who seek release from jail, claiming that there are no charges pending, that there are no apparent grounds for charges, or that their constitutional rights have been impaired in some other way. Actually, habeas corpus may apply to civil cases as well. It can be used by a mother to regain custody of a child, for example, or by a person committed to a state hospital to gain his release.

# CRIMINAL RECORDS

After you have had your trial (which will be discussed later), or after charges against you have been dropped, or you plea-bargained, what of the paper trail you have left behind in the criminal-court system?

Criminal records can be damaging, for they can be used to disqualify you from employment opportunity, from holding public office, or from professional status. Felony convictions may cause you to lose some of the rights of citizenship, such as the right to vote. They can block admission to clubs or societies. They are used by judges in determining the punishment to be imposed for any subsequent conviction. They may also influence the setting of bail in the event of a subsequent arrest. And some disgrace is plainly attached to them.

Criminal activity is recorded in various places. The police keep arrest records and descriptions of disposition. Court records reflect convictions, acquittals, and bail. Probation and parole records are generally available both to judges, when sentence is to be passed, and to prison authorities, when parole is to be considered. Prison administration records encompass activity during imprisonment.

## Arrest Record Not a Criminal Record

You must distinguish between records of arrest and charging instruments, on the one hand, and records of conviction, on the other. By the book, arrest and accusation are not criminal records. They are neither convictions nor legal indications of guilt, and are of no legal import when they do not lead to conviction. However, the theory that where there is smoke there is fire sways the judgment of many laymen and even some judges. A record of many arrests becomes suspicious in itself.

Many job application or enrollment forms ask whether you have ever been convicted of a crime. In answering, disregard arrests and accusations. Disregard convictions for such minor offenses as spitting on the sidewalk, marching without a parade permit, or violating the building code, which under local law are only violations and are not felonies or misdemeanors. Your answer is always negative to a question about your criminal record unless you have been found guilty of a felony or misdemeanor by conviction after trial or by a plea of guilty.

Official questions about whether you have ever been arrested or charged with a crime are improper. Government questionnaires may not elicit this information, and the government cannot lawfully take advantage of it, except perhaps as a matter of national security. Private questioners can always ask; how you respond depends on the kind of fuss you are willing to make under the circumstances.

### Expunging a Criminal Record

Because of the prejudice to which conviction, and even arrest records, may give rise, many states have procedures for expunging (erasing) arrest or criminal records. The procedure is usually a matter of statute, but if there are no statutes, there may be court rules that enable judges to direct expungement of a criminal record.

Most states do not allow a person who has been convicted of a serious crime, such as murder, rape, or kidnapping, to have his criminal record expunged even after completion of a sentence. Unless there are unusual circumstances, a convicted felon's request for expungement is not often granted. Expungement is granted only when the offense is minor, when the offender has successfully completed a drug rehabilitation program, for instance, or when there are special extenuating circumstances. Many states—among them, California, New York, and Pennsylvania—and the federal courts are generous here.

A person exonerated of all charges brought against him will be more successful than a convicted person in expunging a record, but unless a state statute makes it mandatory, courts are still reluctant to grant complete expungement of all arrest documents. In general, judges believe that the compilation of records in the course of an arrest is useful to the police as an investigative tool and for limited use in identifying an accused. In place of complete expungement, many courts allow an arrestee's record to be amended to reflect later exoneration, or the courts may seal the arrest records from public sight, thereby sharply restricting their use. Sometimes a court will order the deletion of the arrestee's name from all identifying police or court documents. Among the states that may provide such relief are New York, New Jersey, Illinois, Washington, Florida, Minnesota, and Texas.

Whereas most states expressly prohibit public access to the records of juvenile or youthful offenders, the outright expungement of a juvenile offender's criminal record is within the discretion of the juvenile or family court. Generally, the records of an arrested or convicted juvenile offender are nonpublic and are sealed. The reason for sealing, rather than expunging, them is that if the same offender should later commit another offense, these records might be relevant.

## THINK ABOUT IT

You have just walked through the maze of the criminal justice system, and have seen it is a twisting path crowded with risk and unpleasantness. Better to stay clear of it! Carefulness in your conduct and in your choice of friends and associates is the best safeguard against coming afoul of the criminal law.

# Chapter Five

# Where You Live

Real property (land and buildings) is one of the most traditional subjects of the common law. In early times in England, when cities and commerce were in their infancy, rights and ties to the land were dominant concerns of the common law. Real property was traditionally in the hands of royalty, the church, and the nobility, so that rules establishing rights and uses in property were oriented in favor of property owners, and against those challenging them. Only in relatively modern times have such social doctrines as conservationism, environmental protection, permissible land use, and civil rights come to challenge the rights of the owners of land and buildings. Home is no longer a castle.

Real property continues to be a lively legal subject, and law cases arise in the areas of buying and selling property, rights of lenders, and relations between landlords and tenants. In addition, there are now a myriad statutes and administrative rules at every level of federal, state, and local government. Together, they form a vast body of law.

Wherever you live, the law is your close companion. Acquiring a place to live, occupying it, and moving away from it may be the most intensely "legal" activities that affect the average person. Knowing what to look for in leases and contracts can save you money and can help you to put the law on your side.

## RENTING

The most common form of rented dwelling in this country, particularly in cities, is an apartment. Buildings that have a specified minimum number of apartments are often called "multiple dwellings" or "apartment houses," terms that distinguish them from a two-family house, for example, in which the owner lives downstairs and rents out the upper floor. There are over 56,500,000 one-family homes in this country. There is half that number of apartments in multiple dwellings. But most housing regulation and rent-control regulation by state and local government is directed at the problems of multiple dwellings.

## Customary Lease Provisions

If you own a building, you are known as the "landlord," or "lessor"; if you rent an apartment, you are known as the "tenant," or "lessee." The lease is a contract entered into by landlord and tenant, which describes the place being rented and declares their mutual rights and obligations. There are leases for all kinds of residential, commercial, industrial, and business uses of properties. Apart from government regulations, leased real estate is generally similar in legal concept whatever the use.

### Elements

The three most important elements of any lease are the description of the place rented, the term (duration) of the lease, and the amount of rent to be paid. Most residential leases run for one to three years. Other particularly important provisions of leases include any renovations to be done, permitted uses, services provided, appliances and fixtures, and provisions for rent increases.

Rent is paid in advance. Leases generally provide that the rent is to be paid monthly to the landlord, at the beginning of each month. The cost of utilities, such as gas, electricity, water, and fuel oil, may or may not be added to the fixed rent. Whether you approach a lease as the landlord or as the tenant make sure the responsibility for heating and utilities is clearly expressed. Compare what is included in the rent with your understanding of the services expected and who is to pay for them—they may amount to a substantial cost when taken as a whole.

Landlord and tenant alike must review their lease carefully to see who is responsible for such items as repair, painting, maintenance, and cleaning. As a general rule, landlords are bound to make structural improvements, such as roof or foundation repairs, but a business or commercial tenant, or a person who rents an entire home, has the obligation to make ordinary repairs and to obtain cleaning services. Apartment tenants under ordinary leases are not obligated to make repairs, generally, but must do their own cleaning. Single tenants of an entire building usually pay for their own heat, as well as other utilities.

Apartment practices vary greatly according to the terms of individual leases, since the general practices and rules may be altered by the parties by their specific agreement. Some government regulations protect tenants by requiring compliance with the lease's promised services—that heat be provided, for example, when the outside temperature falls below 55° F.

Other than for apartments, net leases are common. In such cases, the tenant pays, in addition to rent, all taxes and the costs of ordinary repairs and maintenance. In net net leases, the tenant pays everything, including the debt service on the property and the insurance.

As a landlord, you will want your lease to have an escalation clause that provides for percentage rent increases after the first year of the lease. With this, you can pass along to the tenant your building-wide cost increases, such as real estate taxes or rises in maintenance costs during the term of the lease. Again, relative bargaining power dictates the strength of your hand. These escalation clauses require reference to a base year. Base-year costs are compared with those of the lease year in question, and if there has been an increase in costs over those sustained in the base year, that increase can be passed on to the tenant. You will want to use a previous year as the base period because taxes and costs have been going up steadily, and you will want to start from the lowest possible base for escalation purposes. As a tenant, you will want to try to get the first full lease year as the base period, since that will yield the highest beginning figures. Escalation clauses are more customary for commercial and industrial properties than residential.

### Importance of Reading Your Lease

As a tenant, read your lease, as you would any other contract. You may have no bargaining power and therefore no ability to force a change, but at least you will know what you are expected to pay for and what the landlord must do and pay for. If you do have bargaining power, because there is an abundance of space for rent or you are interested in a poorly located building, ride your advantage.

Insist on the written insertion in your lease of all of your rights and benefits. The probability is that you will get nothing that is not written out. Do not rely on oral assurances, particularly those of an agent, who will earn a commission if you lease the unit.

## Options to Renew or Purchase

Options giving you, as the tenant, the right to renew your lease for specified periods, even if at a higher rent, are valuable. Although residential landlords resist them, try to obtain, wherever possible, without added cost, an option to renew your apartment lease. Landlords of office or commercial buildings are usually more willing to grant renewal options, since they recognize that commercial or business tenants may make substantial investments in altering space to fit their needs.

An option to renew enables you to stay on at a rent that might prove favorable in the future, but also to leave if rents drop in the marketplace. These options are favorable to you if you are the tenant, and unfavorable to you if you are the landlord.

Options to purchase are typically not found in apartment leases, but they do appear in leases of homes and commercial and industrial structures. These are always good to get, because they put you in a position not only to protect your occupancy, but also to profit from an increase in the value of the property.

## Security Deposits

Leases often provide for security deposits. A security deposit is a sum of money delivered to the landlord upon the signing of the lease for the purpose of assuring the payment of rent and the tenant's observance of all other provisions of the lease, such as leaving the place in good order at the end of the lease. The amount of the deposit is sometimes limited by statute, but it is frequently equal to one month's rent. In many states, the landlord must keep the security in trust, separate from his own funds. An increasing number of states now provide that the landlord must place the security deposit in an interest-bearing account and pay the interest to the tenant.

Upon expiration of the lease, assuming that it is not renewed, the security deposit is returned in full, unless there are valid claims against the tenant. If your tenant leaves your apartment filled with debris or in need of repair, you may be entitled to get from the security deposit an amount that fairly reflects the cost of cleaning or repairing the premises. Since security deposits have often been wrongfully retained by landlords, some states have enacted laws to aid tenants in their return.

A practical stratagem that many tenants employ against landlords they distrust is to fail to pay the last month's rent, in effect using up the security deposit in rent. There is no legal basis for this practice, but the short period involved gives the landlord little practical choice, and the tenant has the benefit of arguing with the landlord over the final condition of the premises, with the security-deposit money, in effect, in his own pocket, not the landlord's.

## Sublet and Assignment

In the absence of an express provision to the contrary in a lease, a tenant may assign or sublet his apartment. The two terms are almost synonymous in use. According to either, the tenant remains liable to the landlord for the rent even though the person he deals with owes him the rent. Technically, an assignment by a tenant is a transfer of his entire interest in the lease, whereas a sublet is allowing someone to use only part of the premises or perhaps to use all of them for a shorter period than the full term of the tenant's lease.

Most leases, however, do provide that the lease cannot be assigned or sublet without the landlord's prior written consent. If that is the case, secure the landlord's permission in writing before you put someone else in possession of your apartment. Many leases provide that the landlord's consent cannot be unreasonably delayed or withheld. Always try to have a provision included in your lease (or, for that matter, in any other kind of agreement into which you enter), if you must have consent, that the consent will not be unreasonably delayed or withheld. This helps avoid an arbitrary withholding of consent, delay, and possible controversy later. In some states there are laws that require a landlord to be reasonable in giving consent, particularly in leases of residential property.

If you die, your surviving spouse takes over your lease without the landlord's consent, as does your estate if you have no spouse. Children resident in the apartment can normally stay on. Generally, no other friends or relatives have legal rights to take over a lease that cannot be transferred without the landlord's consent.

## Landlord-Tenant Relations

Any friendly relations between a landlord and a tenant understandably evaporate when either party fails to perform his obligations under the lease.

The most obvious and frequent problems are failure to provide service by the landlord and nonpayment of rent by the tenant. Tenants may refuse to pay their rent when they claim that the landlord has failed to provide heat during the winter or has neglected to make necessary repairs. In rent-control areas, largely big-city metropolitan centers, municipalities maintain housing offices, bureaus, commissions, or departments that will investigate tenants' complaints. They are generally empowered to punish landlords for their failure to remedy violations that have been discovered. In some municipalities the board of health has jurisdiction over unhealthy apartment conditions.

Lease obligations are sometimes referred to as covenants, and one of the most important with which the landlord must comply is the warranty of habitability. A warranty of habitability guarantees the tenant that during the term of the lease no condition will prevail in either the building or the apartment that would render it unfit for human habitation or detrimental to life, health, or safety. Courts have interpreted this covenant broadly to include cracked walls, peeling paint, and leaky faucets. In some states, regardless of specific lease provisions, a warranty of habitability is implied from the landlord-tenant relationship.

Before withholding any rent, as a tenant, make sure you have given the landlord written notice of any problems that exist in the apartment. Make a copy of this notice for your own files. Either deliver the notice personally or send it by certified mail, return receipt requested. Keep the receipt clipped to your copy of the notice, so that it will be easily available, if needed. If you have not received satisfaction from your notice, check to see whether there is a housing authority in your area that processes the complaints of tenants.

Most leases provide that rent may not be withheld because of dissatisfaction with service. In the absence of a protective statute, you are taking a chance by withholding your rent because of a service complaint. If the landlord wants to play rough, he will bring eviction proceedings against you for nonpayment of rent. You may incur legal expense and face the upsetting prospect of being put out of your home. But your only alternative to withholding rent because of the landlord's failure to perform is suing him, unless a local government housing or health office will help you.

### Eviction

If you, as a tenant, fail to pay your rent without legal justification, a court can evict you under statutory eviction proceedings.

Eviction—ordering a person to vacate his dwelling by a certain date—is among the harshest of court decisions. If the apartment or building has not been vacated by that date, many jurisdictions empower the sheriff or marshal to remove physically both the tenant and his belongings from the apartment. A sympathetic court might give a tenant a number of days' leeway to pay or might decree a schedule of payments over a period of time. An unsympathetic court might order immediate eviction if payment is not made by 5:00 P.M. that day. These possible consequences are good reasons not to withhold rent for trivial causes.

Some states require the landlord to notify the tenant of any violation prior to terminating the lease. The tenant then has an opportunity to cure his alleged violation within a specified period.

Unfortunately, some aggressive landlords may decide to take the law into their own hands and, without serving any kind of notice, throw all the tenant's belongings into the street and change the locks on the apartment door. Although such behavior may have been acceptable many decades ago, today most states have stiff penalties for wrongful eviction, and landlords do not like to risk them.

A majority of states provide a summary procedure whereby landlords can quickly take tenants to court, both to oust them and to recover overdue rent. A tenant is made aware of this impending consequence when frightening court papers are served on him. These papers give the date and time he must appear, along with the landlord, in court (the "return date") and the date by which he is expected to answer the charges made against him. On the return date, the tenant will be given opportunity to explain why he has failed to pay the rent. If he loses heart at this point and wants to pay the rent then and there, the court will allow it, and dismiss the eviction, unless the tenant appears to be making a habit of it.

Sometimes there are disputes as to whether the rent was in fact paid. If you, as tenant, claim you paid the rent, you should produce evidence of payment. If rent is paid by check, the check should bear a notation that states the applicable month and identifies the apartment. Save your canceled checks. Cash payment should be made only if the landlord gives you a receipt for it. Save the receipt.

### Ejectment

Another type of legal action often brought to court by landlords is commonly referred to as "ejectment," or some local procedural equivalent. Ejectment actions are usually based on case law, not statute, and overlap statutory eviction proceedings. Many jurisdictions permit this action to be brought before the court in summary proceedings—that is, proceedings that take only a few days from start to finish. Ejectment is not brought for the purpose of collecting back rent; it is, instead, an effort to remove (eject) a tenant for failure to comply with a substantial obligation in his lease.

The meaning of "substantial obligation" varies from state to state and from case to case, but one such obligation that is recognized by all states is the failure to vacate the apartment or building after expiration of the lease. As such a tenant, you can be evicted even if you offer the rent. However, as landlord, if you choose to accept the rent, the tenant will become your month-to-month tenant; he may be canceled or cancel you upon one month's notice.

Substantial breaches of lease include subletting your apartment contrary to the terms of the lease, dividing your one-bedroom apartment without permission into a three-bedroom apartment by constructing walls, damaging the property physically, and behaving offensively, such as by dumping garbage in the hallways.

### Rent Abatement

In some jurisdictions, if a tenant can prove that the landlord has neglected to make needed repairs or failed to furnish agreed services, a court may award him a rent abatement (reduction in rent), in an amount that fairly reflects the loss of the benefit of the repairs. Photographs and witnesses not related to you are helpful in such proceedings.

If, as a tenant, you can prove that the building was without water for three months, a court might reduce your monthly rent by as much as fifty percent. Without essential services, such as heat in midwinter, you may be forced to leave your apartment and take up temporary residence elsewhere. If you are justified in moving out, a court would not require you to pay any of the rent during that period.

In some cities, there are government agencies that have the power to reduce the rent or ask a court to do so. Apart from rent reductions, you can secure awards for damage caused by your landlord—for food spoiled in a freezer, for example, if a disruption in the supply of electricity was caused by his negligence, or for alternate accommodations should the problem force you to seek temporary housing elsewhere.

### Vacating Tenant

If a tenant moves out before his lease expires, the landlord is entitled to the monthly rent multiplied by the number of months remaining under the lease. The tenant may assume that, because the landlord can keep his security deposit, he has no further responsibility. Such an assumption may be wrong. If the damages for this breach of lease exceed the security deposit—if, for instance, the apartment remains unrented for many months—the landlord has rights against the tenant, if he chooses to pursue them—and if he can find the tenant.

In contract law generally, there is a rule of mitigation of damages, which in lease cases requires that a landlord must use his best efforts to relet the apartment. Under this rule, where applicable, the landlord would be entitled only to the difference in rent that might be lost from the departed tenant as compared to the rent collectible from a new tenant even though the premises remain vacant. Many states do not require a landlord to mitigate his damages.

Breaches of substantial obligations under leases occur on both sides. Should the landlord fail to observe his substantial obligations under the lease, the tenant generally has the right to vacate the apartment and be released from the lease without any further liability to the landlord. The tenant may even be able to collect damages for the loss of a favorable rent, measured by the difference between his new rent and the old one.

## Expiration of Lease

### Tenant Moves Out

As tenant, when your lease has expired, you must move out (surrender possession) of the apartment, which is customarily done by removing furniture and personal effects and by delivering the apartment keys to the landlord. Your obligation is to deliver the apartment back to the landlord in the condition in which it was given, usually broom clean, subject only to ordinary wear and tear. If there is damage, such as holes in the walls from removing mirrors or appliances, you are liable for the costs of fixing them. If you take property, such as a refrigerator or a light fixture, that belongs to the landlord, you are not only liable for damages, but also may have committed a crime.

### Or Tenant Stays On

An individual who resides in an apartment without a lease, or who stays on after the expiration of his lease, is, depending upon local law, considered a month-to-month tenant. Where apartments are controlled by local housing statutes or regulations, tenants without leases may not be evicted so long as they pay the lawful rents. Such tenants are often referred to as "statutory tenants."

Some states with statutory rent control, including New York, California, and Michigan, may require landlords in designated categories to offer renewal leases to residential tenants at the end of their lease term, with a specified maximum amount that can be charged as rent. In any case, most jurisdictions direct that a landlord provide a tenant with at least thirty days' notice before the landlord can take legal steps to remove him.

## Rent Control and Emergency Housing Regulation

The effect of rent control and housing regulation in urban areas must always be considered in analyzing a tenant's rent responsibility and a landlord's obligation to provide services, quite apart from the law of leases. Generally speaking, housing is considered an emergency need in many places, and municipalities step in to meet this emergency by controlling rents, services, and apartment occupancy (number of occupants), and conditions. Tenants affected are usually those in residence without a lease, those who enjoy a regulated rent, and those whose lease terms are controlled by legal rent limits.

As a tenant, you can go to municipal rent-control offices to complain that your rent is too high or your services are insufficient. For instance, the law may allow you a painting every three years, and you did not get it. As a landlord, you may want to petition for rent increases.

Local rules are intricate and differ considerably from place to place. If you are in a rent-controlled area, do not hesitate to go to your local rent-control office. Rent control is highly political, and tends to favor tenants. There are many more tenants than landlords in the voting booths.

## PURCHASE AND SALE OF A HOME

The purchase of a house, or its sale, may be the largest financial decision of your life and may also be the most emotional, even traumatic, event.

The objectives are simple enough. If you are the seller, you want to sell your home when it is most convenient—usually as soon as possible—and for the highest price. If you are the buyer, you want to acquire the house you choose when you want it and for the lowest price.

If you want to sell your house, you have some idea, perhaps after talking with friends and neighbors, of how much you can expect to get for it. If you want to buy a house, you have selected a general neighborhood and determined how much you can afford to pay. But how do the potential seller and buyer find each other? They can deal directly, through newspaper advertisements, for instance, but most often real estate brokers are involved, and with them comes your first contact with the law.

### Real Estate Broker
A neighborhood real estate broker's office is like a supermarket for homes. Sellers list their homes with brokers, who, in turn, show the homes to prospective buyers. The broker works for the seller, who hires and pays him.

Initially, most brokers will ask the prospective seller to sign a brokerage or "listing" agreement. If you are the seller, handle the broker with care; you may be at legal risk. Read the agreement carefully and understand it, because it will set forth your rights and duties. Look particularly for the conditions under which the broker will be considered to have earned a commission, its amount, and the period of the listing.

### Types of Broker Listing Agreements

The listing agreement may grant to the broker a nonexclusive brokerage, an exclusive brokerage, or an exclusive right to sell. The differences are important, although the precise phraseology and its meaning vary from one state to another.

Normally, under the terms of a nonexclusive brokerage agreement, as a seller you have the right to use as many brokers as you wish and are obliged to pay a commission only to the one who actually makes the sale. With an exclusive brokerage agreement, you agree not to employ any other broker, but you reserve the right to make the sale yourself (to someone not introduced by that broker), in which event you will not have to pay the broker a commission. Under the exclusive-right-to-sell arrangement, if the sale occurs during the listing period, you may owe the broker a commission even if you alone arranged the sale.

### Commission Payable Only on Closing

As a seller, you want to make sure that the broker is entitled to a commission only *if and when* a buyer has actually paid you the specified purchase price. To make this clear, the brokerage agreement should state that if the sale is for any reason not concluded, even if the reason is something that is under your control, no commission is payable. Without this language, if the broker finds a buyer who is ready, willing, and able to close on your terms, you may be liable for a commission even though you have decided not to go through with the sale. Many brokers will not sue you for a commission if the sale is not actually completed, but some will.

### Agreement Terms

The brokerage or listing agreement should specify the price at which you agree to sell the property. In order to induce you to list your property with them, brokers tend to give you an optimistic opinion of the price you can get. Later, when offers below that price start coming in, the broker may urge you to accept a lower offer. In the brokerage contract, you should fix as high a listing price as is reasonably possible. This gives you greater bargaining room when a lower offer comes and the broker urges you to accept it. You have the right to refuse to sell. Sometimes a broker agrees to reduce his commission, which he may do in order to yield to you the net proceeds you want and to make the sale.

The brokerage agreement should specify the commission, which is usually a fixed percentage of the sale price, fixed by local practice. This is normally five to seven percent, but the rate may vary, depending on many factors, including special advertising the broker may do and the state of the market. It is perfectly proper to negotiate a brokerage commission with the broker that is below the local practice in the community in which the home is located.

Specify the period for which the property is to be listed with the broker. It is usually to the seller's advantage to have the shortest reasonable period—say, two months—since the shorter the time the broker has the property, the more industriously he will attempt to sell it.

If the broker tells you that he will advertise your property in local newspapers, make sure that this promise is in the brokerage contract. Promises to advertise often accompany exclusive listing, although sometimes brokers will advertise attractive nonexclusive listings at their own expense.

### Switching Brokers

Switching brokers in midstream is not unusual. If you sign any kind of exclusive brokerage contract, you cannot use another broker during the period of exclusivity without paying two commissions. This is another reason to limit exclusive broker agreements to short periods: it facilitates your switching brokers without liability. If there is no agreement with a broker, you are free to use as many brokers as you want.

With or without a contract, a problem arises when someone buys the house through one broker after having been shown it by another. To avoid getting caught in the middle, as a seller, you should seek to specify in the purchase contract the broker you are to pay, and to ask the buyer to agree that no other broker was involved in your sale to him. If the buyer has himself involved another broker, he should agree to pay that broker's commission. Unless the doubling of brokers is the seller's fault, the seller should not be obliged to pay more than one commission.

### Buyer Beware of Broker

The buyer typically contacts the broker through an advertisement. Or the broker may be an acquaintance or be referred by someone else. But as a buyer, remember one thing *always*: no matter how friendly and forthright, the broker is working for the seller, who pays the commission, and the broker is attempting to sell the house to you to earn that commission. He may gain your confidence, and be very competent, but do not forget that his true loyalty is to his commission.

Take your broker's opinion of the house, or any of its features, or of the fairness of the asking price, with a few grains of salt. And never lose sight of the fact that the lovable old couple selling the house to you are sellers and want your money. Use your own judgment and rely on your own investigation.

If you are not expert at appraising the physical condition of a house, you can obtain honest and objective opinions from professional services, usually staffed by engineers, who will examine and report on the house for a modest fee. Do not rely on the broker's advice in selecting an engineer or a lawyer. They may be perfectly competent professionals, but they may also have a relationship with the broker that serves his interests, not necessarily yours.

## Purchase and Sale Contract

Brokers generally like to keep buyer and seller physically apart in the early stages. If you are a buyer, however, it may be in your best interest to try to talk with the seller. Possible adverse effect on their own interest notwithstanding, many sellers will often be less cautious and more candid about problems that exist in the house than will their brokers.

After seller and buyer have met, or perhaps been in touch only through the broker, they can arrive at a common understanding of the purchase price and what is to be conveyed. For the buyer, this is the best time to obtain the owner's agreement to convey with the house particular items, such as the light fixtures, the appliances, or the garden tools.

### Binders and Offers to Purchase

After a tentative oral agreement has been struck, the broker may ask the buyer to sign a piece of paper known as a "binder." Ostensibly, it is a statement of intention to enter into a contract, accompanied by some relatively small amount, usually $100 to $500. In practice, it is meant to help the broker prove that he has found a ready, willing, and able buyer. Never sign a binder if you can help it, whether you are buyer or seller. If drawn by a clever person, a binder, which may theoretically be meant as a token of good faith, may have the legal consequences of a contract. If you want a binding contract, work through your lawyer. Binders are incomplete documents, and they are bad news. If you are anxious, try to expedite the execution of the contract.

A similar practice to watch out for is an offer to purchase, signed by the buyer, which, in effect, becomes a binding contract if the seller signs in acceptance. Do not sign any such instrument without first talking to your lawyer. If you do, you may find that you have bound yourself into a purchase, and it may be too late to improve or clarify the deal or protect yourself properly. This applies whether you are buyer or seller.

After you have made your tentative oral arrangement, turn to your lawyer. The contract, in which all the terms must be set forth, and mutually agreed upon, is the critical part of a real estate transaction.

It is the enforceable agreement. When it is signed, the oral promises and assurances dissolve, and the later title closing follows from it. Whether you are buyer or seller, do not rely on a broker, who may hand you a printed contract form with the specific terms of sale typed in and ask you to sign it. Rely only on your lawyer.

### Negotiating the Contract

In most areas, the seller's lawyer will usually draft the contract and pass it on to the buyer's lawyer for comment. It is fairly common for contracts to be negotiated entirely by the lawyers, who will talk and exchange drafts, after consultation with their clients. The contract itself might be signed by each side separately and exchanged by mail through the lawyers. Sometimes the parties and their lawyers will meet and hammer out the contract. These face-to-face contract signings can be emotionally charged. The parties, their lawyers, the broker, possibly the parties' spouses and children, and even in-laws may be present, and all of them may be arguing, fighting about particular points, expressing dismay lest the deal fall through. There may be threats to pick up and leave, and briefcases may be slammed shut. But in the end all is usually worked out. If you are a strong-willed person and confident of your own negotiating ability, this is the occasion that can be most profitable to you. On the other hand, if you are not such a person, let your lawyer do your negotiating.

Your lawyer will advise you fully as to what should be in the contract, but there are some items to which you should give special attention. The most important part of the contract is usually the price; but, surprisingly, that is usually the least-negotiated point, because it has already been agreed upon in the oral consensus leading to the contract.

MANNER OF PAYMENT. The price to be paid is usually made up of two components. The first is the down payment, the amount of money the buyer gives the seller upon signing the contract. This is sometimes known as the "payment on contract." The amount may vary and is negotiable, but it is usually ten percent of the total purchase price. The contract itself should specify how that down payment is to be handled. If you are a buyer, you might want to ensure that the down payment is held in trust or in escrow by the seller's attorney, so that it can be more easily recovered if for any reason the deal is not closed. On the other hand, if you are the seller, it is to your interest that no such restriction be placed on the down payment. You might need that money for the down payment on your new house. If an impasse is reached here, the seller usually prevails.

The second payment component is the amount that will be paid on final closing, or settlement, when the deed is actually given to the buyer. As buyer, unless you have sufficient cash available to pay the contract balance in full, which is not usual, you will need a mortgage. If getting a mortgage is a condition of the contract, see that the contract specifies the nature of the mortgage, particularly its amount, term, interest rate, and prepayment right.

INSPECTION.   A common contract provision is a clause giving the buyer
an opportunity to have the house examined by an engineer or other
expert, if he has not already done so. Such a clause might state that
if the examination discloses some structural defect, the buyer has the
right to cancel the contract within a specified period of time and obtain a refund of his down payment. A similar clause applies to inspection for termites.

WHAT IS INCLUDED.   The contract should specify exactly what goes
with the house. As a buyer, do not rely on the seller's oral assurance
that the light fixtures in the dining room will "of course" stay. Make
sure that the contract says so. Similarly, the contract should provide
that any guarantees obtained by the seller will go to the buyer. There
are often builders' guarantees, for example, or guarantees by manufacturers or installers of boilers, foundation, roof repairs, appliances,
exterminator services, and the like, which should be assigned to the
buyer.

TIME OF CLOSING.   The contract must specify a date on which the
closing will occur, usually one to two months after the contract has
been signed, thus leaving time for the title search, inspection of the
house, and making arrangements for financing. If you are not prepared to close on the appointed date, the courts will not normally hold
you in breach of the contract, but will allow you a reasonable extension. If, on the other hand, you have some pressing need for the closing to take place on a precise date, the contract can provide that time
is "of the essence," a phrase that will usually cause the courts to
hold both parties strictly to the agreed date.

POSSESSION.   The buyer usually takes possession at closing. Arrangements that allow the seller to remain in possession are troublesome.
You may have to go to court to evict him. Get possession on closing.

FORM OF DEED.   The contract should specify the type of deed the seller
is expected to deliver upon closing. There are three kinds.
    Under a full covenant and warranty deed, the seller guarantees that
he is conveying good title to the property. He also guarantees that he
has not placed on it any lien (which is an encumbrance), such as a

mechanics' lien to secure payment of a bill for work done on the property.

A bargain and sale deed, usually "with covenant against grantor's acts," is one that does not warrant title, but promises that nothing the grantor did or will do will prejudice the title.

A quitclaim deed provides that the seller is conveying all of the property but guarantees nothing, not even that he actually owns it.

The theoretical legal differences among these types of deeds and variations of them are great. As a practical matter, however, the differences are unimportant if the buyer has obtained adequate title insurance.

### Mortgages

Mortgages constitute a large subject. Basically, in the purchase of a house, two types of mortgage are available. The most common type is a home mortgage commitment from a third party, usually a bank, to make a loan to you, the buyer, which will be secured by a mortgage, which is a pledge of the house. The mortgage money will go directly to the seller at the closing.

A less familiar mortgage is a purchase-money mortgage, which is a loan by the seller to you, the buyer, to help you complete the purchase price. Essentially, he sells the house on terms—cash. That kind of loan is secured by your mortgage to the seller. A purchase-money mortgage often has the advantage of saving the buyer the fees and other costs incident to obtaining a loan from a financial institution.

From the seller's point of view, of course, it is usually preferable not to have to take a purchase-money mortgage. He would obviously like to have the entire purchase price paid to him in cash at the closing instead of extending credit in the form of a purchase-money mortgage. Customarily, sellers expect all cash, part from the first mortgage on the home given by the bank and the balance made up by the buyer. Sometimes, to facilitate a sale, the seller will take a purchase-money mortgage as a second mortgage, one that is subordinate to a first-mortgage loan by a bank, because the buyer does not have enough cash of his own to close the purchase.

A standing mortgage is one due in a fixed number of years, with no payment of principal until the final due date. For instance, you borrow $70,000 under a mortgage with the stipulation that five years later it becomes due in one lump sum. During the term, you pay interest only. With an amortizing mortgage, you keep paying interest but also pay regular installments of principal. For instance, if you borrow $70,000 for thirty years under such a mortgage, you may have monthly installments of principal and interest to pay of $774.30, calculated to pay up the principal at the end of the thirtieth year, with all interest also being paid. The payments, called "level" payments, are so calculated that they are the same each month, although their interest and principal components vary each month. In the beginning, the interest component is much higher than the principal; later on, the principal payments are greater. In the example, at the end of the first loan year, ninety-seven percent of the loan is still owed, so the interest paid for that year was about ninety-seven percent of your payments. At the end of the twenty-ninth year, the principal component of each monthly payment is almost eighty-eight percent, and so the balance of the payments in the last year will be almost all principal.

You may see the word "points" as a charge when you take out a mortgage. Points are percentage points and are nothing more than disguised interest deducted from your loan in advance. They increase the true interest rate you pay. To illustrate, if you borrow $34,000 and your interest rate is thirteen percent per annum and you pay three points at the mortgage closing, your true interest rate will be thirteen and four-tenths percent. This is because the interest you pay annually is $4,420, but after the three points are deducted (or $1,020), you receive only $32,980 in net loan proceeds. Therefore, if you pay annual interest of $4,420, that is thirteen and four-tenths percent of the $32,980 you actually received. The practice is legal.

The contract should clearly specify the mortgage arrangements that are to be made. From your point of view as a buyer, there should be an escape hatch through which the deal will be canceled and the down payment refunded in the event that you are unable to secure your mortgage. If a home buyer is dependent on getting a mortgage to make his purchase, his contract should, by its specific terms, enable him to drop out if his written financing commitment is not in place by a specified date. Do not take anyone's oral assurance.

You may buy a home on which a mortgage already exists. If you take advantage of this mortgage, and keep it in place, you buy "subject" to the mortgage. The cash otherwise payable for the home is reduced by the mortgage, on which you then make payments. Your home remains security for that mortgage. It can be foreclosed if you fail to pay. You are not personally liable for the mortgage debt unless you "assume" the mortgage. "Assuming" means that you become personally liable for the debt (as if you took out the mortgage originally), and the mortgagee can rely on your general credit and other assets, as well as the home, to satisfy that debt. In either case, the prior owner, who took out the mortgage, remains personally liable. Thus if you sell your home subject to a mortgage you took out, you remain personally liable for the mortgage unless the bank specifically releases you (which it will not do). Be careful about your buyer.

As buyer, always try to get a mortgage with a reasonable prepayment clause, which gives you the right to pay off the mortgage at any time. If interest rates drop, you may want to replace the mortgage with one calling for lesser payments.

### Good Title

Another clause commonly embodied in a contract is the requirement of the passage of good title by the seller to the buyer. There are "abstract" companies who search filed land records, sometimes using one of the lawyers representing the parties. They report any problems in the seller's title, such as a "covenant running with the land," for example, which gives a local property owners' association a prior right to purchase the property on the same terms as the buyer ("right of first refusal"). There are title-insurance companies (sometimes overlapping abstract companies), which issue policies that insure the adequacy of your real estate title. Most third-party lenders, such as banks, require that their mortgage loans be covered by title insurance.

Regardless of whether the lender requires title insurance, it is a good idea for you, as buyer, to obtain such insurance for yourself. Compared to the value of a home purchase, it is a reasonable expenditure. After you have purchased the property, if it develops that the seller did not actually own it, or that the electric company had the right to put up utility poles in the middle of your lawn, or that there is a footpath across your back yard that others have a right to use, the insurance company will compensate you for the loss in value.

Rights of way over your property are known as "easements." They give other people limited rights to use your real estate. Easements not accepted in your contract are defects in title and legitimate grounds for the buyer to refuse to go through with the contract.

It is useful to obtain a survey, or map, of the property, so that you will know exactly what you are buying, and the accuracy of the survey should be insured as well. When you plant a tree or build a sidewalk, you will want to know that you are doing so within your own property lines. Conversely, you do not want to find that your new neighbor's fence has been placed on your land.

## After Contract Is Signed
### Results of Title Search
The lawyers have the title search made after the contract has been signed. Important defects compel attention, of course. It often happens, however, that the search reveals some trivial defect, such as a neighbor's fence that is three inches over on your large property, or the house inspector finds some defect in the physical condition of the house, such as a leaking roof, that might technically be a breach of the contract and entitle the buyer to refuse to close the deal. If the defect is not major (or perhaps even if it is), you as buyer might be willing to overlook it, perhaps if the seller either agrees to correct the problem or reduces the purchase price. Often, contracts are renegotiated, usually to the benefit of the buyer, as a result of information gained from title searches and other inspections.

### Breaking the Contract
Sometimes people regret their home purchase or sale contract and seek to break it. If the contract has been properly drawn, the possibilities of breaking it are not good, so be careful *before* you sign. Remember the saying about acting in haste and repenting at leisure.

A real estate contract is uniquely enforceable, because real estate is stationary, ownership of it is officially recorded in a government land record office, and it is the classic example of a situation in which the courts will order the contract to be performed according to its terms as opposed to assessing damages payable only in money. A special feature of real estate litigation is the ability of a suing buyer, simply by filing a *lis pendens* (an official notice of an action pending that questions title to the property), to block the sale of the property until the suit has been resolved. This notice stays in effect unless and until it is lifted by court order or replaced by a surety bond. Anyone who deals with you for your property is alerted by a *lis pendens* to the possibility that you do not own the property. This normally chills any buyer.

BY YOU, AS BUYER.  The seller's failure to give good title, the poor physical condition of the property, and your failure to obtain financing are typical failures that allow you to break the contract. Misrepresentation of zoning or building codes may also be grounds for your refusal to consummate a purchase agreement.

If you merely change your mind and do not want to buy after all, you usually must throw yourself on the seller's mercy. The probable result is that you forfeit all or part of your down payment. Sometimes you can lessen your forfeiture if you can plant a doubt in the seller's mind that his contract is enforceable. Unfortunately, a defaulting buyer of low moral standards and high access to legal talent can frustrate a seller who has rights to enforce but who wishes to avoid incurring legal bills or tying up his property. This is yet another reason to deal only with people who seem trustworthy.

BY YOU, AS SELLER.  You may regret having made a deal and wish to sell to someone else for a higher price. If the contract is clear, however, you are legally bound by it so long as the buyer pays your price on time.

Sometimes sellers seek to buy their way out of contractual liability by offering money to the buyer, and sometimes they turn to the same kind of moral abuse of the litigative process that is open to buyers who have turned unwilling.

It is harder, in general, for a seller, than for a buyer, to break out of a well-made real estate contract.

### Title Closing

Once all the problems have been overcome, the closing, or settlement, will finally take place. In most states, this is done in a lawyer's office, usually that of the seller or of the bank that will hold the first mortgage. In some states, the title-insurance company or the abstract company may close, and your lawyer is not necessary. This reemphasizes the importance of the contract.

The seller executes the deed, which is given to the buyer or his attorney or to a representative of the title company. The attorney or representative records the deed in the county clerk's office, then returns it to the buyer or his lawyer. Obviously, the balance of the purchase price must be paid, usually by certified check or cashier's check.

### Adjustments

Numerous financial adjustments are made at closing to account for taxes, utility, water, and fuel bills. In addition, there may be adjustments for such items as oil that remains in the tank. In principle, the seller pays for all the taxes, services, and fuel from which he has already benefited, and receives credit for payments he has made that will cover the buyer's occupancy. The buyer should come to the closing with checks or money enough to cover these adjustments. In practice, there is usually an adjustment balance in favor of the seller.

### Insurance

As a buyer, arrange for your own homeowner's insurance coverage, including liability insurance, before the title closing or during it. You walk out of that closing a homeowner. You are then responsible.

## COOPERATIVES AND CONDOMINIUMS

The terms "cooperative" and "condominium" are heard more often every day, but many people confuse the two or use them interchangeably. You should be aware that, although both are a cross between owning a house and renting an apartment, they are very different from each other.

### Distinctions between Them

Cooperative apartment ownership is the ownership of shares of stock in a corporation that owns an apartment building. Ownership of the stock entitles the shareholder to the use of a specified apartment in the building under a long-term proprietary lease from the corporation. The corporation owns the common areas and facilities, such as halls, basements, gardens, walks, and laundry.

Condominium ownership is outright legal ownership of a specified apartment in an apartment building and of an undivided interest in all the common areas and facilities. There is no lease, although there are articles of association that define owners' rights in the use of their apartments and the facilities much as a lease would.

A holder of a cooperative apartment is a shareholder and a tenant of the corporation; the owner of a unit in a condominium owns both his apartment and a share of the common areas and facilities.

In both cases, the occupants are apartment dwellers, and their relation to the building entity is substantially that of tenants. They are assessed for the costs of operating the building and the common facilities, although the condominium owner pays his own mortgage and taxes directly. The interest and taxes attributable to both condominium and cooperative apartments are tax deductible. Neither the shares of stock in a cooperative nor the apartment in a condominium can, in most instances, be sold without the prior consent of the board of directors of the project.

The compelling difference between them is in their financing. In a cooperative apartment house, there is one mortgage on the whole building, and if a number of tenant shareholders default, the entire building is threatened. The other tenant shareholders must then take up the financial slack or the building may be foreclosed (sold to satisfy the mortgage). As more tenant shareholders default, the load on the survivors is increased proportionately. During the Great Depression of the late 1920s and early 1930s, many cooperative buildings reached the breaking point, went into receivership, and left the reputation of the cooperative form of apartment holding tarnished for three decades. Condominium units, on the other hand, are separately mortgaged, apartment by apartment. If the owner of an apartment defaults, his mortgagee forecloses his apartment only, so no one else is similarly threatened. If too many mortgagees take over, the level of service in the building is often reduced, since banks take less kindly to voting for assessments to upgrade living conditions than more self-indulgent resident owners.

## Pluses and Minuses

There are various economic and social pluses and minuses in cooperative and condominium ownership. Compared to a free-standing home, they afford ease of maintenance, security, companionship, and cost benefit. On the other hand, houses have more room, individuality, privacy, and no "partners."

As between condominiums and cooperatives, the differences are less clear-cut. Given equal quality of buildings, condominiums are considered economically safer than cooperatives for an individual apartment holder; each apartment holder has his own mortgage liability and is in no direct danger of a default on the overall mortgage on the building. Cooperatives are considered to be better managed, as a general rule, than condominiums, because the proprietorship has direct control over the whole building, and not merely supervision of a confederation of apartments. Their boards tend to be stronger, because the corporation can mortgage the building, including the apartments, to raise funds. Cooperatives are somehow considered to be more "exclusive," in some fancied ability to preclude undesirables (often read "minorities") from the building, although condominium associations can also preclude apartment transfer.

## What to Watch for in Buying

Buying and selling cooperative and condominium apartments is much like buying and selling one-family houses; most of the same practical and legal considerations apply, including the broker, the contract, the engineer, the procurement of title insurance and the closing.

Condominium apartment financing is directly comparable to one-family home mortgage financing. But a loan for a cooperative apartment is a loan against the stock in the apartment house corporation and the proprietary lease. However, many banks in areas in which cooperatives flourish will now freely issue cooperative apartment mortgages. Again, the obtaining of a clause enabling prepayment of the mortgage without penalty is salutary.

An important distinction between cooperatives and condominiums, on the one hand, and free-standing homes, on the other, is the subjection of the apartments to articles of association or incorporation and bylaws of cooperatives and condominiums. Both cooperatives and condominiums are forms of communal living. The apartment documents must be read carefully before you sign a purchase contract. If there is no time for that, you should have an escape clause, in case a reading before title closing reveals some onerous restriction. For instance, rules usually forbid pets or limit the number of occupants. There are restrictions on permitting other people to use the apartments by sublet or otherwise, even limitations on permitting sustained use by relatives. There are limitations on occupancy depending on age or marital status, which can be ticklish. Many of these restrictions seem unconstitutional, but they go largely unchallenged, doubtless because the residents like them.

The financial condition of a cooperative corporation is important, because its debt and its ability to service it is of great concern to the shareholders. Condominium associations typically have less or no debt, because the apartments are not mortgaged centrally. In any event, it is good to look at the operating figures of all apartment operations, condominium or cooperative, to gauge the amounts paid for services, the amount of help employed, and the generosity with which the staff is treated. This will give some idea of the substance of the operation.

The monthly-charge statement to a cooperative tenant includes his share of mortgage interest and amortization, taxes on the whole property, and carrying costs for the common areas and facilities. A condominium owner's statement covers only the cost of the common areas and facilities (including mortgage and tax costs, if any, relating solely to them), since he pays his own mortgage and tax costs separately. Although both parties should insure their personal furnishings and effects, the condominium owner should also insure his apartment physically.

Check all assessments that may be forthcoming. Before you buy, you should check all taxes and carrying charges for common services and common-area maintenance. In addition to an engineer's report on your own apartment, you should get an engineer to review the whole structure for major deficiencies that may result in assessments later.

## NEIGHBORS AND NEIGHBORHOODS

In buying a house, you acquire real property in which you have legal rights, but also, in some instances, obligations to others. Your boundary lines delineate your property. As others cannot intrude on your property, you cannot intrude on theirs.

## Easements

Easements, as mentioned earlier, are rights that allow others to use your property for some purpose, such as a path to walk across. They are strictly limited by their terms. A utility company that has a right of way for poles and wires is nevertheless not justified in erecting a shed; if there is a footpath across your property, to drive an automobile on it would not be permissible.

Utility lines and poles, sidewalks, and rights of way are by far the most common easements.

If you permit someone to use your property steadily for fifteen years, without any objection, that person may get permanent rights to use your property, known as "adverse possession," even though there was no easement. A customary example is a fence put on your land, and left there without your objection for over fifteen years. Your neighbor becomes entitled to locate the fence there permanently by right of adverse possession. In major developments, such as Rockefeller Center in New York City, which have internal sidewalks integrating with public streets, metal plaques are set into the pavement declaring ownership, thus negating adverse possession through acquiescense in use. Closing the walks to the public occasionally is another way to deny adverse possession.

Do not let anyone else use your property regularly if you can help it. Express your objections by letter or through a lawyer. Make a record. Take removal action, if necessary, through legal proceedings.

## Common Driveways

Common driveways are a form of joint ownership that cause much trouble. Whereas you and your abutting owner can drive your cars on the driveway, neither of you can obstruct it or cross over to the sole property of the other, even by an inch. Obviously, in the course of ordinary living, cars remained parked on driveways and block them, and bicycles and tools may litter them. It is easy, particularly in bad weather, for your car to slip off a driveway onto the lawn or a flower bed of the other, technically trespassing on the other's property.

If neighbors cannot get along, common driveways keep their fires of resentment burning bright. Sharing arrangements for driveways are usually troublesome, especially when it comes to deciding upon and sharing costs of improvement or repair. Theoretically, neither can alter the driveway without the consent of the other.

## Neighborhood Irritations

If your neighbor's branches hang over your property, you can cut them back to your line. If your tree falls on his property, you are obliged to remove it, but you are liable for any damage caused by it only if you are in some way at fault. You are not responsible for high winds or other acts of God that uproot trees and knock down fences.

Utility companies are liable for their poles and their wires.

You cannot alter the grade of your property to cause rain water to accumulate on your neighbor's property. With the growth of chemical use on home properties for weedkilling, pool decontamination, and other things, chemical users are becoming liable for the effects of their chemicals on their neighbors' properties or pets.

## Homeowners' Insurance

The best protection against the consequences of legal liability, whether you are being damaged or doing the damage, is a comprehensive homeowners' insurance policy.

Keep your home insured with comprehensive homeowners' insurance, including adequate liability insurance, covering you for damage to your property or damage by you to someone else's property.

There are many forms and alternative coverages. Carry enough fire insurance to meet any coinsurance clause that may be included in your policy. This clause limits your insurance recovery for partial fire losses if less than the stipulated percentage of full value of your property is insured. For instance, if you have a ninety-percent coinsurance clause, you will need to be insured to ninety percent of the full value of your property to recover in full for a partial loss. To illustrate, if, on your $100,000 property, your insurance is only $45,000 and you have a $30,000 fire loss, you will recover only $15,000. The formula works this way: [$45,000 (insurance) ÷ $90,000 (90% of value)] × $30,000 (loss) = $15,000 (recovery).

In addition, be sure you have coverage that insures the replacement value of your home, without reduction for depreciation or demolition of a burned-out structure.

## Dangerous Conditions

The general rule at common law is that no homeowner has any duty to keep the neighborhood beautiful or to maintain his property in any certain way. If a piece of property is kept in dangerous condition, however, and children are attracted to it and hurt themselves, the owner may be liable for personal injury caused by an "attractive nuisance." A deserted house that is not properly boarded up, for example, often appeals to children as a play area. If the steps are decayed and collapse under the children, the owner may be liable. An unfenced swimming pool is a common hazard that gives rise to liability.

Most communities have statutes that require owners to take measures to correct dangerous conditions. Many communities, moreover, have ordinances against the burning of leaves and requiring the clearing of ice and snow.

## Zoning

The principal way that municipalities protect neighborhoods is through zoning laws, which set forth the uses of properties that are permitted and the amount of land area that can be covered with buildings or other structures. They typically specify the distance that a structure must be from a road or a neighbor's property. They classify property as commercial, industrial, or residential, with various subclassifications of each. Exceptions to zoning laws may be granted to applicants in the form of variances or permitted uses.

Zoning laws are generally enforceable unless they are unreasonable or discriminatory. In a block of two-family houses, for instance, a zoning law restricting the only remaining vacant lot to a one-family house is of doubtful enforceability, as is the denial of permission to build an office building on a street otherwise solely of stores and office buildings.

## Aesthetics

Few statutes protect the aesthetics of neighborhoods, but interest in maintaining historical landmarks and protecting heritages is growing.

Many deeds contain restrictions on the use of property; these are generally enforceable unless their effects are violations of civil rights. Houses built on a single tract by a developer often have deed restrictions to preserve the quality of housing in the neighborhood, as do those that are part of associations, such as a lake colony.

You have no general legal obligation to your neighbors to mow your lawn, nor do they have to mow theirs, as far as you are concerned. However, a number of municipalities, on penalty of fine, require landowners to keep their lawns and shrubbery cut below maximum heights.

## Chapter Six

# Lot of the Working Man or Woman . . . and the Boss

The legal rights of employees form an evolving and expanding subject. Historically, employees have had few legal rights unless they were provided by express written contract. The employers laid down the work terms and conditions, and the employees did what they were told. But increasingly, social legislation has served to improve employment rights and working conditions, and courts have shown willingness to extend economic fairness to employees with or without protective contracts.

You should be familiar with the principal legal effects of employment and the ways in which you can, as employee or employer, conduct yourself to put the law on your side.

## LEGISLATION

### Federal Government and Unionization

*National Labor Relations Act of 1935 (Wagner Act)*

Statutory protections for unions and collective bargaining came in 1935 in the form of the National Labor Relations Act, also known as the

"Wagner Act." This legislation was designed to permit and regulate union activity, to give unions the right to bargain collectively and to make contracts with employers for the benefit of employees, covering areas such as pay, working conditions, job tenure, and strikes. These contracts are known as "collective-bargaining agreements."

The National Labor Relations Board, known popularly as "the NLRB," was created under the act. This board is charged with hearing grievances under federal labor legislation. In addition, the states have their own agencies and departments to deal with labor matters that fall within their jurisdiction, largely those employers not engaged in interstate commerce.

Arising during the New Deal of the first Franklin D. Roosevelt administration, the Wagner Act encouraged unionism and threw the weight of federal enforcement into its growth.

### Labor-Management Relations Act of 1947 (Taft-Hartley Act)

The Taft-Hartley Act was a reaction to fears of big unionism and government support of it. It was a shift from governmental benevolence toward neutrality in labor-management affairs. It forbade such labor practices as secondary boycotts, featherbedding, jurisdictional strikes, coercion of employees to join unions, imposition by unions of excessive or discriminatory fees, and striking to force employers to hire union members. It protects the rights of individual employees not to strike, and provides for grievance presentation without unions. Significantly, it was directed against the closed shop. An important addition of Taft-Hartley was the provision of an injunction section empowering the President to direct the Attorney General to seek in Federal Court to enjoin, for an eighty day "cooling-off" period, strikes or lockouts affecting a substantial part of an industry in interstate or foreign commerce which, if permitted to occur, would imperil the national health or safety.

Whereas federal law now outlaws closed shops, those in which only union members can be hired, it permits union shops, those in which nonunion workers, once hired, must join a union after a stated period of time. A third of the states, some in the South and others in which there is only low industry density, have enacted "right-to-work" laws, which make it illegal to fire employees who are not union members even if the union contract has a union shop provision.

*Labor-Management Reporting and Disclosure Act of 1959 (Landrum-Griffin Act)*

This act requires stringent financial disclosure by union officials, remedies for financial abuses by union officers, and provides for democratic procedures in the election of union officials.

## Fair Labor Standards Act

The federal Fair Labor Standards Act, first enacted in 1938, and amended in 1974 and 1977, fixes minimum wages and maximum hours. Almost all states have at least some similar provision to cover employment that does not come under federal jurisdiction, although there are significant variations among them concerning wages, hours, age, and payment for overtime. Nine states do not specify any minimum wage—Alabama, Arizona, Florida, Iowa, Kansas, Louisiana, Mississippi, South Carolina, and Tennessee.

## Occupational Safety and Health Act

The federal Occupational Safety and Health Act (OSHA), first enacted in 1970, and amended in later years to take account of increased knowledge and growing concerns among the public, is administered by the Department of Labor. It establishes standards that employers must follow for the health and safety of their employees.

All states have departments of labor or public health that also address themselves to work safety. Usually, when structural safety conditions, such as building codes and fire regulations, have been violated, complaints directed to the appropriate state agency are effective. But where sophisticated hazards prevail, such as radiation or chemical infiltration, the federal Department of Labor may be a better place to turn for results. There are regional offices across the country.

## Equal Employment Opportunity Commission

The 1964 Civil Rights Act set up the federal Equal Employment Opportunity Commission (EEOC) to deal with complaints of discrimination in employment. Most states have their own civil-rights or human-rights commissions, too. They act, in various ways, to protect workers against discriminatory practices in hiring, job conditions,

tenure, promotion, discharges based on color, religion, race, or ethnic or national origin, and similar matters. All states except Alabama,
Arkansas, Florida, Louisiana, Mississippi, North Carolina, Virginia,
and North and South Dakota have fair employment practices acts
covering work done within their borders. There are also federal and
state statutory prohibitions against discrimination by reason of age and
physical handicap, among others.

### Where to Complain

If you have a complaint of discrimination based on a violation of your
civil or human rights, the best place to go, unless you have a union
resource to do it, is a regional office of the EEOC, which will assist
you in the preparation of a formal complaint and refer you to a state
agency, if it is appropriate to do so. Some states have complaint,
hearing, and enforcement procedures, the efficacy of which varies,
but most defer to the EEOC. There are requirements as to the timing
of complaints and proceedings based on them.

Both the EEOC and state agencies tend to be proemployee and
prominority where industry is concerned. Their determinations may
bring about reinstatement of jobs, restoration of back pay, damages,
or fines of the employer.

### The Stacked Deck against Employers

Awareness of the stacked deck in civil-rights and human-rights commissions is growing among employers, many of whom now go to great
lengths to avoid being called upon to justify their practices. This means
greater sensitivity in hiring, promotion, and firing, and toward sex,
color, religion, age, and ethnic considerations. There is now, rightfully, more employer concern as to "how it will look."

For their own protection, employers should maintain manuals in
which standards of conduct are established, and should promote strict
adherence to them. Discipline should be as nearly uniform as circumstances permit; leniency in some cases and not in others sows the seeds
of discrimination charges. If it is feasible to do so, records of attendance and production should be kept. Reporting of all incidents and
investigation of all complaints should be required. Employers of large
numbers of people now commonly maintain compliance sections to
perform investigations, interview witnesses, marshal proof, and pre-

pare for government hearings. Employees should be sensitive to their advantages here.

## Workers' Compensation—State Concern

Every state has some form of workers' compensation legislation, most of which functions in conjunction with industrial codes to provide for industrial safety and for financial compensation for work-related injuries. Workers' compensation was discussed above.

Where no protective union mechanism is in place, complaints about unsafe or unfair working conditions, improper withholding of wages, and the like should be made to the state labor or industrial commissioner. Many states have local offices at which these complaints can be made.

# IF YOU ARE FIRED

## Union Protection

If you are a union member, you should report promptly to your union officials all known or suspected infractions of your employment rights under union-negotiated agreements.

Collective-bargaining agreements stipulating that employees may not be discharged without good cause are enforced by the courts.

## Nonunion Employees
### Employment at Will

Employees without access to union protection, or to individual employment contracts, or to a protective antidiscrimination statute can be fired at the will of their employers, and usually cannot do anything about it.

Employment "at will" means, in legal context, that employment can be terminated by either the employer or the employee at any time, without prior notice and without reason. The employee can quit whenever he wants, but, more important, he can be fired at any time and for any or no reason. These are the long-established common-law rules.

*Abusive Discharge*

In 1984, fourteen states recognized some limitation to the discharge of employees "at will." They were: California, Connecticut, Illinois, Indiana, Maryland, Massachusetts, Michigan, New Hampshire, New Jersey, Ohio, Oregon, Pennsylvania, Washington, and West Virginia. The cases that have limited employers' rights to discharge employees at will have come to form the new legal doctrine of "wrongful" or "abusive discharge." The word "wrongful," when it applies to discharge of employees who serve at will, is ambiguous, for obviously employees discharged in breach of an employment contract are also wrongfully discharged. For clarity, "abusive discharge" will be used here.

The doctrine of abusive discharge is still in a conceptual stage. One problem with it is its lack of a general formulation; a number of different contract and intentional-tort theories are invoked in its support, sometimes within the same state. New York, for instance, does not recognize the doctrine, denying that any implied contractual promise of fair dealing is built into a simple oral at-will employment relationship. But the state is perfectly willing to find an implied contract, prohibiting discharge except for cause, under specific circumstances. For instance, employee manuals have been used in New York courts to spell out a contractual right not to be fired except for good cause.

Discharges of people who stand up for their rights or who call for enforcement of the law may be held to be abusive. This includes retaliatory discharge of whistle-blowers—the firing of those who report wrongdoing to the government. It includes employees who have been discharged for objecting to unsafe working conditions, for refusing to engage in illegal acts, such as falsifying financial records or cooperating in price fixing, and for refusing retaliatory transfers of work place. In one state, an employee who reported to the company's board of directors an illegal overcharge on an installment loan was protected from being fired. There have been cases in which courts have ruled in favor of employees who were fired in retaliation for filing claims for workers' compensation.

An employee discharged simply to forestall the vesting of pension benefits has a good case. To illustrate one, if an employee has two weeks to work before receiving a pension for a twenty-year career, most courts will not allow that person to be fired simply to cut off his pension. If an employment manual provides for severance pay after a prescribed length of service, a precipitous discharge designed solely to avoid that severance payment may be overturned. In cases in which employees are found to have been unfairly deprived of pensions, severance pay, or other benefits, court awards restore the employees' full rights, as if the firing had never taken place.

Some states, Massachusetts being one, have recognized a tort theory as grounds for remedying a wrongful discharge—that is, they have assumed that the employer intended to inflict distress on the employee. In one case, the court stepped in to protect waitresses whose employer was firing people in alphabetical order until a presumed thief among them confessed. California recognizes a tort by a third party; a court there found that a competitor who paid another's cashier to quit during a busy sales period wrongfully interfered with an at-will employment relationship. California, generally a front runner in protecting employees, may even award punitive damages in this kind of situation.

Employees who fail or refuse to take lie-detector tests may be protected from discharge. New York prohibits employers from requiring a psychological stress test—a form of lie-detector test that relies only on voice fluctuations.

Despite such advances, however, the overall prospects for legal success for at-will employees who are discharged now are few. Statistically, an at-will employee who is terminated is unlikely to find the court in his favor. Since upsetting termination is a long shot in most places, the possibility should not be relied upon unless you are threatened with exceptional deprivations, such as forfeiture of accumulated pension rights or severance pay.

Getting your job back after an expensive lawsuit is of little solace if your employer, with a bit more caution, can fire you again. It is, however, good to be alert to claims that you can assert. Sometimes a claim with some substance, even if it is inconclusive, will bring you enough satisfaction in settlement terms of back pay, bonus, vacation pay, severance pay, or pension payments. Your boss may even change his mind.

## SEXUAL HARASSMENT

Title VII of the Civil Rights Act of 1964 is the principal law prohibiting sex discrimination in employment. Every state except Alabama, Louisiana, Mississippi, Texas, and Virginia forbids sexual discrimination in employment, either by state constitution or by statute. Under case law, sexual harassment amounts to discrimination.

### Definition

Sexual harassment in employment is a condemned practice, although it is not always easy to define. EEOC publishes *Guidelines on Discrimination Because of Sex*, which defines sexual harassment in terms of "unwelcome advances," or oral or physical conduct of a sexual nature, when submission is a condition, express or implied, of continued employment, when employment decisions depend on doing or not doing requested sexual conduct, or when the conduct interferes with work performance or creates "an intimidating, hostile, or offensive working environment."

### Difficulties of Accusation

A charge of sexual harassment may be at once a sword and a shield. Although sexual harassment in employment may be actionable under civil-rights or human-rights legislation, it is known to be all too easy for a woman to make a false charge to threaten or jeopardize a man's position. People, somehow, are titillated by sexual charges and like believing them, at least on the theory that "where there is smoke there is fire." Women may be subject to humiliation by being accused of having encouraged the advances. The charges alone can be damaging to innocent parties.

You should be alert to the hazards, and not accuse, or open yourself to possible accusation, if it is avoidable. Many men and women are harmless touchers, for instance. It is good to keep in mind that a person of the opposite sex may not consider your touch irresistible, or even friendly, and may resent it, and it is also good to keep in mind that a touch may or may not be an invitation.

## Offensive Conduct

Overt sexual advances—direct requests for sexual contact at the pain of being discharged—are the most obvious, and the charge most likely to be sustained, if provable.

Women have won sexual-harassment cases involving their refusal to date employers or supervisors. Sexually oriented conversation can constitute harassment. Patting of various parts of a body, inquiries into the sex lives of women employees, and lewd comments have been found to be harassment in many cases.

The reference to "unwelcome" advances in the EEOC guidelines is important. If a woman is flirtatious, initiates or freely participates in lewd dialogue, or aggressively or suggestively encourages sexual conduct toward herself, she will not be able to sustain sexual-harassment charges.

There is also the phenomenon of reverse harassment, as in a recent federal court case, where one woman, who had never been approached sexually in her employment, was passed over for promotion in favor of another woman, who had agreed to her supervisor's sexual conditions. The woman who had never been approached won her case.

## Liability of Employers

Employers who sexually harass are obviously liable for their misconduct. If an employer knew or should have known what his employees were doing, he can be liable for their harassing conduct, particularly that of supervisors. EEOC and the courts are strict on employers, and are quite willing to find that an employer knew or should have known what was going on.

Employers must be particularly careful in this newly sensitive area of the law. They should make clear that they will not tolerate sexual harassment. They should investigate carefully any sexual harassment they hear about, document their records, and take whatever remedial measures they can to avoid, or be successful in, formal proceedings. A mechanism should be established to look into grievances, and prompt remedial action should be taken.

Defenses by employers vary with the circumstances, but normally involve denial of harassment or alleged encouragement by the "victim,'' and they often interpose such nondiscriminatory grounds for discharge or lack of advancement as poor work results, incompetency, or insubordination.

### Actions in Response

If you feel you are being harassed, the best first step is to speak right up to your harasser; make your feelings known clearly. This usually ends it. Suffering in silence does not. To the extent that you can, avoid giving opportunity for harassment. If that fails, speak to the offender's superior, if there is one.

If all else fails, go to your local EEOC office and file a charge. If you have suffered economic loss, you can go to court to recover it.

## HOLDING BACK ON PAYMENT OF WAGES

### Employer Who Fails to Pay

Many states provide criminal penalties for the employer who fails to pay or is late in paying earned wages.

If there is a bona fide dispute over whether the wages have actually been earned—that is, whether the employee's work was done—they then may become the subject of a lawsuit, and need not be paid until an adjudication has been made.

If the employer goes bankrupt, claims for unpaid wages have priority over the claims of general creditors, such as suppliers.

### Garnishment of Wages

Most states, notably excluding Texas and Maine, permit creditors of an employee to seize his wages to satisfy overdue debts. In Pennsylvania, wages can be seized only for alimony and child support.

Seizure is accomplished through a court order known as a "garnishment," sometimes as an "attachment." The verb is "to garnish." Your employer, known in this capacity as a "garnishee," must then hold back a percentage of your income and pay it out as directed by the court. Governments sometimes garnish the wages of delinquent taxpayers.

All states that permit garnishment exempt some percentage of the wages, so that the employee and his family will have money to live on; otherwise they might become public charges. Exempt percentages generally range from seventy-five to ninety; some states exempt flat sums.

The practice of garnishment is now being carefully scrutinized by the courts; they are particularly concerned that an employee be given sufficient notice that wages will be garnished. New York prohibits employers from firing an employee upon notice from creditors that his wages are being garnished—another instance of the trend to curtail arbitrary firings.

# EMPLOYMENT CONTRACTS

When an employee has an employment contract with his employer covering his work arrangements, normal rules of contract law apply. Contracts of employment for a year or less may be oral, but if they are for a longer period, they must be in writing if they are to be enforceable in court.

## *Importance of Written Assurances*

Customarily, employment contracts set forth salary, job description, period of employment, working conditions, expense allowances, and fringe benefits such as vacation and sick leave, medical insurance, and retirement, disability, and death benefits. They may call for equity incentives, such as stock options. Employment contracts usually have clauses dealing with early termination by the employer for causes specified, and they often restrict the employee during employment, and sometimes for a period after termination of employment, from competing with the former employer, or from luring personnel or customers away from that employer. Confidential information and trade secrets are commonly protected by contracts.

Your employment contract should specify every assurance you want. Do not rely on side oral assurances.

When a written contract provides for termination only for cause, the grounds constituting "cause" are normally specified as gross neglect of duty, dishonesty, and criminal or immoral conduct. Even when there is no specific provision in a contract for termination, employment can be terminated if the employee breaches the agreement.


## Breach of Contract

If an employer breaches the contract and fires the employee, the employer is nonetheless legally liable to continue the compensation called for in the contract.

### Mitigation of Damages

The employee, in this situation, usually has a legal duty to minimize the employer's payment by making a reasonable effort to find comparable employment elsewhere. This is called "mitigating of damages," recognized in all states but Hawaii, Nevada, South Dakota, Vermont, and Wyoming. The breaching employer is entitled to credit any new wages that are, or reasonably could have been, earned against what he would have had to pay otherwise. For this reason, employees in jurisdictions that require mitigating damages, are well advised to look for other work immediately, keeping a record of their efforts. This is because the employee might find that the employer is able to subtract sums which *could* have been (but were not) earned in mitigation.

If your employer fires you in breach of your contract, you should keep records of advertisements placed and answered, of listings with employment agencies, and of job interviews. You are not expected to accept just any job, however; it must be a suitable position, comparable to the one lost.

### Employment Contracts Favor Employees

On balance, formal employment agreements for specified terms are written with the interests of the employee, not the employer, primarily in mind. Employers generally agree to written employment contracts only because they must in order to attract or hold valuable employees.

If an employee quits, there is not much the employer can do to recover money damages, and the courts will not compel employees to work. The practical best the courts will do is order the employee not to work for a competitor or a party adverse to the employer. If an employee does not want to perform at an optimum level, he can hang on by minimal compliance and cannot be fired without the payment of damages. Long-term contracts encourage complacency in employees. For this reason, among others, incentives such as percentage compensation or bonuses based on profits or sales are built into employment contracts, as are stock options or other equity incentives.

### Covenants Not to Compete

Contracts do help employers if the employee promises, when the employment ends, not to compete with the employer or lure away personnel or customers. If reasonable, these clauses, or restrictive covenants, are generally enforceable. "Reasonable" is usually defined by the courts in terms of a limited time for noncompetition, perhaps six months to three years, lack of geographic proximity—the owner of a men's retail clothing shop in New York could not reasonably prevent an employee from opening a men's retail clothing shop in Portland, Oregon—and whether the employee received sufficient consideration in return for agreeing to the restriction.

There is always the factual question of whether an employee left his job voluntarily and then went to work in another business for a former associate, or whether the former associate lured him away.

Restrictive covenants are regarded with suspicion by the courts, because the policy of the law is to allow people to continue to earn their livelihood the best way they can. California is particularly strict in barring agreements that restrict the opportunity to work; so is Michigan. The degree to which restrictions are enforced often depends on the circumstances that gave rise to the contract containing the restrictive covenant. Ordinary employees, for example, are given more competitive leeway than one who sold the store, then became an employee of the new owner. The purchaser of a business is understood to have an interest in restricting the former-owner-turned-employee, as a way of protecting his bargain.

If you are an employee, seek a written employment contract, but try to resist or limit the inclusion of any clause that restricts your competition after expiration of the contract.

If you are an employer, try to avoid a long-term employment contract unless you require protective covenants against actions of your employee during or after employment.

## *Corporate War of Nerves*

A drama often played in the executive suite involves the employee who is under contract and whose number is up. Your employer may want you to make the break and to forfeit any contractual rights in the process, but is unwilling to fire you because your salary will still have to be paid. If you want to stay in place, you must be patient, put up with much that is trying, and not provoke your superiors or give them grounds for discharge. The employer may be seeking to break your resolve. The importance of specifying job functions in your contract in the first place looms large here, for it may prevent your employer from assigning demeaning duties to you or relocating you in an unfavorable site. Your employer can reduce you to idleness if your employment contract does not specifically prevent it, so long as he keeps paying your salary.

Enough harassment by your employer may constitute a breach of contract. A favorite tactic of employers, in these strained-relations cases, is to lock the employee out. When the storm clouds gather on the employment scene, it is a good idea to take home all your valuable personal effects and memorabilia. But be careful not to take any of your employer's property or business records. This may in itself constitute a breach of contract on your part and make you vulnerable to legal action.

Similarly, as an employer you have your own fences to watch. Your employee should not be allowed control over important or sensitive business records. He should be allowed neither to take work home nor to stay late with access to the office files and duplicating machinery.

# CONFIDENTIALITY

Agreements that prohibit disclosure of trade secrets and confidential information are generally—but not always—enforceable. This is a difficult and particularly uncertain part of the law. A confidentiality agreement may be enforced by a state court if the employee uses a secret ''customers list'' compiled by the employer to lure away customers, for example, but that court will not prohibit the former employee from soliciting customers whose identities are readily available from trade directories or the phone book. Confidentiality agreements thus may raise difficult questions of proof. When is a customers list confidential? Everyone in an industry has access to the same trade directories.

One way an employer can improve his position is by establishing internal practices that support the confidential nature of what he seeks to protect. One employer runs a manufacturing plant and uses a chemical process that he regards as a trade secret. His plant has special rooms in which this process is used, and access to these rooms is restricted to certain key employees, who must sign a register every time they enter or leave the rooms. A practice of this sort makes it plain that the process really is a ''secret'' one—and woe betide an employee who goes into competition using it.

Confidentiality of trade secrets is not restricted to employees under written contract. Although state laws vary greatly in degree, all employees have a duty of loyalty and obligation to refrain from disclosing or using confidential information to the employer's disadvantage. For instance, an insurance underwriter cannot disclose the names of the insured of his former employer and their coverage. A beautician cannot disclose the color formulations for the hair of individual customers. Courts will enforce these obligations. An employee can, however, transfer any expertise developed in one job to work done for another. Compelling an employee not to compete after leaving the job is not part and parcel of employment at will, or even of a general employment agreement. It requires a specific agreement.

## PROPRIETARY RIGHTS TO INVENTIONS AND IDEAS

Proprietary rights to inventions and ideas developed during a person's employment are often litigated. Without a contract restriction, whatever employees develop on their own time, in their own place, with their own equipment, belongs to them. The situation is less clear when the developing is done on the job or with the employer's facilities. Whatever is done on an employer's premises within the scope of an employee's job usually belongs to the employer.

Since courts lean over backward to favor inventors and creators, it is wise for employers who hire people to invent, research, create, or develop, to require, as a condition of their hiring, a written agreement assigning to the employer all rights in any inventions or creations developed by the employee during the period of employment, including patents, trademarks, and copyrights.

If you are an employee who invents or creates, you should engage in your creative activities away from your place of employment and without using your employer's materials. If you have sufficient bargaining power, you should insist on a written agreement in which your rights in your inventions or creations are spelled out. This may be done by providing for registration of patents or copyrights in your name, a common practice of independent writers and inventors. You can also ask for a royalty—a percentage of the price or a fixed sum for each unit produced on the sale of your product, or, alternatively, a percentage of the profits from the sale. There are many contractual protections that can be devised, but bear in mind that contracts are not self-enforcing. To hold a balky employer to your contract, you may have to take him to court.

As an employer, seek to have all inventing, artistic, research, and development personnel assign to you in writing all products developed on your time or at your facilities.

As an employee, seek to have a written agreement protecting your rights in your inventions, artwork, research, and development.

## PRINCIPAL AND AGENT

A person who acts for another person can cause that person to be legally liable, or may unwittingly become liable himself. This involves laws of agency.

In legal jargon, the employer is the principal, the employee the agent. As agent, the employee may have two kinds of authority, actual and apparent. The distinction is important in determining whether the principal / employer is responsible for the acts or contracts of the agent / employee. "Actual authority" is that authority which is expressly delegated, as when the owner of a business tells the employee to buy a specified machine. In that instance, a purchase contract that the employee signs on behalf of the employer to buy the machine will be binding on the employer. "Apparent authority" is the authority that outsiders may assume an agent possesses judging by that agent's title or position. If you are, for instance, the president of a corporation, you are assumed by virtue of your high office to have the authority to buy that machine for the corporation, even though a resolution of the board of directors, unknown to the seller of the machine, may have deprived you of that authority.

Commitments made by employees acting within the scope of their actual or apparent authority bind—that is, create legal obligations upon—their employers. If the employee has in fact exceeded his authority, and has wrongfully caused the employer to be liable to a third party, that employee may be liable for damages to the employer. If a salesman employed by a fire-insurance company issued a policy that the insurer told him not to issue, and if a fire loss occurred causing the company to pay to the insured the proceeds of the policy, the insurance company might turn around and sue the salesman for the amount of the loss it paid. Similarly, if the president of a corporation was authorized by resolution of the board of directors to spend $30,000 for machinery and spent $50,000, he might be liable to the corporation for the $20,000 difference. Conversely, an employee held personally liable to pay money for an action taken within the scope of his agency may recover his money from his employer.

In many cases, those who furnish professional or personal services, such as architects and insurance agents, may procure insurance to cover errors and omissions; thus they protect themselves against liability for damages that their mistakes, or their failure to do something in the course of the work, may cause others. Such insurance is comparable to the malpractice insurance of doctors, dentists, and lawyers.

When an employer is released from legal liability for the activities of any of his employees, it is prudent to have the terms of the release explicitly cover not only the employer, but all his agents, directors, employees, and affiliated companies and their personnel, as well. Liability-insurance policies of principals should, if possible, cover their agents and employees as well.

# Chapter Seven

# Get It in Writing

When you go to the movies, order a meal in a restaurant, or board a bus, do you feel the need for a written guarantee of satisfaction covering what you are to receive? Of course not! These are small everyday transactions, which are never considered in legal terms. You trust people and take your risks.

You may venture even into more complex relationships without written agreements. You may allow a repairman to move your expensive hi-fi equipment to his own shop. You have no assurance as to what parts he will use, who will do the work, when or whether the equipment will be returned, or how well it will work when you have it back, if you have it back. You buy a fur coat for $6,500 by simply handing over a check to the furrier; you may even have given him a $2,500 deposit, with no written assurance whatever from him. A contractor may build for you, under an oral agreement, a bluestone wall at a cost of $1,700. He measures, digs up your lawn, leaves messy debris on your grass for weeks, eventually constructs the wall, and restores the condition of the grounds. You like him, you like the wall, you like the price, you like the way he cleaned up; happy ending.

But the ending is not always happy; you may have complaints about the job that was done or the goods that you received. How do you go about getting satisfaction? How do you establish, even in relations with an honorable person, that the two of you were in accord as to the precise subject matter of your transaction when all you have are differing recollections of a conversation?

Suppose all that exists is a simple receipt showing a down payment of $2,500 on the price of a "fur coat, mink, $6,500." You say you ordered a black mink coat. He says you ordered the natural ranch mink coat that he now has ready for you, and he really believes it. If you are a good customer or if the furrier finds you to be an appealing, sincere person, he may give ground and make a black mink coat for you, or he may offer you a discount if you will accept the natural ranch mink coat quietly, but he may do neither. He has made a fur coat, tailored to your measurements, and he has your deposit money. He wants the balance of his money. You do not want the natural ranch mink coat. What do you do? One option is to give up, take the natural ranch mink coat, and pay the balance, saving a lot of wear and tear on your emotions. Natural ranch mink coats have their occasions, too. But suppose you really want that black mink coat. Is a lawsuit in order?

If you had had it in writing that you specified a black mink coat, the furrier could only, in honesty, concede that you are right. If you had to haul him into court, you would have proof of your claim in hand. Written agreements thus serve two purposes: they memorialize the mutual intent of the parties and they supply proof of what was agreed upon.

Of course, no written agreement guarantees you a happy ending. The furrier might go bankrupt, close shop and run, or even produce three witnesses who will swear that during a later trip to the shop you changed your mind about the coat. It is hardly worth paying a lawyer $7,500 to try to recover a $2,500 deposit or to obtain a $6,500 black mink coat, particularly if you might lose the case. Thus written agreements are not everything, but they do help.

## CONTRACTS

### Elements of a Contract

Most people think of a contract as a neatly typed sheaf of gleaming white paper, with all its terms set forth. When the parties to it sign, the contract springs into effect, binding both parties simultaneously. This is not necessarily true, however. A contract may be oral, and, even if written, it may be entered into in stages.

Legally, a contract requires an offer, an acceptance, and the furnishing of consideration. An offer is an expression of an intent to contract, on specific terms, communicated to the offeree, the one receiving the offer. The offeree's acceptance must be responsive to the offer, absolute, unconditional, and brought to the offerer's attention. Consideration is what the parties give, do, or promise to do, for each other—the value exchanged, whether money, an object, an act, or forbearance from acting.

If, to illustrate, you call me and ask me whether and for how much I will paint your apartment, with two coats of white paint supplied by you, I tell you I will estimate the cost and let you know. You have invited me to make you an offer. Later on, I call you back and say, "I will paint your apartment tomorrow, two coats, with the white paint you will supply, for $575. That is my best offer." You then tell me, "Great! I accept. You have the job. I will pay the $575 and supply the white paint. Start tomorrow." We now have a contract. My offer is the promise to paint tomorrow for $575 with the white paint that you agree to furnish; your acceptance is your expression of agreement to the offer. The mutual considerations are that you give me $575 and that I do the painting. The precise words—"offer," "acceptance," and "consideration"—are not in themselves significant; it is the fair meaning of what is said that counts. Before I actually start painting, we really should have, for our mutual protection, a letter signed or initialed by both of us or a memorandum of our terms, particularly mentioning the sum of money and the two coats of paint.

Offers may be revoked before they are accepted. In the example, suppose that after calling you with my offer to paint but before you accepted it, I call you again and say that I have accepted another job and therefore cannot do the painting for you. My offer is thereby revoked, and we have no contract. If I had said, however, that I had made an error in calculating my price and must now raise my asking price to $850, that is a new offer, and my original offer has been revoked. An acceptance must be unconditional; if you now say that $850 is too high but you would pay $700, you are declining to accept but are, in effect, making a counteroffer. If I say, "O.K., I will do it for $700 and I will start tomorrow," a contract has again been made.

This simplified example sets forth the basic ingredients of contract law, which, as a subject, is perhaps the most important in the civil branch of American law. There can be, to be sure, many ramifications as to what was offered, what was intended, and what was accepted. There can be sophisticated distinctions to be drawn, moreover, between promises and conditions, and between bilateral and unilateral contracts, and there are countless other legal complications.

Bear in mind that the words "contract" and "agreement" are synonymous in the law. They can cover complex arrangements or the simplest of transactions. But the principles always remain the same.

Although oral agreements are generally enforceable, with the exceptions noted below, it usually pays to put them in writing, if only in the form of a letter or memorandum initialed by the parties. Just as good fences make good neighbors, careful notation makes good contracting partners.

## When Contracts Must Be in Writing

Some contracts are not legally enforceable unless they are in writing. If the contract at issue falls within certain types, it does not matter whether five clergymen will swear to having heard the oral agreement; the court will throw the case out unless there is a written contract.

According to the original English common law, there was no requirement that a contract be written. In early times, written contracts were a rarity, since literacy itself was not general. But in 1677, the English Parliament enacted the famous Statute of Frauds, which changed the English law and became part of our own legal heritage. It decreed that specified types of contracts must be written to be enforceable. The ancient expression is so prevalent among lawyers that when you hear one mutter today, "Statute of Frauds," he is pondering whether a particular contract must be in writing in order to be legally valid, even though that exact phrase probably does not appear anywhere in the United States as a statutory heading. He is not talking of a case in which someone is accused of defrauding another.

The requirement of a written contract does not necessarily mean that the contract must take any particular form. The actual legal requirement is simply that there be enough in writing to establish an understanding, signed or acknowledged by the party who is to be held to the promise.

### Involving Real Estate

Contracts for the sale or leasing of land must be in writing. In many states, agreements to pay brokers' commissions or finders' fees—except to lawyers, brokers, and auctioneers—and for sales of real estate and businesses must be in writing.

### Performed over Extended Time Period

Any contract that cannot, according to its own terms, be fulfilled within one year of execution—three years in some states—or within the promiser's lifetime, must be in writing.

### Guaranteeing Debts

Agreements to pay the debts of another, including an executor's or administrator's agreement personally to pay the debts of a decedent, must be in writing.

### Other Occasions

The three categories just mentioned are the most common circumstances compelling written (not oral) contract. There are, however, a miscellany of other situations.

Contracts to make a will or a trust, or that promise something upon marriage, must be in writing. In almost all states, a contract for the sale of goods worth $500 or more must be in writing, unless the purchaser accepts delivery or pays for all or part of them when the agreement is reached.

Because of the harshness of the writing requirement in particular cases, a body of exceptions to the strictness of the Statute of Frauds has grown up in the various states—particularly when possession of real estate or goods has been delivered pursuant to an oral understanding or when there has been partial performance of an oral contract for services.

In modern courts there is a growing awareness that the original purpose of the Statute of Frauds was to have solid assurance that a contract was in fact intended and entered into, and that such assurance can sometimes be given other than in written form.

## Unenforceable Contracts

Some contracts, whether written or oral, are not enforceable at all. Contracts entered into by minors, for instance, are usually not enforceable against them in court and can be disavowed by them at any time until they come of age—nineteen in Alabama, Nebraska, and Wyoming; twenty-one in Colorado, Mississippi, and Pennsylvania; no age specified in Missouri; eighteen in all other states and the District of Columbia. If the contracts continue in force after that, these former minors are presumed to have adopted them as adults and become bound by them. If minors leave home and are not supported by their parents, they become "emancipated" and can generally be held to contracts for their necessities, such as food, housing, clothing, education, and medical expenses.

Mental incompetents are not held to contracts, except for necessities, and their legal guardians can disaffirm their contracts.

In contracting with a minor or an incompetent, secure the guarantee of a responsible adult to guard against disaffirmation of that contract by the minor or the legal guardian of the incompetent.

### Fulfilling Your Promise on Time

Sometimes it is important that the thing to be done under a contract be done exactly on time. For instance, if an item is being bought for resale on a certain date, or if several arrangements must be dovetailed, as in selling and moving out of one home and buying and moving into another, the buyer must be ready to act by the promised date.

Contracts should provide for the time by which they are to be fulfilled. In the absence of a specific time provision, courts will allow reasonable time to act. Courts are willing, however, to extend even a specified time limit to a period that is reasonable under the circumstances. If it is essential to you that a contract be performed within the time stated, without any adjournment, you should make sure that it says "time is of the essence." This is a legal phrase that signifies that a genuine deadline is intended. In this case, courts are unlikely to extend the deadline. Keep in mind, however, that in specifying that time is of the essence, you must be ready to act on time yourself.

### Patents, Copyrights, and Trademarks

Transfers of patents and copyrights must be in writing. In this intricate area of the law, registration of the rights with the federal government and written agreements are practical necessities.

If you are an inventor, artist, writer, or other creative person, you move in a sophisticated legal world, one in which written notations, official and private, are particularly critical. On top of that, the legal rules are difficult. As described in the nineteenth century by Justice Joseph Story, of the United States Supreme Court, "Patents and copyrights approach nearer than any other class of cases belonging to forensic discussions, to what may be called the metaphysics of the law, where the distinctions are, or at the very least may be, very subtle and refined, and sometimes almost evanescent." Ordinary mortals would seem to have little chance here; they should turn to lawyers with specific experience in this field.

The law branches three ways: the first deals with the mechanics of registering your patents, trademarks, and copyrights; the second with infringement and misuse by others of what is yours; and the third with any contracts for the sale, licensing, or other economic exploitation of your creation.

According to the Constitution, the federal government retains sole jurisdiction over patents and copyrights. Information particularly useful to laymen is available from the Commissioner of Patents and Trademarks and the Copyright Office of the Library of Congress, both in Washington, D.C., and in all regional libraries of government publications and many public libraries.

### Patents

Patents apply to useful new processes or newly assembled objects. Patents are in the form of documents, issued by the U.S. Commissioner of Patents and Trademarks, which grant exclusive rights in inventions, usually for seventeen years. Design patents, which last for ten years, are given to novel designs of a wide range of articles.

The patenting process normally begins with a search of the Patent Office records to see whether a patent has previously been issued for a comparable invention. Once you are satisfied that your innovation is unique, you file an application for a patent. This entitles you to proclaim "Patent pending," which may scare off would-be infringers, who will not wish to be stranded with machinery or inventory when your patent has been issued. It is a federal offense, with a fine of as much as $500, to state "Patent pending," for the purpose of deceiving the public, when a patent is not in fact pending and no application is on file.

To exploit a patent, you can go into business for yourself or you can sell it to another party. You can also license your patent, in writing, permitting someone else to use it as you specify.

Unauthorized use of your patent is an infringement and may entitle you to an injunction, which is a court order to the infringer to stop using it or pay damages or both. The statute of limitations on enforcing patent rights is six years.

### *Copyrights*

Copyrights apply to the broadest definition of writings: books, poems, short stories, novels, song lyrics, musical compositions, motion pictures, sound recordings, maps, drawings, paintings, photographs, computer programs.

As the author of one of these writings—or the one to whom the author may have assigned copyright—you must give consent before your writing may be copied, reproduced, or printed. If you have assigned all of your copyright to a book publisher, who publishes your manuscript in hardcover, another publisher, who wishes to publish it in soft-cover, must obtain a license from the hard-cover publisher.

A copyright springs into existence on the creation of a work in a tangible medium of expression, such as manuscript, film, recording, or sculpture, and it can be protected simply by putting a notice on all "published" copies of the work in a location where it is reasonable to expect that it will be seen. The preferred notice consists of a *c* in a circle (©), the date, and the copyright holder's name. Do not distribute your work publicly without notice of copyright on display.

Failure to use the copyright notice, plus failure to correct your omission on copies subsequently distributed after the omission has been discovered, plus failure to register the copyright with the Copyright Office within five years of the omission, will cause forfeiture of your claim to copyright. The copyright notice is doubly important because it also assures protection under the Universal Copyright Convention, which is in force in more than fifty countries.

As soon as possible after creating your work, certainly before publication, you should register it, in writing, by means of the official forms supplied by the Copyright Office. A new copyright law went into effect at the beginning of 1978. Before that, registration was not available for unpublished prose, such as books, novels, short stories, and radio, television, and film treatments (as distinguished from dramatic works, such as plays, which are characterized by dialogue, and which could be registered in their unpublished form). To protect themselves, authors in the past mailed themselves registered letters containing their unpublished prose or deposited copies of them with the Writers Guild of America in order to have proof of date (or priority) of authorship. That procedure is no longer necessary and, in fact, is less desirable than registration in the Copyright Office. In a judicial proceeding, the certificate issued by that office is prima facie evidence of authorship and creation. You cannot do much better than that.

For works created after December 31, 1977, the duration of copyright is the author's lifetime plus fifty years. For creative works that are done for hire, and which from their inception belong to someone other than the author, the copyright lasts for one hundred years after creation of the work or seventy-five years after its publication, whichever comes first.

Infringers of your copyright can be enjoined (made subject to injunction) and be liable to you for your damages as well as their own profits as defined in the statute and refined by the courts. Note, however, that if you have failed to register an unpublished work prior to infringement or have failed to register a published work prior to infringement *and* prior to three months after the first publication, you will have lost the right to obtain statutory damages or counsel fees in the event of infringement. The copyright law allows the successful copyright owner to elect to recover statutory damages. This is frequently the best choice, since the infringer's profits can seldom be ascertained, nor can your own damages, usually your lost profits. The court fixes the amount, generally in the range from $250 to $10,000, but if the court determines that the infringement is "willful," the amount can be as much as $50,000.

The statute of limitations for copyright infringement actions is only three years.

Not all unauthorized uses of a copyrighted work are unlawful. Unlawful uses are only those uses reserved to you as copyright owner as part of your bundle of rights—the right to make copies or derivative works, for example, such as translations and film adaptations, the right to perform the work publicly, and the right to display and distribute the copyrighted work or its derivatives. Although you may not duplicate a copyrighted sound recording by a well-known singer, the copyright law does allow you to imitate his style and voice. You can read or perform a play before an audience of your family and social circle in your home without infringing anyone else's rights. Similarly, lawyers use copyrighted textbooks in their law libraries and even copy extracts from them into their briefs.

There are several uses, such as performance of a religious musical work during services, that are exempt (permissible) by statute. In addition, a use must be substantial to be an impermissible one. It is not possible to lay down a rule that five lines of a novel or ten lines of a history textbook may be freely used, but that the taking of six or eleven lines of poetry or another type of work will constitute an infringement. Determinations must be made case by case, depending always on both the nature and the amount of the material the publisher chooses to utilize.

FAIR USE OF MATERIAL.   Fair use is a potential line of defense available to an accused infringer. Under the doctrine of fair use, the public has a special interest in materials such as news commentary, scholarship, teaching, research, and criticism that limits the exclusive rights of copyright owners. It is permissible, for example, for a teacher to make multiple photocopies of a current magazine article for classroom use, whereas a commercial organization could not make and distribute such photocopies to its nationwide sales force.

This fair-use limitation permits newscasters and commentators, whether in educational format, such as a historical motion picture, or by way of entertainment, to use a substantial amount of copyrighted material, though they must do it within legal guidelines set by the courts that are quite technical and generally require an expert's hand. Even expert lawyers frequently disagree as to the application of the doctrine in any particular situation.

SUBSIDIARY RIGHTS.   Assignment of copyright in a work includes not only the right to reproduce the work but also disposition of the other rights in the copyright bundle, such as the right of adaptation to other forms—transforming a novel into a play, motion picture, or even a comic strip, for example. You might, however, prefer to parcel these rights out separately to different users in different marketplaces. You might grant to a book publisher exclusive book-publication rights, and transfer the exclusive right to adapt the novel for a motion picture and to make and distribute that film separately to a film producer. Foreign rights may be distributed among a number of different parties. All this points to the need to negotiate your contract terms carefully.

The complications in piecing out the various rights to creative works contribute to the desirability of employing an agent, essentially a business agent, whose job is to locate publishers and to achieve maximum realization of all the licensing potential.

### Trademarks and Trade Names

Trademarks are distinctive identifying symbols that serve to distinguish your goods and services from those of others. They are often confused with copyrights. The mark can be a word, a phrase, a drawing, or a combination of these. Rights to them are acquired through use, provided the mark is not a descriptive or generic term. For example, "lite" for beer has been held by the courts to be descriptive and not subject to the exclusive use of one brewery.

You should, generally, have a trademark search made before adopting a mark for use. If the search shows no previous close use, you may use the mark on your product or in connection with your services. If you use it in interstate or foreign commerce, you may apply to the Commissioner of Patents and Trademarks, in Washington, D.C., for federal registration of your mark. Federal registration is good for twenty years and can be renewed for successive twenty-year periods. The advantages of written registration are largely in connection with lawsuits, including immediate access to federal courts and the ability to get nationwide injunctions.

Trade names are distinctive names that can be protected under general laws of unfair competition. They do not have trademark status, but once they have developed public meaning and acceptance, substantial rights grow out of them.


# REMEDIES FOR BROKEN CONTRACTS

A contract that is broken is said to have been "breached"; when you sue someone for breaking a contract, you sue for "breach of contract." Contracts are breached in one of three ways: one party fails to live up to its promises; one party prevents the other from performing; or one party repudiates the contract—anticipatory breach—by stating that it will not comply.

The awards provided by the courts for breach of contract are known as "remedies." They are essentially either money damages or orders for specific performance, which is when the court orders the breaching party to carry out the contract.

### Money Damages

The usual judicial method of dealing with proven contractual breaches is to award money damages. In theory, the blameless party is only to be "made whole"—that is, to be put in the position that would have been reached had the other fulfilled its part of the bargain—not to profit by the breach.

If your contract is broken by the other side, you may be awarded the money difference between the contract price and the cost you expected to incur in performing as agreed. Sometimes this is referred to as "recovery of lost profits" or as "collecting the fruits of the bargain." In the earlier paint example, if it would have cost me $375 to paint your apartment under our $575 contract, your breach of contract, by refusing to let me paint, deprived me of a $200 profit, and I may recover that amount from you. On the other hand, if fulfillment of the contract would have brought me a loss, I have no case against you for damages.

The nonbreaching party, it must be warned, usually has a duty to mitigate damages, or minimize his losses. If you have breached our contract to buy my goods, for example, I must make a reasonable attempt to sell those goods to another buyer; if I succeed in doing so, you are entitled to a credit for what I have received. When the other side breaches a contract, keep a written record of your efforts to mitigate your damages.

Contractual money damages, meant to be purely compensatory in the sense of giving you the benefit of your bargain, are referred to as "general" damages. "Special" or "consequential" damages are collectible only when the probability of "specific" damage was, or should reasonably have been, known by you at the time of entering upon a contract. Examples of possible special damages are the value of special equipment purchased for and usable only under the broken contract or, a more usual example, the value of contracted goods that you know your buyer was liable to resell to a third party.

When there is only a minor deviation—say delivery of a hundred cases of tomato juice that includes two defective cases—a court would not deem the entire contract breached. For that to happen, the breach must be "material," which is legalese for "significant," "substantial," or "very important under the circumstances." The court might award as damages the cost of going into the market to replace the two bad cases of juice.

There are, however, important variations of awards based on circumstances of equity. Suppose, for example, that you built a road under a contract with me; I knew of the existence of many subsurface rocks that would make the actual cost of constructing the road twice as expensive as the contract price. I had falsely told you that I had the ground explored by a geologist and assured you that the subsurface was all sand, clay, and gravel, typical of the area. Under these circumstances, you could "rescind" the contract, in which case you could recover the fair value of your work, unrestricted by the contract price. Your recovery may exceed the contract price by a measure that bears a Latin designation, *quantum meruit*, "as much as deserved."

## Specific Performance

In cases involving things that are considered unique—land, buildings, works of art—money need not be the remedy for breach of contract. The court may order "specific performance"—that is, if a seller refuses to comply with his contract with you for the sale of the unique item, a court may order him to make the sale and to turn the item over to you. In short, the court forces the seller actually to complete the contract in accordance with its specific terms.

If you desire the remedy of specific performance on the purchase of a business, for instance, your contract should contain a clause stipulating that the business is unique and that the contract may be specifically enforced. If the business in question is a bookstore, it might be specified: "The parties agree that the business of MAW's Book Shop, Inc., is unique, and this contract for its purchase may be specifically enforced."

If you wish to be assured that a sale will go through, write into your agreement that the contractual subject is unique and that the contract may be specifically enforced.

Generally speaking, courts will *not* specifically enforce personal-service contracts, because of the difficulty of regulating human actions and reactions. If you agree to work for me as an employee, and then you refuse to, the courts may award me money damages, but will not force you to work for me.

## DEFENSES TO CLAIMS OF BREACH OF CONTRACT

When any lawyer is called upon to defend a client against a charge of breach of contract, he seeks reasons, called "defenses," which justify why his client need not carry out his end. The possibilities are many. One, already discussed, is the failure to reduce the contract to writing under the Statute of Frauds.

### Construing the Contract
The principal defense is that there was no breach. The terms of the contract are construed, or interpreted, and cited to show that you, the suing party, are mistaken, and that, in fact, I have complied with my contractual obligation. This defense most often arises when the contract is ambiguous or has gaps in it. For instance, if the contract calls for thirty tons of "Grade A" paper, the issue may turn on whether the paper supplied was in fact Grade A as meant in the contract. Be clear in your contractual specifications.

### Payment
An obvious defense to an action for breach of contract is that the price demanded has already been paid. It is good practice, on making final payment, to obtain some acknowledgment of that from the other side. Pay by checks and endorse them with such information as "Paid in full for work under contract of November 14, 1984."

Canceled checks are proof of payment. Save them for reasonable periods. When it is convenient, a friendly letter, with a copy retained, describing the purpose of the check is a good idea.

### Failure of Consideration

The reverse of payment as a defense is "failure of consideration." This means that the suing party did not himself fulfill his part of the bargain. A classic defense to a lawsuit for breach of contract is that the goods or services for which payment is sought were never supplied or were not as contracted. Avoid written praise of a contractor until you are completely sure that all went well, lest it later be held against you.

### Release

"Release" means that the complaining party earlier released you from contractual liability. It is another way of defending yourself against a claim of breach of contract.

Releases are documents that state that the party being released is no longer legally liable to the releaser. General releases cover all liability for acts from the beginning of the world to the date of release. Special releases apply to transactions specified in the release instrument itself.

Releases should always be in writing; there is a special legal mystique to them, and courts are jaundiced about claimed oral releases. Written releases, in many jurisdictions, do not require consideration.

### Accord and Satisfaction

Sometimes a discharge of another from contractual liability comes under the heading of "accord and satisfaction." This kind of discharge is important in daily life.

The most familiar application of accord and satisfaction is in the form of a check endorsed "Payment in Full." You and I are arguing over an amount due to you, say. I take the bull by the horns and send to you a check for the low amount I want to pay and I write "Payment in full of any and all obligations of Bertram Harnett under contract of January 3, 1985" on the back of the check. My hope is that by cashing the check, you will be deemed to have consented to accept it in full payment of your claim. The common-law rule, in force in New York, New Jersey, Georgia, Alabama, Utah, and most other states, is that cashing the check is agreement to settling the dispute. Your striking out the endorsement before cashing would be ineffective. Writing "Accepted without prejudice" would also do no good.

For the sender, a letter specifying that the enclosed check is in full settlement is useful.

When you get my "Payment in full" check, you have to make a decision. Can you live with the sum or should you return it? Do not endorse and deposit the check unless you are satisfied with it, for you will likely be deemed to have accepted it as payment in full. There is an exception, however, under the Uniform Commercial Code, if a check is tendered to you as payment for the purchase of goods and marked "Payment in full." You can cash that check without agreeing to full settlement if you write "Accepted without prejudice" over your endorsement on the back before you cash it.

All compromises that settle contractual disputes are further examples of accord and satisfaction.

## Statute of Limitations

If you are too late in bringing a lawsuit for breach of contract, you will lose if you bring the case to court. This is the "statute-of-limitations" defense, designed to eliminate stale cases where proof is no longer feasible and to place a time limit on possible disputation. Although time limits vary in different states and different circumstances, the most common state limiting period is six years from the execution of a contract. A contract is considered to have been executed on the first date that all the parties to it have become bound.

## Equity and the Chancellor's Foot

A whole series of defensive moves, classically known as "equity" or "equitable defenses," which may be in the form of counterattacks, may serve as justification for not going through with a contract.

The concept of equity arose in English church courts in medieval times and was later shifted to the secular system of the common law. Originally, the common-law rules and judges were strict and formalistic, and the king, acting through his chancellors, sought through equity a forum for more flexible remedies. Contrary to the old English common law, which was supposed to adhere strictly to prior case authority, equity was seen as a more individualized sort of justice, bringing fairness and common sense into judicial rulings. Since equitable relief was, in a sense, based on appeal to the chancellor's individual sense of fairness, the rationale of an equity case was said to have been the result of measuring the size of the chancellor's foot.

Although you may have seen references to defenses "in law" or "in equity," equity is an anachronism today; law and equity run through the legal mill together as the law.

*Rescission and Reformation; Fraud, Mutual Mistake, and Duress*
Two requests for relief under equity headings are rescission, or canceling (calling off) the contract, and reformation, which means rewriting the contract in accordance with the original mutual intent of the parties. They can be your defenses when you are sued, and can be the basis for a separate lawsuit initiated by you. Either fraud, duress, or mutual mistake of fact in your undertaking the contract may form the basis for your rescission or reformation.

Fraud is generally misrepresentation of a material fact on which you relied to your detriment, or concealment of material facts that you would not be likely to discover on your own. An example of fraud is touching up and selling a brand-new chair and representing it as an antique.

Charges of fraud often involve the sometimes difficult distinction between sales talk or "puff" and outright misrepresentation of specific facts. A statement that this is a "great" chair is just sales talk. A statement that the chair is real mahogany, when it is only stained pine, is a misrepresentation of fact. Fraud cases often turn on whether the statement was one of fact or one of opinion. Opinions are not considered representations of fact.

If both you and the seller thought a new chair to be an antique, a mutual mistake of fact has been made, and rescission may be had.

You alone may be mistaken; the seller may know that you are relying on a mistaken fact, to your detriment, and remain silent. If this is discovered, you may, in some jurisdictions, be able to rescind the sale and recover your money.

Since the facts in individual cases are critical and substantially related to the knowledge and the motives of people carrying out their business, the judicial results in rescission and reformation cases generally vary widely and are highly unpredictable.

Duress is a defense that excuses you from performing your part of a contract on the grounds that you were forced into signing the contract against your will under threat of harm. If I threaten to hit you if you do not sign my contract, and you sign in fear of me, that contract is not binding upon you because of the duress I exercised.

### Unconscionability

Unconscionability is a fairly new defense in equity cases. Where there is disparity of bargaining position because one party has a great advantage, and he does take advantage of the other, the other may not be bound to perform something to which he agreed. Assume you are an uneducated laborer, and you agreed in writing with me, a lawyer, to work for $150 for six months. You meant $150 a month for six months. You should win if I claim you breached the contract by not continuing to work for the six months. It would be unconscionable if I, the lawyer, had you work for me for six months for $150.

The classic unconscionability cases involve mail-order overcharges, high-pressure door-to-door selling, and retail installment-sale prices entailing terms of sale so unreasonably high or so weighted in favor of the seller that to enforce them would offend the conscience of any reasonable member of the community.

Unconscionability does not apply simply because you feel you cannot complete the contract without losing money or you regret having made the deal.

### Impossibility

Impossibility as a defense, where it is permitted, means that by virtue of altered facts, circumstances, or laws no one could possibly fulfill the terms of the contract legally. A person's death, for instance, is sufficient excuse for not fulfilling a contract to sing at a series of meetings.

If a contract is made for the delivery of certain medicines, and the law is then changed to ban their sale, the contract may be voided.

Suits to collect the proceeds of an illegal contract are unenforceable. Contracts to lend money at usurious rates of interest are unenforceable, and the usurious lender cannot even recover his principal.

### Plain-English Statutes

Many states have enacted statutes to require that consumer contracts and insurance policies be written in "plain English," so that you will know what you are contracting to buy, and they bar suits brought on contracts that violate this requirement.

# BUYING AND SELLING GOODS

The Uniform Commercial Code, a model statute drawn originally by law professors, has been adopted in one form or another in every state. It modifies in specific respects the common-law rules of contract law that govern the buying and selling of goods. It is often necessary, therefore, to know precisely how the rules are modified in each state. The rules are all in the statute books of the states, but the subject is quite detailed. You will need your lawyer if you have an important question. Some of the more common questions are answered in general here.

If merchandise is lost or destroyed in a store or in transit, who bears the risk of its loss? If you bought the goods outright and took them out of the store, the risk of whatever happens later, fire or theft, is yours. If a store is to deliver the goods to you, you do not have title or the risk of loss until they have been delivered. If, as a condition of sale, you have the right to return the goods within a stated period, they are still at your risk. But if you take them out of the store on approval, they remain at the store's risk until you have advised the store that you will keep them or you have kept them for an unreasonably long time without notifying the store.

Shipments involving delivery by common carrier have special language. "C.I.F." means "cost, insurance, and freight" and "F.O.B." means "free on board." In F.O.B. "place of shipment," the buyer pays the carrier and assumes the risk when the goods are actually delivered by the seller to the carrier. In F.O.B. "place of destination," the seller pays the carrier and bears the risk of loss until he delivers, or if the buyer refuses delivery when the goods are tendered to him. C.I.F. means that the price includes in a lump sum the cost of the goods and the insurance and the freight to the destination named. "C and F" is the same except for the insurance. Under both arrangements, the seller bears the risk of loss until he actually tenders delivery.

Rules of title refer to risk as between seller and buyer—whether the seller or the buyer must pay for goods sent in good condition but not received in good condition or at all. But they do not relieve the carrier, who may be liable to the title holder who takes the loss.

# WARRANTY OF QUALITY OR USE OF GOODS

When the goods you have received prove to be of poor quality, what do you do? In pondering your possible remedies, first discount the effects of the sales talk you swallowed about the great value, many uses, unusual comfort, and high style of the goods and the envy they would arouse in your neighbors. The courts will consider you to be an adult, and adults are not supposed to believe everything they hear.

Warranties are another matter and offer hope of success in making legal claims. They represent a departure from the old doctrine of *caveat emptor*. The maker and the seller have more responsibility now. Warranties are assurances that products are of a specified kind, quality, or usability. They are promises that the products are as represented. Warranties may be either express or implied.

## Express

A sales statement that says this automobile is a brand-new 1985 Ford sedan automobile is an express warranty. If it turns out that the car is an unused 1984 Ford sedan, the warranty is breached. You can either return the car and recover the purchase price, refuse to accept the car and sue, claiming breach of the express warranty, or keep the car and sue for the difference between its actual value and the price you paid.

Express warranties can be oral, but they must, of course, be provable.

## Implied

The field of implied warranties is one of the great modern legal improvements over the jungle code that used to prevail in the marketplace. Today, goods carry an implied warranty, which is a promise, deemed by operation of law to be made, that they are reasonably well suited to the purposes, and safe for the uses, for which they are sold. Other implied warranties include: that the seller has clear title to the goods he can pass on to you, and that if a sample was shown, the goods supplied will match the sample.

As stated earlier, there is a growing doctrine of strict liability for defective products that breach an implied warranty. Under contractual warranty breach, you are entitled only to money refund. If your claim can be based on tort, you may have a right to recover for damages for personal injury. To illustrate, if your new car has a defective engine that makes the car operate poorly and impairs its value, you can get your money back under implied-warranty-contract principles. However, if the engine comes loose because of its defectiveness and causes an accident in which you break both your legs, you can recover under rules of tort for your medical expenses, loss of income, and pain and suffering.

### Disclaimer

The law permits a seller to disclaim all warranties. Be alert to this possibility, because purchasing "as is," with no warranty, means you are taking an extra risk. You take the full risk of the condition of the purchased item.

## CREDIT SALES

The field of credit sales is rife with abuse of consumers. Whenever you purchase on credit, make sure you understand all the terms, including the hidden charges.

Many states require companies to tell you the actual rate of interest and any other charges that make up your credit transaction (such as delivery charges and alteration fees). States also limit the interest and penalties that can be charged, and, in some instances, forbid compulsory "tie-in" sales—for instance, a requirement to pay for life insurance as part of a car purchase on credit. The vice of tie-in is the requirement that you buy something you do not want to get something you do want, thereby adding to your true cost burden.

Most states have enacted retail-installment-agreement laws, and there is also a federal Consumer Credit Protection Act. Both require disclosures—complicated though they may be—of your rights in credit sales and credit card transactions, your entitlement to periodic statements, and your protection against misleading advertising and false labeling.

Take good care of your credit card and be careful whom you allow to use it, because you are liable for purchases made on it, whether by you or by someone else. If your card is stolen, you may be liable up to a maximum amount specified on the back of your card, although you may be insured against this harm for purchases made before you notified the credit card company. There are credit card coverages available in connection with homeowner's insurance policies. Fraudulent use of a credit card is in some instances a felony. Report all lost credit cards to the issuer *immediately*. Keep a record in a convenient place of your credit card numbers to facilitate reporting loss of the cards.

A chattel mortgage, comparable to the real estate mortgage on your home, can be placed on personal property. Automobiles bought on credit used to be subject frequently to such mortgages, which made the car collateral for repayment of the car loan. The mortgages are filed in a government office, usually with the county clerk. Any subsequent buyer of the car would be subject to that mortgage. Conditional sales agreements, whereby the dealer actually owns the car until you finish paying for it, are now more common. These agreements are also recorded, and if you fail to make the payments on schedule, the seller is able to seize the car summarily, since he is already the owner. Chattel mortgages, on the other hand, require a foreclosure sale for the dealer to get the car.

Government agencies, including the Postal Service, the Food and Drug Administration, the Federal Trade Commission, and local consumer protection offices in the states and cities, monitor abusive sales practices, receive complaints, and often act on them. There are enough agencies and laws regulating credit sales and credit cards so that if you feel abused, you can attract sympathetic attention—and even results—if you seek help. With this kind of problem, you do not need the help of a lawyer.

## MOVING YOUR THINGS

### By a Friend

If a friend who has a private van is carrying your property to another town purely as a favor and not for any charge, he is not liable for any damage incurred on the way, unless he is grossly negligent in handling your property. If that same friend, who is not a professional hauler, should charge you for the service, he is responsible for any damage that arises as a result of his own negligence—that is, of failure to exercise the care that a reasonable person would have taken under the circumstances. You should have a receipt from him.

Do not ship valuable property by friends who are willing to do you a favor, even if you pay them.

### By Common Carrier

The most usual questions of responsibility for damage arise when property is in the hands of a common carrier—an airline, a trucker, a railroad, or a shipping line. A common carrier is in the business of transporting people and property for money, and, with several exceptions, is absolutely responsible for any loss or damage to the goods or for any unreasonable delay in delivery of them. The exceptions are centered on those events known in the law as "force majeure"—acts beyond the carrier's control, such as storms, riots, strikes, and government seizure.

Have the shipping papers describe, in as detailed manner as feasible, the goods shipped, and have the shipper sign a receipt for them. The carrier is not liable for damage to goods that you have packed improperly. It is a good idea, if possible, to let the movers pack your valuable items, thereby increasing their responsibility.

To the extent permitted by government regulations, the carrier sets its own terms as to what it will carry, and it can establish limits, within reason, to the damages that it will pay. When you ship property by truck, for instance, you will see these limits on your bill of lading. If you are taking goods with you on an airplane, your ticket tells you that the airline bears only a limited dollar responsibility, although the notice may be in fine print, forcing you to resort to your latest prescription eyeglasses if you want to know what it says. Save all ticket receipts and claim checks until the journey is finished and you are satisfied that you have all your property, in the condition in which it was shipped. You can usually buy additional insurance from the carrier to cover your property, but do not overinsure, since you cannot recover more than the fair value of the goods.

# GETTING AROUND

## *Travel*

If you want life insurance for plane flights, carry travel-accident insurance year round through your regular agent or broker. It is the best buy if you fly frequently or travel a great deal generally. Trip insurance in air terminals is more expensive.

By treaty, the Warsaw Convention, the legal limit of air carriers on international flights for loss of life is now $75,000 on a flight beginning, stopping, or ending in the United States. Claims that can be made for property damage on international flights are severely limited. See your ticket.

Overbooking is a common practice of airlines. When you are told there is no seat for you on your scheduled flight, that the plane is overbooked, show your ticket and insist on your rights, which are a seat on the next practicable flight or a refund of your money. Many airlines, as a good-will gesture, will offer a cash bonus to volunteers from an overbooked flight who are willing to switch to another flight.

## *Hotels and Restaurants*

Theaters, stores, restaurants, schools, sports stadiums, and other public places are responsible only for property checked with them, and then only if they fail to exercise the care imposed on them by local law, subject again to posted dollar limits to responsibility for loss or damage to personal property. They put in writing their limits of liability. Many local laws and statutes impose special rules and obligations on these businesses, even to the extent of overriding attempts to limit liability for loss or damage to personal property. You may have more rights than those you see on the posted sign or claim check. If a problem arises, inquire. And always be sure that you are given a claim check, which is essentially a receipt.

Hotels are liable for negligence on their part that causes loss or damage to the person or property of their guests. Some states limit the property liability by statute. In all states, however, hotels may, and do, limit their liability further by posting a written schedule of limitations, usually on the doors of the bedrooms, and by providing a vault for safekeeping of valuables. In addition, there is usually a posted written limit on the value of property that the hotel will keep in its vault, and that limit applies unless the hotel exercises gross negligence in caring for these valuables. You can inform the hotel of the excess of the value of your jewelry over the posted schedule, and the hotel may agree to be responsible: if it does, get it in writing. Where there are no posted limits, the public places are fully liable for their negligence. It is still better to have your own personal insurance, however.

Hotels habitually overbook, counting on the law of averages to protect them. If you are in the lobby when the law of averages is repealed as to you, you have a problem. Your best protection is to have written confirmation of your reservation from the hotel, not the travel agent, in your hand. This will usually secure you a room. If you have prepaid for your room, in whole or in part, have your receipt with you. With confirmed reservations, prepayment, and a confident manner, with determination to match, the problems can normally be worked out. Sometimes acceptable accommodations are available elsewhere. Your legal rights are thin. You are at least entitled to a refund of any prior payment you may have made, and if you suffered some unusual damage, such as a nervous breakdown or a miscarriage, you might have a case for your physical or mental injury in some places, but not for your ruined vacation. In many states, unless the fine print in your reservation packet does you in, you may have a breach-of-contract action against the hotel, for whatever it may be worth. If you are the sort who will sue for the value of occupying a hotel room, you might receive in court whatever justice you may have been denied at the hotel registration desk.

The principal effect of rules of safekeeping by hotels, restaurants, and other public places is to deter carelessness and provide some barriers against theft. These operators have no absolute liability to you, and they are not treated as common carriers.

The moral of the story is, deal with reliable concerns and people, check your valuables whenever it is possible, and carry your own private insurance. If you are not inclined to do all this, leave your valuables at home or in your vault. Indeed, it is a good idea not to carry your valuables around—period. In putting the law on your side, there is not much room for mobile valuables. There is a labyrinth of local rules, inconspicuously posted limits of responsibility, and great difficulties of proof. The law is not hospitable. Remember that in most of these situations you are on the move and probably a stranger in town. You will be leaving soon.

## REPAIR WORK AND STORAGE

People who agree to repair, clean, or otherwise work on your property must take reasonable care of it. They may limit their liability, however, by advertising a schedule in their office or on your claim check or receipt. Make sure you have a receipt or a claim check, so you can prove you left your property there.

When property is left in storage or parked in a garage, the guardian is liable to you for negligence in care and handling. Your property may not be used unless it becomes necessary to move it. Be sure to keep your warehouse or garaging receipt or claim check in a safe place.

## PROPERTY INSURANCE

It is a particularly good practice to keep all your personal property insured throughout the year by a "personal property floater" with an insurance company. This is the form of policy that insures against destruction or theft of the personal effects you carry around with you, without regard to the limitations of the law and the establishment with which you may deal.

## GET IT IN WRITING

Get it in writing does not necessarily mean a contract, although, as indicated earlier, it is wise, and sometimes essential, to have a written contract in important undertakings. Even fragmentary writings can serve as a reminder of what was intended or can perhaps be used later to help prove a case.

A basic rule is never to surrender an object of any value or significance without receiving a descriptive receipt or at least a claim check.

Not only does a receipt or claim check facilitate finding your article, but it also establishes you as a serious claimant.

When you seek a receipt for a letter or a document, the best procedure is to submit a photocopy along with the original, and the receipt acknowledged on the face of the photocopy.

When you are party to a transaction in which a paper is signed by any party, always obtain a copy for yourself. Keep copies of letters and any other papers, including envelopes, until you are sure the transaction has been completed. Remember, you can be sued for breach of contract up to six years later.

Read carefully all documents you are called upon to sign, even the fine print. If you do not understand a word, a phrase, a sentence, or even an entire paragraph, do not be embarrassed to request an explanation. If the other party says, "It doesn't mean anything" or "It's not important," cross it out. Obviously the other party cannot object to the crossing out of meaningless and unimportant provisions. Do not leave any blanks open on the page; line them out.

You will occasionally be asked to sign credit card slips, form agreements, blank checks, and even blank pieces of paper. Turn them all down, unless it is one of those times when you really have no choice. Suppose there is only one car-rental agency for miles around and you need a car urgently and immediately. The manager will not rent you a car unless you sign a blank credit card slip so that he can insert the exact charges later, on the basis of actual time and mileage. You must decide whether you want that car badly enough to take the chance of being cheated.

# Chapter *Eight*

# *Minding Money*

If money is not the root of all evil, it certainly underlies most of the legal patch. When people are not suing each other or divorcing over money, they are scrambling to get it or to give it. The lawbooks tell tales of working, cheating, manufacturing, investing, lying, selling, swindling, planting, robbing, insuring, extorting, consulting, gambling, writing, and more—all for money.

Unsurprisingly, much of the law deals with such subjects; money and law do seem to go together. Here is an area in which you will want to be particularly sensitive to your legal rights and duties. Not only does available money enable you to acquire your necessities and niceties, but it also enables you to fund your later years. Money—handle with care!

## BANKING AND CURRENCY TRANSACTIONS

### *Cash Payments and Receipts*
Cash does not care who owns it. It passes just as it is, with no concern for creditworthiness or need for identification. On the other hand, cash is susceptible to loss and theft, and, unlike canceled checks, its passage leaves no evidence. This is a drawback. In any important transaction, pay by a check drawn on a financial institution that returns your checks to you with a monthly statement. If you must pay cash, get a receipt.

Be wary of anyone who asks you to pay or receive cash for services or for goods, and will not give you a receipt or take one from you. There are dishonest people who will hide from their employers the cash they receive from you, or who will not declare the cash on their income tax returns, or who are paying you from stolen funds. You are on notice that these are troublesome people. They are chary of receipts, which put beyond their control documentary proof of their connection with the money. Some of them may offer you a discount to participate in a traceless cash transaction.

Remember, when you pay cash and have no evidence of it, you are at risk. You might be called upon to pay twice. If you knowingly purchase stolen goods, you may be committing a crime. If you pay cash in a questionable transaction that is not provable, your chances, if you are bilked, of obtaining satisfaction by taking your seller to court are slim because of difficulties of proof and your own voluntary and unsavory participation.

There are no general laws that prohibit paying or receiving cash. Retail stores, for instance, which deal regularly in cash, usually have no problem (unless some extraneous hand is in the cash register), because they accept cash in the ordinary course of their business, and they issue receipts or sales tickets, presumably keep track of all their receipts, and honor their tax obligations and other legal and accounting obligations. Service or professional people may accept payment in cash for services and deposit and report the cash in their regular accounts under their regular systems of accounting notation. There is no legal harm in that. Illegalities, if any, arise from failures to account for the cash, often for tax evasion.

Banks and other financial institutions may be required to report to a governmental agency their receipts of specified amounts of cash, or to report the receipt of cash from foreign sources.

## Checks
### Bad Checks
If you issue a check for which you have insufficient funds in the bank, it will eventually be returned by your bank, stamped "Returned for insufficient funds." Bad checks, sometimes called "rubber" checks, which "bounce" back to you, are not funny. They can be more than embarrassing. They are not light technicalities. They damage your credit. They can cause a breach of contract. Obtaining goods and services with a check you know to be bad may also constitute larceny by false pretense. If your bank honors your check with insufficient

supporting funds—an overdraft—it is, in effect, lending you the money. Banks often do this for valued customers, but may charge fees for doing it.

### Forgery

You can have a checking account in your own name or in a joint account with another. You can empower another to draw from your account as a "deputy." Keep in mind that if you have a joint account or deputize another person with the power to withdraw money from your account, that other person can clean out your account. Be guided by that sober fact in limiting your account and who you trust to draw checks on it. Even if you disapprove of the purpose of the withdrawal—even though the money is being stolen from you—the withdrawal is effective and not forgery. The bank is thoroughly protected in making the payment.

Forgery of a check means affixing the signature of the maker (the one who writes the check) or the endorser (the one who signs the check on the back), or altering the amount for which the check is drawn, all without authority. If someone signs your name to a check without your authority, that check is no good and your bank cannot charge you for it. If someone receives a check signed by you, and then without your consent alters the amount or changes the payee, your bank again cannot charge your account for it.

Under the Uniform Commercial Code, however, if, by your negligence, you contribute to the alteration of a check, or to the making of an unauthorized signature, you may be liable to your bank for the amount of that check. Classic examples of negligence that will cause you to suffer the consequences of forged checks are: leaving signed blank checks unguarded, failure to safeguard devices used to sign checks, and failure to take action to prevent further forgeries after you have found that one has taken place. It is essential that you review your bank statements punctually and regularly and report to the bank any unauthorized signatures or alterations.

Check writing should be precise. You should fill all spaces in which the payee and the sums are indicated, either with flush written text or by drawing a line from the finish of your text to the end. Leave no room for names or digits to be added.

With the advent of computerization, checks are identified in bank processing by their imprinted number. You may fill out a check, inadvertently leave it unsigned, and pay a bill with it. The check may slip by the one who took it in payment, and your bank will pay the check, but you are still responsible for it.

### Endorsement

A check endorsement is a signature on the back of a check. If the endorser's signature appears alone, without qualifying language, it is known as an "endorsement in blank" and has the effect of making the endorser the guarantor of the check, which means that the guarantor either has to make the check good or return the money given to him, for instance, on endorsing and cashing a check made payable to his order. The endorsement facts of legal life calls to mind one of my favorite legal anecdotes. In a paternity suit, the mother claimed that John Brown was the father of her child. Brown freely admitted having had sexual relations with the mother of the child but proved conclusively that these took place only during the fourth month of her pregnancy. After the evidence had been submitted, the judge pondered the case, then ruled that Brown was the father of the child. Brown was thunderstruck.

*Brown:* Your honor this is just not humanly possible.
*Judge:* It is the law!
*Brown:* Which law?
*Judge:* Section 3-414 of the Uniform Commercial Code.
*Brown:* What has that got to do with a case like this?
*Judge:* If the maker cannot be found, the endorser will be held liable.

An endorsement qualified by some words is a restrictive endorsement. The least restrictive is "Pay to the order of Philip A. Newman," followed by the signature of the payee (the one to whom the check is made payable on its front). When it is delivered to him, Newman is free to negotiate that check to whomever he wants, to deposit it in his own account, or to cash it. If a payee wishes to turn a check over to another person but not to guarantee that it will be paid, he can accomplish that purpose by writing "Without recourse" above his signature. This may happen when the payee wishes to accommodate a third party who is willing to take the maker's check, but the endorser does not wish to take the risk that the check might not be good.

"Deposit to the account of John Payee" is a common restrictive endorsement made by the payee himself, as when he deposits the check in his own bank. The endorsement is for the restrictive purpose of depositing in the bank. A recipient of that check cannot lawfully do anything else with it. Banks will not always insist on endorsements for deposit to be signed physically by the endorser. They will often accept his name signed by someone else or even rubber stamped.

If you agree to accept a check that must be endorsed to you, it is well to have that check endorsed in your presence. If it has already been endorsed, have it signed again by the endorser to see that the endorsing signatures match. The maker of a check is not liable for forged endorsements.

A check with a blank endorsement is almost the same thing as cash. Do not endorse a check until you are ready to transfer or deposit it.

### Certified and Bank Checks

A certified check is one stamped by a bank to indicate that funds are on deposit to cover it and that the bank has set aside funds for payment of that check. A bank or cashier's check is a check issued by a bank directly to a payee who wants special assurance that he is getting a good check; the bank, of course, charges the account of its own customer who caused the check to be drawn.

Certified checks and bank or cashier's checks are normally used in real estate purchases, whenever a seller does not want to pass title to his property without a firm assurance that the buyer's check is good. But their use is not limited to real estate. They are also used whenever the payee does not quite trust the maker of the check. Bank checks are also typically used in transactions where the true identity of the buyer is being concealed—through, for example, a corporation that has no business or assets.

Your safety is diluted if you accept a certified or bank check made out to a payee who then endorses that check over to you. The bank has no direct obligation to you, and you may suffer if some action of the endorser causes the check to become impaired—for instance, he files for bankruptcy before you cash it.

*Stopping Payment*

Where a check is mislaid or goes astray, you may want to stop payment on it. Stop-payment orders on checks are common. Your bank will ask you to sign an indemnity first, to keep itself out of trouble, and it will take no responsibility for any slip-up. It will also charge you a fee for its services in the stoppage. It is your transaction all the way.

People dissatisfied with purchases or services often try to stop checks. If a stop-payment order reaches the bank too late, after the check is cashed, the order is totally ineffectual. When you receive a check, deposit it in your bank as soon as possible. The sooner that check is deposited, the sooner it clears the maker's bank, and the sooner you know you have the money. A bank may dishonor a check that is more than one month old. Endorsing a check to another keeps it in circulation; it is better to go to the bank and deposit it, thereby initiating the collection process. Pay others with your own checks.

Although stopping payment on checks is common enough, the practice may bring countercharges of crookedness from the other side. If you are a respectable citizen and have a plausible complaint justifying your stoppage, these charges will have little legal effect, although the charges may be annoying and harassing if pressed. Stopping payment on a check may open you to charges of larceny or breach of contract under sufficiently grievous circumstances. All in all, only. stop payment on a check if you are replacing a lost or stolen check, or if you are in the mood for trouble.

Although few realize it, it is possible to stop a certified check, possibly even a bank check, but to do so requires indemnities and the cooperation of the bank, and it should not be undertaken except on your lawyer's advice.

## Lending and Borrowing Money

*Improving the Terms of Your Loan*

If you are an average person, borrowing money from banks or other lending institutions usually means taking it on the terms offered. You do not have the bargaining alternatives open to big corporations and wealthy investors, who can secure better interest rates, longer repayment periods, liberalization of restrictive provisions, and collateral terms that lenders habitually seek to impose. Big borrowers and big lenders deal on more or less equal terms; each has what the other wants.

Small borrowers are individually of little interest to most lending institutions. Nonetheless, since many banks compete for their class of business as a whole, a would-be borrower can, to some extent, shop among banks for the best terms. Some may charge less interest or have more liberal time-payment terms than others, including the right to prepay the loan.

When you seek to borrow and are presented the bank's form of note, there is little, if any, room to negotiate, except to verify whether the amount to be lent, the interest, and the date payment is due are stated correctly. The document itself is, typically, a long sheet of paper tightly printed in small type on both its sides. If security (collateral) is to be given to the bank, such as shares of stock or accounts receivable, their enumeration should be reviewed carefully.

Try to remove any language that allows the lender to demand payment if it "feels insecure." The terms of repayment should be very clear.

One thing you definitely can do is find the part deep in the fine print where you agree to pay the bank's expense in collecting from you if you fail to pay, including its legal fees, sometimes expressed as a percentage of the loan amount. Most banks will let you qualify the phrase "legal fees" with the inserted word "reasonable" and will agree to strike any references to percentages. This limits your liability to the bank's lawyer for collection costs to his "reasonable fees." If you should happen to default on the loan, and the bank must resort to legal collection procedures, this little maneuver could save you five to twenty percent of the amount of the loan, depending on how long your default continues and the complications of collection, of which your own defenses may be part.

One important benefit to seek on any loan of more than a year's duration is the right to prepay the loan without penalty, as mentioned earlier. A penalty is essentially a bonus to the lender for permitting you to get out of the loan. If interest rates drop, you can replace your loan, so you should have the ability to pay off your initial loan at any time you want. Many lenders, however, will not allow prepayment unless a minimum amount of interest has already been paid or the debtor is willing to pay the bonus to the lender.

### Personal Guarantees

If a loan is requested by a corporation or an individual who is not wholly creditworthy, and there is not adequate collateral posted, the lender may seek someone else to guarantee the borrower's note. If you sign as a guarantor, your guarantee usually continues as long as the borrower is indebted to the lender, even on loans made after the one for which you gave your guarantee. Be sure there are provisions in the guarantee document you sign that allow you to absolve yourself by revoking the guarantee as to any loans that may be made after you stop the guarantee. This becomes particularly important if you should terminate your association with a business; you might, for example, sell your interest to those who continue it.

Guarantees can be limited to specific property pledged for repayment of a loan. Under these circumstances, if the borrower defaults, the one who has pledged property will lose it but will not be liable to the lender for anything more.

If friends or relatives borrow money from a bank, do not have enough credit, and want you to guarantee their loans as a favor, head for the hills. Guarantees of loans are often made by means of an endorsement in blank on the back of a note, similar to the endorsement on the back of a check; little formality is necessary. Accept with skepticism all assurances that you have nothing to worry about. The request to guarantee should worry you all by itself. There is good reason for the old saw that "a guarantor is a fool with a fountain pen." Be miserly with any personal guarantees of the loans of others.

You may be asked by a relative or a friend to lend money to them. Be careful, because you may not be able to compel payment upon default, since you may not want to sue a relative or a friend, and you certainly might not have the stomach to foreclose the home of such a person if you took a mortgage as collateral. Would you really put their children out on the street? Lending money to a relative or a friend is often an unwilling gift. If the urge to lend overpowers you, instead of providing your own funds consider arranging a bank loan for the amount desired, and then guarantee the bank's loan. The borrower is more likely to pay the bank than to pay you, and the bank will push for payment in ways you would not.

Shakespeare knew this: "Neither a borrower nor a lender be; / For loan oft loses both itself and friend, / And borrowing dulleth edge of husbandry." (*Hamlet*, I, . . . .)

### Usury

All but a handful of states have laws restricting the rates of interest that can be charged on loans to individuals. These range, in most states, between six and twelve percent a year, sometimes higher. Impermissibly high interest is called "usury."

The civil penalty for usury in loans to individuals is severe. Not only is no interest payable, but the usurious lender forfeits his principal as well.

In general, there are no restrictions on interest rates charged to corporations, except that in some states charging excessive interest, such as twenty-four percent a year, may be a crime.

Usury rules are often confusing, however, since there are significant exceptions, primarily having to do with loans from banks or automobile finance companies, who are separately regulated by the states in their lending activities. In addition, accredited small-loan companies and pawnshops can charge much higher rates of interest. Were it not for these statutory exceptions, the loans of these companies would be usurious.

The practice of taking payment of interest in advance has the effect of raising the true (real or effective) rate of interest charged. If, for instance, $1,000 is lent for three years at eight percent and the whole interest, $240, is subtracted in advance from the loan proceeds (taken off the top), the amount of money actually lent would be $760, and the effective rate of interest would, by actuarial count, be nine and six-tenths percent. In addition, permissible charges on credit card balances and installment purchases average one and one-half percent a month, or an effective interest rate of eighteen percent a year.

When taking out a consumer loan where the interest is discounted in advance, or buying goods on time, ask the lender or seller to advise you in writing of the true annual interest rate you will be paying.

After you learn the true interest rate, you may want to take the money anyway, but at least you will know what you are getting into. Under federal truth-in-lending legislation, you are entitled to know the true interest rate charged by discount lenders, credit card companies, and installment sellers.

### Collateral and Security Interest

Loans are either secured or unsecured. Secured loans involve collateral, such as a home mortgage, an automobile, furniture, or appliances. If a loan is unsecured, the lender relies only on your general promise to pay.

Mortgages and liens (notices of a debt for which property is security) on movable items are recorded in a government office (usually the county clerk's) to give public notice that the property is already pledged. If you default on a secured loan, the lender may, subject to local law, foreclose (take away your right to redeem) your property and sue you for any balance of the loan not covered if the collateral is sold—that is, for any deficiency. If there is a surplus—if more is realized on the collateral than the amount owed—you are entitled to it.

There is provided under the Uniform Commercial Code a special status called a "security interest" in enumerated assets. If the lender wishes a security interest in assets of yours, he specifies them in the notice-of-loan forms you execute, which he files with the appropriate government office. If you default, he then has a lien on the assets enumerated. There is an important distinction between security interest and collateral, even though collateral is commonly referred to as security. The conjunction of the word "interest" with "security" is the key. If a lender has collateral, whoever acquires or holds the property is subjected to priority of the lien even if there has been no loan default. He cannot defeat the interest of the mortgagee in the property by transferring it away. However, under a security interest, you have no lien on the assets covered unless and until there is a loan default.

## MAKING YOUR MONEY GROW (OR WATCHING IT SHRINK)

The words "savings" and "investment" are really synonymous. With inflation, currency fluctuations, and all the effects of the global economy, the simple stashing away of dollars in the proverbial mattress may not be saving at all, because the dollar tucked away in 1955 may, in 1985, buy only a quarter of what it would have in 1955. That same dollar put into the stock of a leading corporation might be worth many times the dollar invested thirty years earlier. What is the *real* course of saving?

## *Risk*

Never lose sight of the fact that the return on your investment is always a function of risk; there is always something wrong with the deal that is *too* good. Investments are guaranteed only in exceptional circumstances, so be careful with yours. Dealing blindly with strangers, acting on tips, and looking for fast bucks are invitations to a fleecing—yours—and perhaps to the law courts later.

### *Legal Protections*

Recognizing that risk is inherent in investment, the law concerns itself with whether the true nature of the risk was fairly communicated to the investor. So long as the risk was fairly disclosed to you, you have no legal recourse if you lose your money simply because the prospect did not pan out. Under the federal securities laws and those of the states, you are entitled to be informed properly. There are also significant federal protections against manipulative practice in the sale of securities.

You are entitled to a fair shake in whatever prospect there was. The honesty and prudence of those who handle the funds of others are subject to much legal scrutiny. If there is dishonesty, highly imprudent management conduct, market manipulation, or improper inducement to make investments, there is likely some legal remedy.

### *Where the Law Does Not Help*

You take the business risks of your investments. The law does not protect your from your own investing imprudence.

Even if technically you have legal redress for a failed investment, your money may well be lost to you. Outright swindlers and crooks have infinite ways of causing the evaporation of the funds of investors they entice. If honestly run businesses do go broke, there may be little on hand for the stockholders after any remaining assets have been picked over by creditors.

If you must gamble, you should understand that being in a game in which someone else is throwing loaded dice is not gambling. And even the best ideas are not automatically translated into successful business; economic practicality, good management, sufficient capital, timing, and the ability to withstand competition are also required.

## Bank Deposits and Money Funds

The most low-risk way to invest is to deposit your money in the bank. Bank accounts offer greater security than stocks or real estate, require no expertise or attention, and can accommodate any amount. However, their investment return is conservative, and they offer no chance of capital appreciation. Bank accounts grow only through further deposits and interest accumulation.

Accounts in commercial banks and savings banks are insured by the Federal Deposit Insurance Corporation (FDIC) up to $100,000 for each depositor. Similarly, accounts in savings and loan associations may be insured to $100,000 by the Federal Savings and Loan Insurance Corporation (FSLIC).

Money market funds—a form of mutual funds—have come to be regarded as alternatives to bank accounts. They are not, however, federally insured, so the banks are safer. A middle ground is a fund that invests only in federal debt obligations. Bank accounts that pay interest at money market rates are not mutual funds, and are insured.

## Stocks and Bonds

There is a whole range of investment opportunities, from the highly conservative to the sheerly speculative, in the securities markets. Stocks and bonds are collectively known as "securities."

A bond is a loan from you to a government or a corporation. It is evidence of a debt. If you hold one, you are a creditor; the issuer of the bond is a debtor. Stock, on the other hand, is ownership in a corporation—called "equity." Bonds normally call for regular interest payments and repayment of the amount lent (face amount) at a stipulated time. Stockholders receive dividends when and if they are declared by the board of directors of the corporation.

Bonds resemble bank accounts in that they are fixed-interest-bearing obligations. Usually they are riskier than bank deposits, but they offer higher rates of return for longer periods. Since bonds may be publicly traded, a limited capital-appreciation opportunity arises if you resell the bonds after market rates of interest have declined. Conversely, you lose on resale of bonds if interest rates rose after your original purchase.

Common stock fluctuates in value directly in relation to the value and appeal of the business, without limit. It is the riskiest class of securities investment. Much of the potential profit in stocks comes from trading in the marketplace, buying low and selling high. No dividend is guaranteed. You are an owner, not a creditor with a fixed right to interest. Your fortunes are at the risk of the business and the stock market.

Preferred stock is a hybrid stock and bond, although, strictly speaking, it is equity and not debt. Holders of preferred stock usually receive priority in the payment of dividends over holders of common stock, but they do not share in the accumulated earnings or growth of the corporation. Preferred stock may often be redeemed (required to be sold back to the corporation) at a price specified on the stock certificate itself.

### Bond Features

United States Treasury notes or bills (due within a year) or bonds (due on longer terms) are the safest debt securities, because they are government obligations as to both interest and principal. There is always an active public market for them. They are "liquid," which is another way of saying that they are easily salable in a public trading market where there are more than a few buyers and sellers. Their sale price depends on general interest rates at the time. Corporate bonds are less secure, but their yield is usually somewhat higher than that of government bonds.

One feature to consider about corporate bonds with favorable rates is whether they are callable, which means that the issuer has the right to pay them off on the call date, at a specified price. The call feature works against you as a borrower, for if market interest rates decline, your bond is called and you lose your favorable return. If interest rates rise in the marketplace, you are bound (locked in) to the interest-rate return provided on your bond, which is then not favorable. The same principles apply to redeemable preferred stock.

Not all government bonds are federal. Some are issued by states, some by municipal subdivisions, both of which are known as "municipal bonds." They form the basis of tax-exempt bonds. The interest on tax-exempt municipal bonds is exempt from federal income tax and further exempt from the state and local taxes of the state or municipality issuing them. Interest on federal bonds is exempt from state income tax. An obvious advantage of tax-exempt bonds lies in the tax savings resulting from their tax exemptions. Be sure your income makes worthwhile the lower rates paid by municipal bonds than you would receive on safer U.S. Treasury bonds. Investment in mutual funds or trusts that offer only tax-exempt bonds is a good way for relatively small investors to diversify into tax-exempt bonds under expert management.

In investing in tax-exempt bonds, find out whether all the debtor's assets are available to satisfy the debt (general obligation) or whether the bonds are secured only by defined revenue (revenue bonds). A general obligation bond is safer (with less return comparatively), because it is a debt of the government effectively supported by its taxing power, whereas a revenue bond is payable only out of the income of a designated project, such as highway or bridge tolls.

### Investing in Common Stocks

Common stocks are the popular vehicles for income, for capital appreciation, and often for market speculation, depending on their nature and quality, although as a class they are riskier than bonds. Less volatile stocks, like those of utility companies, tend to pay higher dividends and have less appreciation in the market than, for instance, stocks of high-technology companies. Risk and return are mutually related.

Stocks are bought through commission brokers, either on organized stock exchanges or over-the-counter. Although there are many exceptions, companies listed on the major stock exchanges tend to be more substantial than those not listed and their stock tends to have more value as collateral for loans. The stock exchanges, which are organized administrative bodies, are under the regulatory authority of the federal Securities and Exchange Commission (SEC).

MARGIN BUYING. Stocks may be purchased for cash outright, or on margin, which means borrowing part of the purchase price, usually from the broker, and leaving the stock with him as collateral for the purchase loan. Leverage is using borrowed money to make more purchases, and margin purchase is the typical form of leverage for stock investments. The word "leverage" signifies that the buyer invests limited cash and then uses credit as a lever to make purchases for which his own cash would be inadequate. Margin buying is risky. If the market price of the stock declines below a certain level, you will be called on to pay more cash to restore the balance between your borrowing and the current value of your stock. If you fail to pay the margin call, the broker can and will sell your stock in the market and repay himself, leaving you with only whatever balance may be left over. Margin buying is a giant step up on the risk scale.

CHURNING. A further risk in stock buying is introduced when you give your broker discretionary power, which means he can invest your money as he sees fit. Letting the broker act on his own discretion is the very purpose of the arrangement, since he is the expert and you presumably are not. You are trusting him—not only his judgment, but his character as well. Unscrupulous brokers are known to exercise their investment authority to "churn" stocks, buying and selling stocks just to make the commissions that they receive on each purchase and on each sale. Churning is illegal, but it is difficult to prove. The indication of churning is a lot of trading and a lot of commissions with little or no profit. Be wary of giving discretionary authority to anyone, particularly one whom you may not know well or at all. Listening uncritically to a rapacious stockbroker who sells you on a stock although he may not hold discretionary authority to act on his own can have the same effects as churning.

MUTUAL FUNDS. Mutual funds have grown up to meet the needs of the average investor who wishes to invest relatively small sums yet have the advantages of expert management and investment diversity. Hundreds or thousands of investors in a mutual fund share ownership of a large portfolio of securities.

In "load" funds, you pay a sales commission to enter. If you invest $1,000 and pay an eight percent load, which goes out as sales commissions, you are in effect putting only $920 into investment activity, and your return will be based on that amount. There are, however, many "no-load" funds, on which you pay no sales commissions at all. Your $1,000 is taken in as $1,000. All mutual funds of stock pay management fees to their investment advisers, typically one-quarter to one-half percent per year of the average invested assets. In no-load funds the entrepreneurial profit is in the management fee alone. Bond funds pay less, perhaps one-tenth percent. Mutual funds and their investment advisers are also heavily regulated by the SEC.

### Securities and Exchange Commission

The federal government, largely through the Securities and Exchange Commission (SEC), regulates stockbrokers, including their employees, who are salesmen or registered representatives, in the sale of both stocks and bonds. If you have a complaint against a stockbroker, you can go to the stock exchange of which his firm may be a member, the SEC (which has regional offices), or the National Association of Securities Dealers (NASD), in Washington, D.C., all of whom have important powers over stockbrokers and salesmen.

You can check up on the activities of public companies in which you invest if they are of sufficient size to be required under the law to file reports with the SEC. These ''reporting'' companies file monthly, quarterly, and annual reports of various kinds. These are generally informative, to an intelligent investor, and are available at the office of the SEC in Washington, D.C., as well as at the SEC's regional offices.

A wide variety of remedies against underwriters, promoters, officers, and directors of public companies is available, for breach of federal and state law and also under the common law. State laws that govern the sale of new securities are known as ''blue-sky'' laws, presumably with reference to the possibly airy and high-flown contents of the offering. They vary greatly in efficacy and scope. All this is heavy legal stuff. Do not back off if you feel you have been treated unfairly. Some lawyers will take such cases gladly, on the understanding that they will collect their fees contingently, only from any recovery that they may bring about.

### New Issues

''New issues'' may strictly be defined in two ways. The usual meaning is stock that is being freshly issued by a company. Although the company may have issued 10 million shares to the public three years ago, if it decides to issue another 2 million shares this year, those 2 million shares become a new issue. The second meaning relates to a company that has never sold stock publicly before. When its stock is sold to the public for the first time, that becomes a new issue. New issues of stock of companies that have no previous record of public stock ownership or sales, and therefore no SEC disclosures, can be particularly troublesome to investors.

"HOT" NEW ISSUES. Sales of stock that has never before appeared in the marketplace are singularly subject to abuse, since many of them are for new (just starting) companies with inflated claims of worth. They are from the sales land of "hot" new issues. There is eternal hope in the breasts of hot-new-issue buyers that they will be purchasing early a Xerox, a Polaroid, or a Texas Instruments of the future, but most often they are disappointed.

PROSPECTUS. A prospectus is a memorandum, usually printed, lengthy, and formidable, that is designed to give a possible investor full information about a newly issued security. Since many companies have had no previous public reporting, the prospectus is the only real opportunity to evaluate them. Theoretically, salesmen are not permitted to sell new issues "away" from the prospectus, which means that they may not give out assurances and promises of company prospects that are not set forth in the prospectus, but unfortunately many do, telling their tales in whispered assurances, side letters, and clandestine financial projections. Some separate literature is legally acceptable, but its leeway is sharply limited. Difficult as prospectuses may be to understand, try your best.

If stocks or bonds are already being traded in the marketplace, they are not new issues. There is no current prospectus for those issues. Prospectuses for currently offered new issues, however, give all investors of a given company a current view of that company's prospects and condition.

You must remember always that although the SEC and the various states require the registration of securities to be sold, the SEC and the states do not approve the merits of any security. Their regulatory mission is to ensure full disclosure. Once you have that disclosure, you are on your own. Unhappily, the disclosure requirements of companies selling stock for the first time ("going public") are often particularly complex, and the prospectuses therefore long and difficult. Issuers and underwriters believe that few investors have the training or endurance to plow through a suitably complex prospectus with real understanding, and they do not rely on prospectuses for their sales. Increasingly, the view is that investors rely on their salesmen and on the investment allure of the issuer and its product, without much hard knowledge; that they believe in catchy phrases and fashionable concepts. This has led some issuers to throw extraneous material into their prospectuses without regard to readability. The expression is popular among issuers that a prospectus is their insurance policy, not their sales literature.

Do not believe that the fearsome contents of a prospectus are meant to be disregarded. Do not believe anything told to you that is not in the prospectus. You can grasp the essentials of most new issues from their prospectuses, if you persevere. If you do not understand the investment from the prospectus, ask yourself why you want to make the investment. Get a good answer before you proceed. If you complain later that you were not told all the relevant facts, you will be charged with knowledge of the contents of that prospectus.

### Private Companies

CLOSELY HELD COMPANIES. Investing in corporations or new ventures held privately—that is, closely held by a very few people—is even riskier in general than investing in public securities, because no useful public information about them is available, and legal enforcement against them is problematic. The SEC and the states effectively regulate only public companies.

If you are a minority stockholder in a closely held corporation, your legal rights are quite limited. Unless you make prior protective provisions in a shareholder's agreement to which you are a party, you have no rights to financial statements, to profit, or even to information about what is going on.

If you suddenly need the money you invested, no one is likely to buy your stock, except perhaps the insiders, who will offer you their price. Your practical inability to sell is known as being "locked in." It is unwise to invest in a closely held corporation without some practical ability on your part to be able to get a fair value for your stock when you want it. Your "way out" can be in the form of a compulsory purchase of your shares by the corporation or the majority shareholders at a formula price, should you demand it. If your demand is not met, there should be provision for compulsory liquidation of the corporation. There should be limitations also on the funds that the insiders can take out of it.

Never invest in a closely held company without receiving a written proposal describing its terms. Aside from aiding your understanding, this will become your basis for establishing the representations and

understandings on which you made your investment, should you have
to sue.

Do not cry later; try now. See a lawyer or accountant experienced
in investment activity before putting any sum you deem significant
into a closely held venture.

Often, people enter into this kind of investment with friends and
are then reluctant to bring up sticky legal questions. Do not be reluctant; it is usually friends who take advantage of your relationship and
stick *you*.

PRIVATE PLACEMENT. There is a halfway kind of financing between
a public offering and a closely held venture: private placement. This
venture typically involves no more than thirty-five investors. A descriptive sales memorandum is prepared, with financial statements,
which is usually more informal than an SEC filing and easier to read,
but not cleared in advance by the SEC for full disclosure efforts. This
memorandum sets forth the understanding of your investment. Private
placement is a favorite way of raising capital in business proposals
that are too small for the expense and trouble of public offerings and
too large for the few people involved to finance by themselves.

The SEC is, nonetheless, a presence in these private placements.
This is because the number of investors solicited is usually large enough
to border on a public offering. The SEC has issued guidelines on the
number of investors and the kinds of disclosures that have to be made
in a private placement to be safe from charges of failing to register
as a public offering. Because there are severe penalties (from refunding the investments, all the way to imprisonment) for the promoters
if a private placement is deemed by the SEC to be a public offering,
there is general care taken to comply with the SEC guidelines.

A usual way out for an investor in a private placement is a right to
compel the company to register his stock for a public offering in the
future.

## Real Estate

Investment in real estate ranges from speculation in vacant land to
renting apartment houses to buying and selling stores, factories, and
office buildings. It is an occupation for experts; it tends to be risky,
in varying degrees.

Many public companies deal in one corner or another of the real estate business, and through their stock they offer opportunities for indirect investment in real estate. A commonplace method of investing in real estate today is through public offerings or private placements by promoters of syndicates, usually in the legal form of partnerships, to buy and operate real estate. Whether it is a prospectus or a private memorandum that you are offered, read the document carefully and investigate those with whom you deal. The comments in connection with all stock investments are applicable here, too. Note particularly carefully how much interest in the property the promoters are taking for how much cash investment, how the promoters will be able to take money from the syndicate, how you can transfer your interests, if you wish, and if you are relying on tax-shelter benefits, get an opinion from your own tax expert. Do not rely on the opinions of the sellers' lawyers or accountants.

Real estate syndications, by the fixed character of real estate, are essentially intrastate, and not in interstate commerce, which is the common basis of federal, and therefore SEC, jurisdiction. Accordingly, many state authorities have moved in decisively to regulate sales. However, once the real estate venture is founded and starts operation, state regulation is largely indifferent.


## The World Out There

The big wide world of investment seethes with commodities, futures, puts, calls, warrants, oil and gas ventures, tax shelters, animal breeding, inventions, and every kind of scheme. Fortunes have been made in all of them, and have been lost in them as well, sometimes by the same investors. The differences in their economic and social worth are beyond imagination.

In approaching all investments, bear in mind that those who are promoting them—from the biggest names on Wall Street to the backers of the tiniest gold mine in Canada—all want your money. They all have something to sell. Do not be naïve.

Legal recourse is a sometime thing, and it is very expensive, particularly when tilting with immoral people. Deal with people you know or trust; suspect the windfall; read all the fine print; know what you are doing; take your chances, but only with your eyes wide open.

# FEDERAL INCOME TAXATION

Hardly good bedtime reading, the Internal Revenue Code, which sets forth the federal income tax and other federal taxes, is often seen in the form of a two-volume paperback set, containing more than 5,000 pages, most of them covered with small print. Though this code affects us all, few would want these volumes, containing, as they do, a statutory compilation of incredible complexity, which is often a source of mystery, not only to laymen, but also to accountants and lawyers who deal with it every day. Simpler tax laws are often called for, but the code seems to become more complicated every year.

## *Gross Income*

The code taxes all the income of a United States citizen, no matter where he earns it. Its definition of "gross income" is simple and sweeping. It means generally all income from whatever source. Your salary and all fees, interest, dividends, rents, and royalties that you receive are part of your gross income, but so are your pension, your gains on stock sales, the money you win in a state lottery, and the valuable necklace you find while digging in your back yard. Even an embezzler's loot is part of his gross income.

## *Offsets to Income*
### *Deductions*

Although essentially all income is taxed, some expenses are deductible in computing your federal income tax. You are entitled to deductions for your business expenses and losses. In addition, there is a range of personal deductions, including interest, state and local taxes, safe-deposit-box rent, investment advisory fees, medical expenses, charitable contributions, casualty losses. In principle, personal expenses are not deductible.

Depending upon the particular facts, an otherwise nondeductible expense might be deductible in your case. The cost of your clothes is ordinarily not deductible, but if you have to buy clothes for a particular job that you cannot wear elsewhere, the cost of that clothing is deductible. Commuting costs are not deductible, but the cost of going from one job to another is deductible. The cost of your meals and lodging is generally not deductible, but if those costs are incurred while you are away from home on a business trip, they become deductible. If you use your car, home, or apartment in your business, there are opportunities for additional deductions.

In effect, the code permits you to itemize your personal deductions separately—but you must be able to prove them—or to rely on a so-called zero bracket amount, which is a uniform minimum personal deduction that does not need proof. Study the instructions to the tax returns; talk them over with your accountant; keep careful records.

### Exemptions

In determining your taxable income you must ascertain the number of your exemptions, which are, in effect, additional deductions for yourself and your dependents.

At present, each person is entitled to an exemption for himself, and further exemptions for age, blindness, and dependents, all as spelled out in the code.

A baby born on December 31 draws any exemption for that entire year, and therefore furnishes a federal tax benefit that may pay for a goodly supply of baby clothes and diapers.

### Tax Credits

Whereas a deduction reduces the amount of income that is subject to tax, a tax credit is applied directly against the tax, directly reducing the amount. The purchase of equipment, such as machinery for your business, gives rise to a credit; so does the purchase of energy-saving items for your home, and part of the cost of child care when both parents are employed.

## Capital Gains

Capital gains are income that arises from the sale of capital assets at a profit. Capital assets are virtually any properties except those that you ordinarily sell to customers in your trade or business. Your securities are usually considered capital assets, as are your automobile and your home.

Capital gains are taxed at the lowest rate of any taxable income that one can have except for tax exempt income. Of the profit from the sale of a capital asset held for more than six months (for property acquired after June 22, 1984—otherwise one year)—a long-term capital gain—sixty percent may be deducted from gross income. Since sixty percent of the gain constitutes a deduction, only the remaining forty percent is subject to tax. With fifty percent the highest effective tax rate in 1985, the net result was that capital gains were subject to a maximum rate of federal tax of only twenty percent (fifty percent of forty percent).

In determining the capital gain that is subject to tax, you begin your calculations with the amount you paid for the capital asset and reduce it by the amount of any "depreciation"—the annual write-off of the useful life of business property. Subtract the resultant figure from the amount you received from sale of the property. The amount of the gain is subject to tax as a capital gain. If the property sold is personal, not used for business (such as your home), or results in a loss, that loss is not deemed a loss for tax purposes. If, however, the sold property was used in business but was not among the things sold in the ordinary course of your business, any loss is a capital loss for tax purposes.

Capital gains and losses are netted against each other each year, and it is only the excess of net long-term capital gain over net short-term capital losses that is subject to favorable capital gains treatment. Short-term capital gains are taxed as ordinary income at regular rates. Capital losses, after they have been used to offset capital gains, cannot be used as deductions against ordinary income except to the extent of $3,000 each year, and may be carried over in $3,000 bites for subsequent years until exhausted. Since capital losses generate such a relatively small benefit if used by themselves, but can fully offset capital gains, it may pay to sell loss assets in the same year as short-term capital assets that have appreciated in value to realize the greatest advantage from the capital loss.

Be alert for capital gains opportunities; they may result in significant savings.

## Tax Breaks on Home Sales

If you sell your home, or cooperative or condominium apartment, and replace it within twenty-four months with a new residence, whether you buy or build, your gain is taxed only to the extent that the sales price of the old residence exceeds the cost of the new. With the substantial increases in the value of real estate during the last decade, many people have used this tax provision to "trade up" one home for another, more valuable, one. Many have done this again and again, each time avoiding taxes. If you keep using this provision, the gain that builds up may be eliminated at your death (because your income tax basis becomes the fair market value of your property at the time of your death), and your spouse may be able to sell the property without paying any income tax on the sale, regardless of intention to buy another. If you sell the new property during your lifetime (and do not replace it), you must use the tax basis of your old property, thereby increasing your then taxable gain.

In addition, a taxpayer who is fifty-five years of age or older may sell his home and elect to exclude up to $125,000 of the gain realized on the sale. Unlike the twenty-four-month provision, which can be used repeatedly, this election, once used, cannot be repeated. It can be combined with the twenty-four-month provision to avoid taxes.


## Tax Returns

Your income tax return for the preceding year is due on or before April 15. You are entitled to an automatic four-month extension of time to file your return if you file an extension form by April 15 *and* pay the estimated amount of tax due.

The code provides a variety of tax tables on which to compute your tax, depending upon your filing status. The most favorable tax rates are available to married persons who file a joint return. The least favorable, interestingly enough, apply to married persons who file individual returns. The head-of-household rate is also favorable and applies generally to an unmarried person who maintains a home for a child or another dependent.

There is now a choice of a long, a short, or a still shorter tax return form, depending upon the complexity of your situation. Though your neighbors may boast about how quickly they "did" their taxes using the short form, using the long form may bring some surprising savings. If your earnings have risen substantially during the past four years, for example, not necessarily in each year, use of the long form allows you to average your income over several years, the result of which may be a considerable saving because of the increase in the tax rate as income increases—the reason some people are in higher tax brackets than others.

## Preparing the Return

A number of choices are available to you when it comes time to prepare your tax return: prepare the return yourself; hire a tax return preparer—either an individual or one of the many companies that provide this service; hire an accountant; hire a lawyer who specializes in taxes.

Unless yours is a very simple return—your salary is your entire income, your deductions are minimal, and you do not use a car or special equipment in earning your living—consider not preparing your own return. The tax laws may be too complicated for you to be able to do the job of ferreting out deductions and credits that a competent professional who does it for a living can do, *unless* you have the ability and the patience and are willing to spend significant time and effort in educating yourself.

Lawyers are likely to be the most expensive of all the tax experts you can use. Their expertise is generally in tax planning and in handling tax lawsuits; few lawyers prepare returns on any considerable scale. If major tax questions arise, they can be called upon to advise your accountant.

The choice between a tax return preparer and an accountant depends on the degree of complication of your return. If you have a business, own stocks and bonds, or are engaged in one or more major transactions in the year, an accountant is likely to be a better choice. If you have your salary, a few deductions, and some interest and dividends, a tax return preparer may be more than adequate, and will probably be significantly less expensive than an accountant. Bear in mind, however, that if the Internal Revenue Service should audit your return, the accountant is more likely to be available and to have greater expertise in handling the audit for you. If a tax fraud issue arises, a tax lawyer should be hired.

If you itemize your deductions, the cost of having your return prepared or audited will be tax deductible.

## Interest and Penalties

### Underpayment of Tax

If you underpay your income tax, interest is charged on the deficiency at a rate that is fixed twice a year by the Secretary of the Treasury on the basis of the adjusted prime rate charged by banks. The interest is compounded daily. It is no longer the bargain to borrow from Uncle Sam that it once was.

If you underpay your taxes as a result of the overvaluation of property—if, for example, you claim a large charitable deduction by overvaluing the property you have given away—a penalty is imposed ranging from ten percent for an overvaluation of one hundred fifty percent to thirty percent for an overvaluation of two hundred fifty percent. There is also a penalty of ten percent for substantially understating your tax. A substantial understatement exists when it exceeds ten percent of the proper tax or $5,000, whichever is greater.

### Failure to File Return or to Pay Tax

If you fail to file a return, there is a penalty of five percent a month, up to a maximum of twenty-five percent, of the tax due—and, of course, the tax is still due. If you file a return but fail to pay your taxes when they are due, there is an addition to the tax of five-tenths percent per month of the tax not paid, up to a maximum of twenty-five percent. In the event of both failure to file and failure to pay, the penalty for failure to file is reduced by the amount of the penalty for failure to pay.

### Negligence and Fraud Penalties

There may be also a penalty of five percent of the underpayment of tax if that underpayment was the result of your negligence. If an underpayment is attributable to fraud, the penalty is fifty percent of the amount by which the tax was underpaid. In cases of negligence and fraud, there is a further penalty of fifty percent of the interest payable on that portion of the underpayment that is attributable to negligence or fraud.

Criminal penalties are provided for "willfully" attempting to evade or defeat the tax laws. Such action is punishable by a fine of not more than $10,000, imprisonment for not more than five years, or both.

To add insult to injury, penalties are not deductible on your next year's return.

## *Statute of Limitations*

The code limits the amount of time the IRS has in which to assess a tax on you. The basic statute of limitations is three years after the due date of the return, or after filing of the return if it was filed late. But if you fail to file a return, the period of limitation never runs out. Always file a tax return, to start your statute of limitations running.

If you do file a return, a special six-year statute of limitations applies if you have omitted items from your gross income that amount to more than twenty-five percent of the amount of gross income reported on the return. There is no time limitation on tax fraud.

Always disclose all your income on your tax return, even if only on a schedule claiming that it is not taxable. This helps you to defend yourself against charges of fraud or negligence (for failing to disclose) and in starting the measuring period of the statute of limitations.

## WHEN FINANCIAL DISASTER STRIKES

When your debts exceed your assets, or your business becomes unable to pay its obligations, relief may be just a swallow away, or perhaps a gulp. This depends in good measure on how you handle your creditors, the laws of your particular state, and, possibly, the federal Bankruptcy Code.

Communicate honestly and quickly with your creditors. Practically all of them will extend at least a month's extra credit. Most will be willing to wait even longer for their money—before suing—if they are convinced that you are trying to pay. They realize that going to court to obtain a judgment against you for nonpayment of your debts, or to seek such special legal remedies as garnishment of your wages and repossession or foreclosure of your property, is a costly nuisance that sometimes boomerangs.

If, however, your creditors refuse to "wait and see," or if they threaten or begin collection efforts, you should immediately seek professional help.

## Deciding What to Do

At your first meeting with your professional adviser, presumably your lawyer or your accountant, be ready to disclose all information concerning your true financial condition and the attitudes of your creditors. Your adviser, to be effective, must be able to determine the approximate amount of your secured and unsecured debt, the nature and value of your assets, the causes of your financial troubles, and your wishes.

The legal choices will be between seeking the kinds of relief that are available under state statutes and common law, or taking the more drastic route of the federal bankruptcy laws.

### Exempt Property

The phrase "exempt property," or "exempt assets," figures prominently in financial stress. In all the states and under federal bankruptcy law, certain property is in varying ways beyond the legal grasp of your creditors. There is a federal list of exemptions, and each state has its own list. These consist generally of your home, furniture, clothing and personal effects, health aids, wages, automobile, life insurance, pensions, social security, and alimony. Property may be wholly or partially exempt, expressed either in percentages or dollar terms, such as ten percent or sums not exceeding $1,500.

### Whether to Take State or Federal Action

Out-of-court settlements with creditors under state laws are normally the cheapest, the quickest, and the most responsive to your immediate needs. The states offer much regulatory help for debtors.

The federal government has a monopoly on bankruptcy proceedings. Since bankruptcy proceedings are expensive, and for some people bear an unacceptable stigma, they are generally used only when all else has failed. You will doubtless realize more money if you sell your property yourself, moreover, than if it is sold by order of a bankruptcy court.

The federal bankruptcy route offers two significant advantages, however. It automatically stays—that is, prevents the carrying on of—most creditors' proceedings in the state courts for a period while the situation is being brought under control, thereby giving you a breathing spell. It may also produce payment plans that enable you to survive, with prospects of succeeding, and that are actually forced on your creditors. In bankruptcy court, you occupy a protected status; you are not at the total mercy of your creditors, with their differences of business outlook, temperament, and financial position. The basic reasoning behind bankruptcy is to give the debtor a fresh start.

## Out-of-Court Settlements with Creditors

### Voluntary Nature

The key to out-of-court settlements within state laws is the voluntary acceptance of proposals by the creditors who hold substantially all your debt. The dissent of one creditor who holds a significant claim may abort a voluntary settlement, because there is no legal authority at this level to compel creditors to agree.

Bring in a lawyer experienced in credit matters. He should arrange meetings with your creditors in convenient locations and ask their assistance and acceptance of your plans to pay them. You must be prepared to disclose your current financial statements and to discuss with your creditors the causes of your financial problems.

Agreements with creditors are juggling acts. Your creditors must be cooperative, they must be agreeable, and they must sit still and not bring state court proceedings against you if total consensus is to be reached. You must handle them with care and constancy. If you find yourself dropping your juggling pins, you may have to take your act onto a federal stage.

### Small Claims

Normally, the fewer creditors involved in the out-of-court discussions, the greater the likelihood of success. Thus, if funds are available to satisfy small claims, they should be paid and eliminated, though you should have the prior approval of your large creditors.

### Types of Plans

Before meeting with your creditors, you should determine whether your financial condition requires an "extension" plan, which provides for the full payment of your debts in the course of an extended period; a "composition" plan, under which your creditors would receive in a lump sum or in installments only a percentage of your total debt; or "liquidation," selling off everything and giving the creditors the proceeds to the extent of their indebtedness, or proportionately less if the proceeds do not cover the whole debt.

When you seek an extension or a composition plan, your projections of your future cash flow should be sufficiently conservative to reduce the possibility of future default. Your creditors will be eager to receive payment of their claims as soon as possible. You must be prepared to negotiate all terms, including concessions for delaying your creditors.

Creditors, such as mortgagees, who hold secured claims against you stand in stronger positions than unsecured, or general, creditors, and they cannot be expected to give up their superior rights easily.

If most of your assets are subject to valid liens, a foreclosure sale by the secured party may be an effective means of liquidation. He will be obliged to pay to your unsecured creditors any surplus that may be realized over and above his debt. Your unsecured creditors will usually demand the designation of an agent to whom the sales surplus, if any, is to be given to insure a pro-rata distribution to them of any excess to which they may be entitled.

### Assignment for the Benefit of Creditors

Under procedures in most states, you may choose to assign—that is, transfer your nonexempt property to an assignee for the benefit of your creditors. Under a properly made assignment for the benefit of creditors, all your creditors are compelled to participate; they can no longer express their dissent through individual creditors' remedies, such as seizing your property themselves. The assignee who receives the property manages and disposes of it for the creditors, and if anything is left over after debts have been paid, it goes to you. In a limited way, this resembles the outcome of proceedings in federal bankruptcy court.

## Federal Bankruptcy

If you want the fresh-start advantage and the protection of the automatic stay that only the federal bankruptcy laws can provide, you must go to a federal bankruptcy court. Although it is relatively simple to start a bankruptcy proceeding—you pay a fee and file certain forms known as a "petition" and a "schedule" with the clerk of the court—

a lawyer with bankruptcy expertise can help you maximize your benefits and minimize the potential pitfalls that lurk within the "simple" forms to be filed.

### Transfers

Many people try to protect their assets by transferring them to someone else before filing for bankruptcy. The hope is that the assets will not be caught by creditors in the bankrupt estate. There are safeguards against this.

Essentially, there are two types of transfer that can be set aside by a judge in bankruptcy court: preference and fraudulent conveyance.

Preference is simply payment on account of preexisting debts that is made within a limited period—usually ninety days prior to the filing for bankruptcy—which give the recipient creditor more than he would expect to receive if your property were liquidated and distributed proportionately to all of your then creditors. If you have made, or want to make, any such potentially preferential payments, you might consider postponing your filing so that the ninety-day preference period expires.

Fraudulent conveyance is a transfer made without the receipt of equivalent value in return, or a transfer made with an intent to deceive or defraud your creditors. Selling your car to your dearest friend at a nominal price even though you continue to use it and hope to reclaim it when your financial troubles have been cleared up is but one example. Fraudulent conveyances may be set aside by the bankruptcy judge, and the assets restored to your estate.

Most bankruptcy lawyers require that you pay them an advance fee before you go into bankruptcy if they are to represent you there. This is because, once you are in the court's hands, no legal fees can be paid for services in the bankruptcy without the court's consent and because the availability of assets to fund the fee may be uncertain. Payments for future services, which include legal expenses to be incurred during the bankruptcy, are not preferential, but are subject to review by the court at any time during the bankruptcy proceeding.

### Plans

If you earn a salary, if you receive investment income, a pension, welfare, or other similar payments, or if you own a small business that is not a corporation or a partnership, there are two principal ways for you to use the bankruptcy laws. You can turn all your nonexempt property over to a trustee, who will generally sell it and use the proceeds to pay your creditors. This is the bankruptcy procedure known as "liquidation." Or you can propose to repay your creditors out of your income in the course of no more than five years, while retaining your property. This is known as a "regular income" plan. Both are governed by the Bankruptcy Code, the first under Chapter 7, the second under Chapter 13.

Government units may not discriminate against you on the basis of your bankruptcy; they cannot, for example, revoke your driver's license because you had your debts discharged.

LIQUIDATION PLAN (CHAPTER 7). The filing of a bankruptcy petition depends on the amount of your property that is exempt, your total debt, its source, the amount that is secured, your current and projected income for the next three years, and your estimated living expenses.

Many people who contemplate filing for personal bankruptcy hold assets most of which are exempt. If this is your situation, liquidation will probably be the quickest way for you to wipe out your old debts.

A Chapter 7 trustee will be appointed to investigate your financial affairs and to liquidate your property. He will send notices to creditors, review their claims, and pass on any objections by creditors to the treatment proposed.

You will be expected to appear at a meeting of creditors shortly after the filing of your liquidation petition. You must be ready to answer all questions about your finances. The trustee will try to determine whether you have transferred away any property that can be recovered for the benefit of your creditors.

A court hearing on the discharge of your debts is held before a bankruptcy judge. If he rules in your favor, the debts that were listed in your bankruptcy petition can no longer be enforced against you. Your creditors must accept the payment made to them from the liquidation or administration of your property in full satisfaction of your debts to them.

Certain debts, however, cannot be eliminated by bankruptcy decree. Those surviving are known as "nondischargeable debts," and they include, in Chapter 7, domestic obligations such as alimony and child support, certain taxes, student loans, and debts incurred through fraud.

At the end of a Chapter 7 proceeding, the trustee sells your property, pays administration expenses, and pays the creditors. Whatever is left, if anything, is returned to you.

REGULAR INCOME PLAN (CHAPTER 13). If you want to keep your property, have a steady income, and are willing to repay a portion of your debts from your income, Chapter 13 may allow you to survive without losing your property.

Only a person with a regular income—defined as income "sufficiently stable and regular to enable such individual to make payments under a plan"—and debts within certain limits can file a Chapter 13 plan, which is a plan for repayment of certain priority debts, such as taxes and past-due mortgage payments, in full, and other debts in part within a stated period. The owner of a small business that is not a partnership or a corporation may qualify. Individuals who file a regular income plan are usually those who own property that has greatly appreciated in value—normally, a home—who believe that they can live within a restrictive budget for the period of their payment schedule, and who have sufficient income to live on and make the proposed payments at the same time.

A Chapter 13 trustee is appointed to investigate your affairs and to oversee that part of your earnings that you will be required to turn over to the trustee periodically if the bankruptcy judge confirms your plan. A Chapter 13 trustee has the same powers as a Chapter 7 trustee to recover preferences and fraudulent conveyances. If your plan is confirmed, your unsecured creditors are bound by it as long as they receive as much of the principal due them as they would if your property were liquidated under a Chapter 7 plan. They have no essential right to object to your plan for any other reason.

There are distinct advantages to the regular income plan. The automatic stay will protect you from actions by your creditors and may also protect those who may be your codebtors, cosigners, or guarantors of consumer debts. If you own a business, you can continue to run it. You may be able, with the approval of the court, to reduce the payments required on your secured debts, except for the payments due under the mortgage on your house.

If you complete the periodic payments required by your plan, you are entitled to a broader discharge than the discharge available in a Chapter 7 liquidation proceeding. This is because the only exceptions to Chapter 13 discharges are domestic obligations and certain long-term debts. You have the right to a liquidation discharge within six years of your Chapter 13 discharge. Even if you are unable to complete your plan, you may be eligible for what is known as the "hardship" discharge, which is substantially the same as a liquidation discharge.

If you qualify, these proceedings are an efficient, relatively inexpensive way of clearing your debts. But be realistic in approaching it; can you make the required payments and still maintain an acceptable living standard?

### Business Reorganization (Chapter 11)

If you are operating a business as a corporation or a partnership, reorganization under Chapter 11 of the Bankruptcy Code may provide the best form of relief.

The reorganization provisions are based on the premise that greater benefits can be realized from continued operation of a financially troubled business than by liquidation of its assets. However, reorganization requires extensive help from lawyers, gives rise to high administrative costs, and requires an asset base sufficient to support what may be an expensive proceeding. You must determine whether your business is capable of being turned around and whether the potential benefits will more than offset the substantial additional costs.

You begin a Chapter 11 proceeding by filing a petition with the bankruptcy court, together with schedules indicating your debts and your assets and statements regarding the affairs of your business entity.

You will be a "debtor in possession" and continue to operate your business, assuming that the necessary working capital is available, unless your creditors demonstrate that you are unfit—that you are a defrauder, for example—and the bankruptcy court finds that a trustee should be appointed. Soon after the filing of your petition, the court will appoint a creditors' committee, which will probably consist of your seven largest creditors. This committee will investigate your affairs and your financial condition and participate in the formulation of a plan of reorganization.

The plan of reorganization is essentially a contract between you and your creditors. Accordingly, you are free to negotiate almost any kind of arrangement acceptable to your creditors, provided, of course, that it meets legal standards. These negotiations, which are central to the whole proceeding, can seem endless.

Your plan will probably divide your creditors into classes to the extent that their claims are similar. It will set forth the way their claims will be treated, such as full payment in cash, partial payment, deferred payment, or debt to be exchanged for stock, and will provide for the mechanics of execution.

You must solicit your creditors for acceptance of your plan, using a court-approved disclosure statement, which must provide adequate information to enable your creditors to make an informed judgment on your plan. You will have the exclusive right to propose and seek acceptance of a plan of reorganization for at least 120 days.

Assuming that you receive the percentage of votes required for approval of your plan—a majority in number of those creditors actually voting and two-thirds in amount owed, both by class—a hearing will be held before the bankruptcy court to determine whether your plan should be approved. In effect, the bankruptcy court will approve plans of reorganization that are in the "best interest of creditors." The standard is that each creditor should receive at least as much under the plan as he would receive upon liquidation. To the extent that a class of creditors has not accepted the plan, the court may force the plan on them—a judicial "cramdown"—if it considers the plan fair and equitable and if at least one class approves.

In an individual Chapter 11 proceeding, the same debts survive as in a Chapter 7 proceeding. As to corporations and partnerships, no debts survive.

Chapter 11 proceedings tend to be grueling. If you have averted financial disaster by virtue of them, you will know your salvation (whether permanent or temporary) did not come easily.

# Chapter Nine

# *On Death and Giving*

Everybody dies. It is no small wonder that the subjects of wills and the affairs of decedents—legalese for those who die—are of such widespread interest.

Although the stark fact of death is made known to the family quite promptly under normal circumstances, that is not always the case. Some people simply disappear. In all states, a person who disappears and is missing for a specified number of years, under circumstances that vary, is presumed dead. The range of years is from a low of five to a high of seven, which is the most common. Only in Louisiana, which has set thirty years, does the number exceed seven.

## WILLS

A will, formally known as a "last will and testament," is a signed writing that disposes of a person's property after death. The male writer of a will is known as a "testator"; the female is a "testatrix."

### *Execution*
#### *Customary Wills*
Ordinarily, your will is typed in a law office and signed by you in front of witnesses there. You must state to the witnesses that the doc-

ument you are signing is your will. Wills do not require paper of any
special size or any particular form. By customary practice of lawyers,
wills follow set patterns and resemble each other in form. Lawyers
traditionally prefer the security and ease of standard legal verbiage,
often in archaic form, but the modern trend is toward greater simplic-
ity. President Calvin Coolidge, renowned for his economy with words,
left a will that read, in its entirety, "I leave everything to my wife,
naming her Executor."

No writing of yours at all should follow your signature to your will.
If it is to be amended after it has been signed, a new writing, separately signed and witnessed, is required.

To be effective, a will must have been witnessed by at least two
persons in most states; some states require three witnesses. A witness
does not read the will, but merely verifies, by signing his name below
yours, that the paper you described as your will was in fact signed by
you.

It is advisable that the execution of a will be supervised by a lawyer, who will act as one of the witnesses. The witnessing requirement
is strict; it is not a formality, but an essential part of a validly executed will. The popular "sign it now, I'll get a witness later" routine, if discovered, can nullify a will. And there is a good probability
of discovery if the will is challenged.

Upon your death, the witnesses may be called upon to testify (as
discussed below) that the will was signed in their presence. If local
practice permits, the lawyer can also prepare affidavits of the witnesses, which dispenses with their appearance and live testimony in
court. In effect, the witnesses sign twice—once as witnesses, then as
"affiants"—that is, as signers of the affidavit.

The formality that surrounds witnessing is but one illustration that
the law considers wills to be important items of social business. They
can work the transmittal of property from one generation to another.
The decedent is unable any more to explain what was meant or wanted,
and unable to protect his intentions. As a protective measure, beneficiaries cannot act as witnesses. There are even rules to discourage
lawyers who draft wills from being beneficiaries. This is to deter unscrupulous lawyers from slipping themselves into wills contrary to the
intentions of their clients who cannot or do not read their wills.

Lawyers specialize when drafting wills in covering every contingency. If you are not comfortable with your will, say so. Insist on reading and understanding every bit of it, because it can doubtless be written in a simpler and clearer fashion.

It is particularly important to read and understand the parts about who is to get what. Your lawyer may not have understood you, or may have set down your intentions in a way you cannot approve. Do not be offhand about the matter; rely on yourself. Read slowly and carefully.

Never sign a will without reading and understanding every word of it.

Only an original copy of a will should be signed. Other copies may be made, with the names of the one signing the will and the signing witnesses, with their addresses, printed.

### Unusual Kinds of Wills

There are two unusual kinds of wills; one dispenses with witnesses, the other dispenses with the customary writing.

Holographic wills are those written by the testator in his own handwriting. In some states they may be admitted to probate, under appropriate circumstances of proof, though they were made without any witnesses.

Noncupative (not written) wills are oral, and are generally deemed invalid. In a number of states, however, if there is sufficient proof that the testator made the oral statement meaning it to be his will, it may be accepted as legal. The statement must have been uttered under special limiting circumstances that preclude the formality of writing, such as being in the throes of terminal illness or on active duty with the armed forces.

## Probate

A will is subject to probate, or proving, before a judge, usually without a jury, for the purpose of establishing that it was indeed signed by the decedent, knowingly, voluntarily, and in apparent sound mind, meaning it to be his will. The procedure is usually routine and can be accomplished simply by affidavits signed by the witnesses, unless there is a challenge. The names of courts with probate functions differ greatly in the various states; they can be probate, surrogate, chancery, orphan's, juvenile, superior, district, circuit, or county.

Challenges to wills are most often based on charges of undue influence, mental incompetency of the testator, existence of a later will, or forgery. Since challenges involve dispute, a real trial may be held. The witnesses to the will figure significantly in challenges. If there is some reason to expect that there will be a challenge, a nice modern touch is the use of video recorders to document the signing. Sometimes in probate of an uncontested will a witness will volunteer that he did not really see the will signed or that the testator seemed to be acting oddly. This may cause the judge to throw out the will.

Courts, as well as families, are usually reluctant to see wills disregarded altogether. Contested wills are customarily resolved by some kind of settlement. If there is a contest, however, an earlier, unrevoked will, properly executed, may be accepted in probate, or the judge may rule that the decedent died without a will.

In one celebrated New York case, a man died at a well-known charitable and social club of which he was a member. In his pocket there was a signed but unwitnessed will leaving substantial money to the club. A retired judge and a prominent lawyer, both elderly, were with him when he died, and they discovered it. As overenthusiastic club members, they then proceeded to sign the will as witnesses. It turned out, however, that another copy of the unwitnessed will was found among the decedent's effects by a policeman. Eventually, the two versions of the will were brought together, the truth came out, and the two lawyers resigned from the New York bar.

Some probate courts go so far as to examine staple holes in an original will to see whether it has been tampered with. If it appears that a signed will has been taken apart, the courts may require, on their own initiative, additional proof of genuineness.

## Changing Wills

Wills go into effect only when the testator dies; they are freely revocable before then. The most common way to revoke a will is to execute a new one that expressly revokes any prior one.

A will may also be canceled by simply tearing it up and throwing it away. Once, upon hearing that a client had died, I asked our office manager to bring the client's will from the safe. To be helpful, she not only brought it, but also opened the envelope. Unfortunately, she used a sharp letter opener and in the process neatly cut the will in half. It took one week and a hearing in surrogate (probate) court to establish that the will had been torn in error and had not been revoked.

A codicil is an amendment to a will for the purpose of changing a specific portion; it is executed with the formality of the original. You can have as many codicils as you wish, but the existence of too many may cause confusion. Changes from codicil to codicil, documented as they are on the court record, can cause bad feelings among relatives and beneficiaries. Continued cross reference between codicils can cause doubts of the meaning to arise if the drafting is not precise. Codicils should be used only for specific changes—for instance, to eliminate a $10,000 bequest to a specifically named person—or as stopgap devices for substantial changes until a new will can be written.

With the clerical advances of word processors, typing a whole new will is now routine in law offices.

## Legatees

Beneficiaries of wills receive legacies, and so are often called "legatees." They may receive their bequests in money or they may be given property—for instance, "my gold wedding ring." Bequests of money need not be made outright; they may be given to a trust set up under the terms of the will. Such a trust is known as a "testamentary" trust.

## Testamentary Trusts

Testamentary trusts, created by a testator in a will, must be distinguished from *inter vivos* trusts, which are created during a person's lifetime by a separate writing and take effect immediately. Both are discussed later. Confusingly, an *inter vivos* trust may be a beneficiary of a will and receive a bequest, which then becomes part of the *inter vivos* trust itself and is administered in accordance with that trust. This procedure is used in wealthy families for tax reasons and has little general application.

# ESTATES

The aggregate of a decedent's property is known as an "estate." Care must be taken to differentiate between "principal," sometimes called "capital"—the decedent's existing property turned over to the executor, which will include any appreciation in value while held by the executor—and any subsequent income, such as interest, dividends, or rents, because beneficiaries may share differently in them, and because taxes to be paid on ordinary income and on capital gains are computed differently.

## *Administration and Accounting*

The estate is taken care of—that is, administered—by an executor, or executrix, who collects and holds the decedent's assets, pays debts, manages and invests the property, files the necessary legal papers and estate and income tax returns, pays taxes, pays out income, and, when satisfied, distributes the net estate to its various beneficiaries.

When the executor is finished, he can file an accounting in court and receive an official approval of his actions and a discharge from further responsibility. This is a judicial accounting, an opportunity for aggrieved beneficiaries to contest the propriety of the actions of the executor. If the beneficiaries are agreeable, they can acknowledge receipt of their legacies and in a properly drafted document release the executor from all further legal responsibility. Although this receipt-and-release procedure is informal, it can do the job more quickly, more cheaply, and with nearly the same certainty (except as to creditors) as a judicial accounting.

Creditors have certain time limits, differing from state to state, within which to file claims for money they believe is due them. These limits range from three to seven months.

Jurisdiction over validity, interpretation, and administration of wills, estates, and trusts is reserved to the states; these are not matters of federal concern beyond the fact that they are subject to federal taxation. There are one-time federal and state taxes, called "estate" (inheritance) taxes, on the transmission of property upon death. There are also income taxes for the duration of estates and trusts.

### *Fiduciaries*

Executors and executrices (feminine form) are known as "fiduciaries." So are trustees. So are administrators appointed by probate courts to manage estates whose decedents have died without a will.

Fiduciaries must exercise great care in dealing with the affairs entrusted to them. They are not free to take the same chances they might take with their own property. There are many restrictive rules governing their conduct, many of which can be relaxed by specific provisions of a will.

Fiduciaries are normally paid by commission according to scales established by statute—for instance, two percent of principal and six percent of income. This fee can be waived.

## INTESTACY

A person who has left either an invalid will or no will at all is said to have died intestate. If this happens, the state steps in to make the testamentary decisions. There are rules governing who gets what.

The administrator, chosen by the probate court, is subject to stricter legal rules than an executor, there being no will granting him greater discretion than the legal minimum prescription of highly conservative fiduciary conduct imposed by the law. A fiduciary bond, guaranteeing the faithful performance of his duty, is usually required of an administrator.

The priority of inheritance in the family of someone who dies without a will is called "intestate succession." If there are no known living relatives who qualify, the property of the decedent may go—that is, may escheat—to the state.

All states provide for division among spouses and children of the property of a decedent who leaves no will. The states vary, however, as to the manner of division, the spouse typically receiving a third to a half and the issue sharing in the balance. If there are children but no surviving spouse, the entire estate is apportioned among the children. When there are no issue, the surviving spouse receives all in some states, but in most the spouse divides with surviving parents of the decedent. If neither a spouse nor issue survives, the parents take all. Lacking these, brothers and sisters or their issue take all. The significance of the word *issue* is described below. Most often it refers to children.

Estates fall under the jurisdiction of the state that the decedent called "home." If there is no valid will, the laws of intestate succession of that state must be consulted. Actually, this concept of home is expressed in law in the complex concepts of domicile, or residence, but these arise only if you live in two places.

Adopted children are entitled to the same intestate share of their adoptive parents' estates as biological children. In Alabama, Arkansas, Illinois, Louisiana, Maine, Montana, New Mexico, Rhode Island, South Dakota, Texas, Vermont, and West Virginia adopted children retain rights to inherit, as well, from their biological parents, if those die without a will. However, adopted children usually do not succeed to an intestate share of relatives of the adoptive parent.

Illegitimate children generally inherit from the mother in intestacy, either in full or in part, or only if there are no legitimate children, depending on the state law involved. They rarely have intestate rights in property of the mother's relatives. Inheritance from fathers of illegitimate children usually depends on whether the father acknowledged paternity of the child or paternity was proved in court.

## SPOUSES' RIGHTS AND COMMUNITY PROPERTY

In legal parlance, a husband or wife is impersonally related to the other as a spouse. In every state there are some protective rights of a spouse in the property a deceased spouse owns at the time of his death. Generally, they apply reciprocally. However, in Alabama, Michigan, and Utah, only wives have specified inheritance rights and protections, although such historical limitations are now constitutionally suspect. Spouses' rights may be waived—that is, voluntarily given up—by the surviving spouse. This is often done when the survivor thinks that the decedent "wanted it that way."

Spouses' rights manifest themselves at four different levels in a bewildering mosaic of state laws. First, there are exempt properties of a limited nature in all states, such as household effects and small sums of money, to which spouses have priority.

Second, in a few states there are special rights in real estate: "dower" for wives and "curtesy" for husbands. These rights, when applicable, mean entitlement to a one-third ownership share. Both dower and curtesy exist in New Jersey, Rhode Island, Tennessee, Vermont, Virginia, and West Virginia. There is only dower in Alabama, the District of Columbia, Kentucky, Montana, South Carolina, and Utah.

Third, there is in most states a right of a spouse to take a statutory share instead of what was provided under the terms of a will. This right is generally known as the "right of election to take against a spouse's will." The amount approximates the intestate share that would have applied had there been no will. This share is usually one-third of the estate outright or the income from a trust of one-third of the assets plus some cash. The right of election is for spouses who are dissatisfied when they are not bequeathed at least the statutory minimum. Sometimes, when dower and curtesy rights in real property exist, the right of election applies only with respect to personal property.

Fourth, eight states have community property laws—also known as "marital property" laws—under which each spouse owns half of any property acquired during marriage, except for gifts and inheritances. When a spouse dies, the surviving spouse need not rely on a will to receive an inheritance, since the survivor is already the owner of half the marital property. However, the decedent may provide for the surviving spouse in his will. The property the decedent disposes of by will is his own separate property. Community property is a continental European concept, which flourishes in Arizona, California, Nevada, New Mexico, Texas, Idaho, Washington, and Louisiana. The subject is highly complicated. In specific situations involving community property, the law of the state in which the couple lived governs.

In general, you should consult a lawyer about inheritance rights. The subject has legal and local difficulties everywhere.

## NONPROBATE ESTATE

Not all assets of a decedent's estate pass through probate. Many people die with small assets that can be delivered physically to survivors without complication, and these affairs are settled pragmatically by the family, perhaps with a lawyer's advice. Wills are even sometimes

ignored if, for any of a number of reasons, the family agrees that probate will be too expensive, or if they agree there should be another
kind of sharing. However, any aggrieved beneficiary under a will or
one who might inherit by intestate succession if there is no will can
take his case to court.

## Lifetime Gifts

Many people give property away before they die; sometimes as gifts
to their children, sometimes to trusts and foundations, often as a result of planning for the purpose of saving estate or income taxes. Much
gift giving, however, is out of a desire to help a child or to reassure
a spouse of financial independence. Property that has been given away
is obviously not on hand for probate, although it may be subject to
an estate tax if the Internal Revenue Service establishes that the gift
was "made in contemplation of death." There are givers who enjoy
tasting the fruits of their bounty while they are still alive. Unfortunately, there are also those who seek to use, often successfully, lifetime gifts to children as a way around the rights of their spouses that
might otherwise arise upon their death.

## Life-Insurance and Pension Proceeds

Life-insurance and pension proceeds are common family assets that
do not go through the probate court if the proceeds are paid directly
to a surviving beneficiary, such as a spouse or a child. In many families, life insurance, pensions, and the family home constitute the real
wealth of the family. If properly set up, life-insurance proceeds need
not be subject to estate tax, or even to gift tax. The rules are so complex that the advice of a professional estate planner and tax adviser is
indispensable.

## Jointly Held Property

Property held jointly is another significant category of property that
stands apart from the probate assets. This is property held in two names
so that the survivor will succeed to sole ownership on the death of
the other. The two most common forms of such joint holdings are
homes and bank accounts. Since the property passes automatically on

death by the very nature of the holding arrangement, no probate procedure becomes necessary to effect its transfer.

In some states, if a bank account is simply entitled "Alice Smith in trust for Jo Black," and only Smith has the bankbook and the right to withdraw funds during her lifetime, Black inherits the bank account directly on the death of Smith.

### Revocable Trusts

Another way to avoid probate is to use a device known as a "revocable trust." Indeed, a best-selling book entitled *How to Avoid Probate*, published several years ago, concentrated on the use of do-it-yourself revocable trusts, and earned its author the vociferous enmity of those members of the legal profession who draw wills and administer estates, although he apparently survived without visible damage.

The idea behind revocable trusts, depending on the local law, is to transfer your property in trust to yourself, or perhaps to some qualified and highly trusted person as trustee, and to retain full rights in the property during your lifetime. The trust property is paid directly to specified beneficiaries on your death, by-passing the probate court. There are no significant tax benefits or disadvantages in the basic revocable trust. The purpose is to avoid the cost and complication of probate; the taxes, on the whole, are inevitable, as is the death that triggers them. The costs of setting up the trust are usually much less than probate costs.

The device may be useful, if cumbersome, under appropriate circumstances, but it should not be undertaken without expert legal assistance and people you trust greatly, since, technically, the trustee becomes the actual owner of the assets placed in trust.

## *INTER VIVOS* AND TESTAMENTARY TRUSTS

Estate planning is the process of disposing of your property in a way suitable to you that minimizes taxes, both estate and income. *Inter vivos* trusts are among the standard devices for these purposes. As in the case of testamentary trusts, they are most often used to give someone, such as a spouse or a child, the use of assets, while at the same time guarding against the folly or inexperience of the beneficiary who might dissipate the property if it were given outright—especially under the influence of a second spouse or a scheming lover. Since the beneficiaries of trusts often do not have investment expertise, trustees can make up for that lack.

### Forms of Trust

Trusts lie in lawyers' country. *Inter vivos* trusts are generally found in complex written documents, often called "indentures." An oral trust requires all manner of proof and legal complication.

A trust is an agreement between a trustee and the person creating the trust, who is normally called the "settlor," under which the latter transfers title of his property to the trustee, who agrees to administer and distribute the property (and the income from it) to the named beneficiaries, in accordance with the trust agreement. As mentioned earlier, trustees are fiduciaries with special obligations under the law.

The assets of an *inter vivos* trust are usually described, from the Latin, as the "corpus" (body). In English, the term is "principal" or "capital." As in testamentary trusts, income is the earnings on principal, and the divisions of principal and income must be strictly observed because of the often differing interests and tax treatments of the beneficiaries.

A common trust arrangement provides that income beneficiaries, normally a spouse or children, should receive the income of the trusts during their lives, and on the death of the spouse, the death of the children, or upon the children reaching a certain age, the remaining principal, then called "remainder," is distributed to the ultimate beneficiaries indicated, usually children or grandchildren. An example is: "The term of this trust shall be until the later of the death of my wife or until my youngest child attains the age of twenty-five years, in which case the then principal shall be distributed to my children then surviving, in equal shares."

In making provision for future payments to beneficiaries of trusts, it is wise to think in terms of shares rather than in fixed cash sums. This is because of unforeseeable changes in future values of property and money. This realization was brought home to me sharply last year, when I was confronted with a testamentary trust to last for the life of a second wife, which provided a life income for her of $15,000 per year. At the time the will was drawn, and also at the time the testator died, the income of the trust property was approximately $15,000 a year. It was his intention to have her receive all the income for life and to have his family inherit the trust property on her death. Accordingly, the remainder of the trust was left to his surviving family, which by then turned out to be remote nieces and nephews. Over the years after the testator's death, the income and principal of the trust increased in value enormously, and, while the widow continued to get her $15,000 a year, the remote relatives shared a windfall annual income in excess of $100,000 a year. This kind of thing can be prevented by providing that the wife gets all, or a large percentage share of the income of the trust. If there is a desire to insure she gets at least $15,000 with any deficit in income being made from principal, the will should say so.

## Rule against Perpetuities

One of the most complex rules of the common law is the Rule against Perpetuities, which determines the length of time a trust can last. The policy of the law historically has been to avoid keeping property tied up in trust for too long—in "perpetuity"—thus restricting its transferability. Under the Rule Against Perpetuities, the permissible duration of a trust is measured by the lives of identified persons who are in being at the beginning of the trust term plus a fixed number of years not to exceed twenty-one. The trust term cannot be made to run more than twenty-one years beyond the death of those whose lives are used for measurement. A trust cannot be provided for a flat fifty years, say, even though that period might, in actuality, turn out to be less than the lives of your spouse and children plus twenty-one years. This is one of the most complicated legal rules afloat, and its application requires local legal advice, state by state.

## Issue

Wills, trusts, and statutes often use the word "issue." It is a legalism if there ever was one. It refers to your whole progeny: your children, grandchildren, great-grandchildren, and so on. But a further definition is needed.

Suppose you have three surviving children and no grandchildren.

A provision for your "issue" is simply construed: it goes in equal shares to each of your three children. But if one of your three children dies before you and leaves two infant children of his own, they are your issue as well as that of your child, their own deceased parent. How then will the bequest to issue be shared? The normal way, and the one generally presumed by law in the absence of any written declaration to the contrary, is called *per stirpes*, Latin for "by the branch," or line of descent in a family. This gives one-third to each of your two living children and divides the remaining third equally between the two grandchildren, who thus receive one-sixth each. This example illustrates a typical stirpital provision, which, properly phrased, might read "to my surviving issue in equal shares, *per stirpes*." Intestate distributions to "issue" are stirpital as a matter of course.

On the other hand, you might prefer that all your issue share equally by head count. If two of your children and your two grandchildren survive you, as in the foregoing example, an equal distribution by head count (per capita) would mean that each of the four would receive a quarter of the distribution. If all your children survive, as well as your grandchildren, all five would receive twenty percent, in a per capita jurisdiction. The classical formulation of that kind of disposition is, "to my surviving issue in equal shares, per capita."

### Time of Payment of Trust Principal

One of the ideas behind a trust is to defer payment of principal to a young person until such time as he is mature enough to handle it. But tying up property too long can be a grave error; the beneficiary may grow into middle age before receiving his share of a trust. He will not have had the opportunity to use the capital during his period of growth. There are, however, tendencies to use deferred payment as a safety measure for beneficiaries who are considered economically incompetent or who are thought to be easily influenced; shrewder beneficiaries may receive principal earlier.

Deferring receipt of principal until a child is forty or more rarely works out well unless huge sums are involved. It has been my experience that payment of principal at the age of thirty or thirty-five works out best. Prepayments of as much as half or a third of the principal at the age of twenty-five or thirty should always be considered.

An important and useful feature of trusts is the discretionary power in the trustee to pay out principal to a beneficiary ("invasion of principal") before it becomes automatically due by the express terms of the trust. This enables hindsight to accelerate payment when need or benefit is great, and hold back when circumstances suggest continued protective measures. Many testators and settlors, however, are unwilling to give sole discretion to any trustee, and they establish standards for invading principal, such as financial need, marriage, the purchase of a home, the desirability of training, or for capital to start a business or a professional practice. No trust should be drawn without some power in the fiduciaries to advance principal.

The desire to provide for invasion of principal may affect the choice of a trustee, for there are adverse tax consequences for someone who can invade principal for himself. A trustee in such a position should have a cotrustee to make the invasion for him. Of course, it is highly troublesome to permit a trustee to invade, for his own benefit, principal that otherwise belongs to brothers and sisters. In some states a trustee may not invade principal for himself.

Trusts involve a certain amount of handling. If the assets are too small, the trust device may be just too expensive and cumbersome to be worth the bother. On the other hand, even a tiny amount of money for an elderly person in need may be worth the trouble.


## HAVING A WILL

### Should You Have One?

You do not avoid a decision by electing not to have a will. You really have made the decision to give away your property the way your state law prescribes.

If you have any property that will pass in a probate estate—as opposed, for instance, to jointly held property or life insurance—you should have a will. If you do not have a will, your property will be given out on your death by the laws of intestate succession.

A will is necessary, too, if you wish to make specific bequests. You may want to give jewelry to your daughter-in-law or a cash bequest to a friend. The division of personal effects can be accomplished by authorizing the executor to make any determinations the family cannot agree upon.

You may not want your spouse or your children to hold property outright; you may want to create a trust to protect them.

You should have a will if you have any minor children, so that you can make provision for guardianship of them. Guardianship can be divided between separate guardians for the persons and for the property of the minor children. Such divisions are common when the desire is to have the children live with a person who may be a wonderful, loving, custodial parent, but may not be good at handling money or property. Someone better informed financially can then be designated as the guardian of the children's property until they come of age.

Remember, you and your spouse could die together in an accident. This is another reason for having a will. In a common accident such as an airplane or automobile crash, it is often impossible to determine who died first. If one spouse has left property by will to the other, with a further provision for children if that spouse should not survive him, the question arises whether the decedent's property is to pass through the estate of the other spouse, who died in the same accident, or is to go directly to the children. The law presumes that where a testator and beneficiary die together, the testator survives. For tax reasons, however, you might want the opposite presumption, namely, that the spouse survived the testator, and you can provide for this reverse presumption.

Making a will enables you, not the probate judge, to name your fiduciary and to determine the latitude of powers of administration. The judge might otherwise pick a political appointee for fiduciary. Further, the judge will normally require the administrator to post a bond to guarantee the performance of his duty, which could cost up to five percent of the value of the estate, an expense you might consider unnecessary and avoidable if you pick a trustworthy fiduciary yourself.

When it comes to putting the law on your side, a will is essential. This is an action you take by yourself, privately, ensuring that things will be carried out as you want them to be, simply by writing a clear prescription ahead of time. With the exception of a few roadblocks, such as a spouse's right of election or too long a trust term, you can run free with your will. You can disinherit some of your survivors who would share if you left no will, penalize some, benefit others, and reward whomever you wish.

### Should You Use a Lawyer for Your Will?

Yes! Wills are important affairs, and it is impossible to reach up from the grave to correct your mistakes. Wills must be right before you die.

Wills are much less expensive than most laymen suppose; they can start as low as twenty-five dollars. Even law firms with blue-chip clientele charge as little as two hundred dollars for simple ones. They are often "loss leaders" for lawyers, who are limited by the competition in what they can charge, and whose real economic interest in drafting your will is the anticipation of representing your estate when your time comes.

Even though you may perceive your affairs to be very simple, you may not be gauging your needs correctly. If you make an error, you will not live to hate yourself, but your family may. If you require a will at all—and if you are studying this chapter carefully, you probably do—why skimp? Use a lawyer to draw your will.

Having a will drafted is a classic way of establishing a relationship with a lawyer on which to trade later for small gratuitous advice, sometimes advice needed in a hurry.

## WILLS AND FAMILY FEUDING

### Estates and Family Trouble

Death of one or both parents has a way of unhinging families, apart from the grief of personal loss. The upset of parental influences can unleash the latent hostilities of children and other relatives, and lead to open combat in the probate court, either when the will is offered for probate, when an accounting is taking place, or upon the need for controversial action, such as invading the principal of a trust. Even if the children can accept an inequality in their inheritances, their own spouses very often cannot. Inheritance builds up the steam that tests every stress mark, every flaw, in the family boiler. It is more the rule than the exception that estates mean family trouble.

When big money is at stake and people are trying to take advantage, legal contest is easily understandable. But dispute over an estate can rival matrimonial litigation in pettiness and meanness. Even the division of the decedent's jewelry, clothing, furniture, and personal effects may be bitter, as the relatives pick over and wrangle about the scraps. Relatives and friends alike search for meaning in the ways they were mentioned, or not mentioned, in wills, and they compare themselves with one another.

The classic testamentary yarn, known by lawyers across the country, involves a wealthy woman who had her portrait painted. She insisted that the artist paint a huge diamond ring on her finger, even though she did not own one. When the artist asked why, the woman replied, "When I'm dead and my husband marries a young woman, I want the question of what happened to that ring to prey on her mind."

## Will Security and Safe-Deposit Boxes

Experience suggests the need to secure your will. There may be a viper in your bosom who will find and suppress a will because he has more to gain from intestate succession. Or he may know of an earlier will more favorable to him, which has been signed and is available. There have been many such villains in families as nice as yours.

You may even lose your will, or put it where it may not be found after your death.

Most people instinctively think that their own bank safe-deposit box, known well to spouse and children, is best for the safekeeping of their will. Sometimes they use a corporate-owned box, which remains unaffected when they die, enabling immediate access without complication at any time. That does not safeguard the will against someone else with access to the box, however.

But the will locked inside a safe-deposit box can cause difficulties. The same is true of the deed to your cemetery plot and your life-insurance policies. The executor believed named in your will or some family member will likely have to petition a court for an order to open the box. Why cause such an expensive nuisance to get at a will? Your will can be secured by depositing it with the drafting lawyer for placement in his firm's vault, or it may be deposited in a bank if that bank is to be a fiduciary, or it may be deposited, sealed, in a courthouse that offers that facility. You should retain an unsigned copy in a secure place for those times when you want to study its contents.

No one will ever know how much is lost in safe-deposit boxes taken out in assumed names of which only the decedent (or perhaps only one other person, who proves most untrustworthy) knew the location and, more important, the ownership designation. The location of safe-deposit boxes can be traced, but you need the name to do it.

## Keeping Old Wills

If you made out a will that was later changed, do not leave the original signed copy intact. Signed originals of old wills are deadly, for they threaten the integrity of the genuine will, the one most recently signed. If there is a change of testamentary heart and a later will is torn up, does the testator mean to reinstate his earlier will? Or is he relying on the rules of intestacy? Can gaps in a later will be filled from an earlier one? Complicated and expensive questions of proofs may arise. Leaving earlier and later wills accessible to an unscrupulous person who can gain more from the earlier one is tempting fate.

Some lawyers favor keeping executed copies of revoked wills on hand, reasoning that if the later will is lost or fails to meet probate for any reason, the earlier one can be offered and is more likely to meet the testator's intent than the intestacy provisions that will arise in the absence of a will. I disagree, except in the very exceptional circumstance that suggests the desirability of retaining an old will. This might happen when a challenge is anticipated to an unconventional disposition. Then old wills can help establish a long-standing intent. If an elderly man, for example, should leave nothing to his only son in a will executed months before his death, a series of prior wills leaving nothing to that son over three decades would help establish the man's intention to disinherit his son, and would be useful in negating charges by the son of senility, undue influence, or trickery if he should decide to contest the will. But lawyers cannot always fathom their clients' minds as to why they make the changes they do.

It is simply common sense not to leave even unsigned copies of old wills lying around loose. They only give people ideas and stir up questions about the reasons the changes were made.

## Construing Wills and Trusts

If a will or trust is ambiguous, it must be construed, or interpreted. Usually family members can settle this among themselves, but if they cannot, they must go to court. They must petition for a judicial construction proceeding.

The best way to head off this difficulty is, of course, to be clear in the first place. Construction issues arise from poorly drawn papers.

Construction proceedings in court are usually nonjury cases. They are decided by a judge alone, on the basis of testimony, exhibits, oral arguments, and briefs of the lawyers. The critical issue is the intent of the testator or settlor. Since the document itself is ambiguous, even taking all its parts as a whole, available outside aids such as letters or statements to determine intent are frequently used. If intent is to be an issue, the decedent's files should be carefully combed for every useful bit of information. As in litigation, preparation and proof are critical and generally go hand in hand.

## SPECIAL FIDUCIARY PROBLEMS

Your lawyer may be a good choice for executor or trustee, but do not automatically appoint him. It is neither required nor necessarily desirable that your lawyer be a fiduciary. If, however, you do have, quite affirmatively, the requisite trust in him, there may be good reason to appoint him.

### *Choice of Fiduciaries*

Selection of fiduciaries may be opening a can of worms, particularly if there are complex affairs, if the estate leads to acrimonious relations among the heirs, or if there are long-term trusts involved. Not only should fiduciaries be named, but also successor fiduciaries, in the event the original fiduciaries either predecease the testator, for some reason do not qualify, die, resign, or become disabled during the course of administering the estate or trust. Testators must be conscious of the relative ages of their fiduciaries and the probable duration of the trusts under their care.

Some people are fortunate enough to have a number of qualified successors to name. Most people do not, however, so a common practice is to make sure that fiduciaries are able to designate their own successors, by filing a form in court, subject to the prior succession that the testator dictated.

If funds are large enough, customarily in excess of $300,000, banks may be good fiduciary alternatives or supplements. This is particularly true if the assets are relatively easily manageable items such as bank and security accounts and real estate. Bank fiduciaries offer continuity, the capacity to give investment advice, and great expertise in all facets of administration. Whereas other fiduciaries may function only part time, for a bank the administration of assets is part of its regular business. Closely held businesses are commonly troublesome to administer, and many banks therefore tend to shy away from stewardship of them.

It is a bad idea to appoint a business partner or his lawyer as a fiduciary, even if the same lawyer is yours, too, because the result can easily be a conflict of interest. A surviving partner may want to take a big working salary and may want to expand, whereas the widow of the deceased partner may want a big unearned salary or liquidation or conservation of the business, without the risks of expansion. A lawyer who represents the surviving partner is obviously in a poor position to represent the competing interests of the deceased partner's widow.

A competent spouse can be a good choice of fiduciary, but children can present problems if their interrelations are poor. If all are appointed, they may fight among themselves; if fewer are appointed, they may fight all the harder.

Commonly disputed issues are the management of family businesses, including compensation and expenses drawn, invasions of principal, investment policy, and commissions earned. If family relations are strained and the appointment of relatives is precluded, the testator must go to the outside—to his lawyer, his bank, his accountant, or qualified friends.

The choice of a fiduciary is a serious one. In addition to doing a good job in managing the estate, making investment decisions, defending the estate against the claims of creditors, and settling tax liabilities, he has a personal responsibility in family intermediation. He has to handle everyone. A fiduciary can give a good financial performance, while unwittingly ruining the fabric of a family, or he can do a bad job and damage the fabric even more. Maturity, judgment, and independence are vital traits for a fiduciary, but he must have the family's confidence as well. Very often, the balance of a lawyer, a friend, or a bank, along with one or more members of the family, is needed to meld professional expertise with human understanding.

Think through the fiduciary issue; be wary of taking the easy way out by naming those whose feelings would be wounded if you did not name them, particularly a number of children. You may find that this gets you out of the personal dilemma while you are still alive, and you need not face the consequences after you are dead. If your family cannot get along, that is their fault and the money is theirs to dissipate; you did what you could! Right? Maybe! It depends on how strongly you feel about the value of your money and the welfare of your spouse and children. Many estates have been squandered in the legal expenses of family fights that could have been headed off by independent, strong, and sagacious fiduciaries with the authority to act. Many beneficiaries are curiously willing to waste estate money in useless legal expense, since none of the estate was earned by them. If the beneficiaries are not fiduciaries, they have to spend their personal money to do estate battle, and they shy away from that. But if beneficiaries are fiduciaries, they have the estate till to support their proclivities. They simply do not connect their own conduct with waste of the estate in the payment of legal fees and other expenses of fighting, and it never occurs to them that to give ground may be in their best interest economically. Too often, the emotions literally rob the roost.

## Fiduciary as a "Nice Guy"

You may find yourself a fiduciary one of these days. You are named. Congratulations—I think. The work of fiduciaries is serious and responsible. It involves looking over everything a decedent had, reading all his papers, investing his assets, and paying his bills and taxes. Accurate records must be kept at all times of all transactions, for fiduciaries may be called to account for them.

Under no circumstances allow assets you hold as a fiduciary to be mingled with your own personal assets. It is ordinarily a crime, and, in any event, such conduct looks suspicious. Do not hesitate to use independent lawyers, accountants, or whatever experts you need to do your job when you have the authority and the funds to retain them.

Beneficiaries are always in a hurry to receive more money. They are willing for a fiduciary to take any shortcut now, but the fiduciary may have to pay later if he prejudices creditors or payment of taxes by depleting the estate in premature distributions. Fiduciaries can be personally liable for their lapses, even if they were made in good faith.

Always consider selling securities to fund the anticipated cash requirements of an estate. Speculating in volatile stock is dangerous conduct for a fiduciary. Woe to the executor who distributes assets, then lets the ebb of the market tide strand him on the beach. The very beneficiaries who applaud premature distributions will be the first to nip at a fiduciary's heels if anything goes wrong later. There are always those, even heirs of heirs, who will feel that a benefit offered to one person worked to deprive them of their own due. Fiduciaries are not chosen to be heroes.

There is normally no set time span during which fiduciaries must distribute the proceeds of an estate to the beneficiaries. If there are ample funds and anticipated expenses are relatively light, advances can be made without court order. If in doubt as to distribution, get an order of approval from the court.

Usually, no funds are distributed until the legal time for filing claims against the estate has passed. Federal estate taxes, if any, are due nine months after death. If there are tax audits, distribution may be delayed for two or more years. In any event, each state has rules as to time limits in distributing assets to beneficiaries.

As a fiduciary, always "go by the book." Invest carefully; use and document advice and reasons for conduct. Do not be a "good guy" and advance money prematurely. Satisfy yourself that all taxes, debts, and claims have been paid or reserved for before making preliminary or final distributions. It is good practice to ask all beneficiaries to whom funds are distributed without court order for personal guarantees against liability—that is, for indemnity. Insurance-company bonds, called "refunding bonds," can be procured in many places to guarantee repayments.

## Commissions

Fiduciaries are paid commissions. All states have standard rules for commission calculation. If there is more than one fiduciary, there may be two or more commissions. Many states limit multiple commissions. But the payment of three or four commissions, which is permissible, can deplete as much as ten percent of an estate. For this reason alone, you should be wary of naming multiple trustees. Often, beneficiaries waive commissions, on which they are taxed, whereas their bequests may be nontaxable.

Commissions can be set at negotiated figures or waived. It is prudent to consider the commission load in determining who and how many are to be fiduciaries.

## TAXES AND ESTATE PLANNING

Before you start saving taxes, make sure you have a tax to save. Under the Internal Revenue Code in 1984, federal estate taxation does not begin until the taxable estate is more than $315,000; by 1988, the exemption is to reach $600,000. In 1986, when all tax brackets will be in place under the present statutory scheme, the maximum bracket will be fifty percent on estates valued at more than $2,500,000. State estate taxes are normally not high enough to be factors; they are troublesome only in California, New York, and a few other states.

Bequests to a spouse qualify for the marital deduction under federal law, which means that a bequest to a wife is deductible. If the whole estate is given to a spouse, there would be no federal estate tax at all until that spouse in turn died, at which time whatever remained of the estate would then be taxable.

Tax planning for estates is an intricate business, to be undertaken with the help of experts. I would like to offer one basic observation here. Many families have come to grief when too much emphasis has been placed on avoiding taxes and too little on the true desires of the testator in using and awarding property. Taxes should be kept in perspective; saving taxes is only a means to an end, that of realizing the best possible net yield for carrying out what you want to do with your estate. Dean William C. Warren, when teaching taxation at Columbia University Law School, was fond of challenging his class. ''I can tell you how to organize an estate and pay no estate taxes at all. . . . Just leave all your money to Columbia University.'' He meant, of course, that the whole bequest to the university would be tax deductible. No taxes would be paid, but the family would then get nothing. His moral was clear.

Planning is not restricted however, to tax measures. Wills should be reviewed periodically for adjustments, since wealth fluctuates, intentions change, and people are born, mature, die, or become alienated. A will should keep pace with the changes in your family, your interest in providing bounty after your death, and your current financial situation. It is also wise to review your will if you move to another state; the laws vary greatly.

# Chapter **Ten**

# *Settle Rather Than Sue*

In the best of all worlds you deal solely with other reasonable and honorable people, and all of you transact your affairs graciously, with carefulness and skill. Things always work out the ways intended, and arguments never arise. But you do *not* live in this heavenly world; none of us do.

Despite the best of initial intentions and information—a dubious assumption to begin with—affairs do unravel. People become careless and injure others. They succumb to greed, to temptations to steal. Families, unfortunately, dissolve; people die or change; they get new loves and new hates. Legal papers meant to describe bargains or to transfer property are imperfectly drawn. Recollections vary of what happened or what was meant or agreed upon. Someone tries to squeeze out of an obligation. The potential for legal mischief is beyond imagination in a complex industrial, commercial, technological, and agricultural country of 240 million people, who number among them 600,000 lawyers, including 30,000 judges. If there were to be a parade outside your front door of all the lawyers in the country, with one lawyer passing each minute all day and all night, the procession would take over a year to pass you by.

In this welter, it is inevitable that disappointment will occur and disputation between people and the companies with whom they deal will arise. Moreover, government wheels ceaselessly into regulatory, enforcement, and punitive actions in the innumerable areas that engage its interest.

Overwhelmingly, people shrug off minor injury or loss of small sums, and they put up with small inconveniences as part of life. Perhaps they complain of shoddy merchandise, undesirable travel arrangements, grasping relatives, or their neighbors' lack of civility. But they usually do nothing about it; they grin or grumble and bear it. Many people will even accept a large loss, rather than fight about it.

There are those, however, who want to do something about their rights, and they start legal processes that may lead to the courthouse. If they are suing—becoming plaintiffs—they must decide whether to act aggressively and launch legal maneuvers to get what they want. If they are being sued—becoming defendants—they must decide whether to resist or to give the other side what it wants, let it have its own way.

Peaceful compromise of a lawsuit, if at all feasible, is invariably a better way than a fight to the litigative death of one side or the other. This is because of high legal costs, the risks of losing even good cases, and the heavy emotional drains of litigation.

Before becoming involved in a lawsuit, whether you are pressing or resisting, think it over. Is it for you? It may cost a lot of money. In the major urban centers of this country, a lawsuit involving a typical business matter, which runs a regular course through pleadings, motions, pretrial discovery, jury trial, and one appeal is likely to cost between $50,000 and $100,000, depending on the aggressiveness with which it is waged by both sides. Proceedings involving the personal affairs of the average person, such as tenants' evictions, accidental injury, and drunken driving, cost less, but can still severely dent the family budget.

You may spend considerable time in lawyers' offices, in courtrooms, and in the corridors of both. Your time will be at the mercy of someone else's convenience; your psyche will be bruised.

Are you sure you would not rather pass?


## GOOD REASONS TO AVOID LITIGATION

### Litigation Is War

You must have the head, the heart, the stomach, the time, and the pocketbook for litigation. A lawsuit may be nonviolent confrontation between people, but it is confrontation nonetheless and bound to be unpleasant. People respond to being sued as though it were the personal attack it really is, even in an auto-accident case involving a friendly passenger suing his car-pool driver for accidental injury, for which an insurance company will foot the entire bill. Do not expect to sue someone and retain that person's good will; you are committing a hostile act. If you seek to enlist a person's future cooperation, suing him is an unlikely way to get it.

There are, to be sure, differences in the personal stresses of a lawsuit, depending on the relationship of the parties and what is at stake. Suits between family members are particularly stressful. Unlike commercial relationships, which are of short duration, family relationships continue for life. The need to get along and to placate common relatives should be a whole meal for thought before entering into intrafamilial litigation. Suits between relatives, friends, neighbors, and business associates (and the categories often overlap) are infamous for generating violent emotions. But, nothing hits home like the possibility of criminal prosecution, with a stiff jail sentence down the road.

At the other end of the scale, the suits easiest to cope with are class actions brought by stockholders or taxpayers on behalf of a whole class of people, seeking relief from corporate misconduct or the wasting of public funds. You may be named a party in such suits but never see or hear from a lawyer or a judge or spend a penny. Accident suits brought against you by strangers and for which your insurer takes care of everything are not troublesome, particularly if the case is settled early. At worst, you may have to be examined or questioned by impersonal insurance-company doctors or investigators, or testify briefly in court.

Between the worst and the best situations lies a whole gamut of situations of intermediate intensity, none of which hold any joy. Cases that pit people against people, not big corporations, and cases that require the loser to dig into his own pocket or suffer some other damage, like losing a home or custody of a child or facing an injured reputation, are bound to become heated, whether they be for breach or contract, stealing, hurting, or failing to control a vicious tongue or animal.

To bring a lawsuit, you must really want to win. This is especially so if you are to weather extended litigation. If the strain promises to be too much, if you have sympathy for the other side, if you have enough qualms, think of settling your lawsuit early rather than late, even if it costs more than you thought. In the end, most cases are settled some way.

## *Practical Litany of Negatives*

Many factors come to bear in deciding whether to sue or to resist. Quite obviously, the amount of your loss contrasted with the unreasonableness of the other side may force you into suing someone. If, on the other hand, someone is suing you and will not let up, you are simply impaled. Equally obviously, the apparent strength of the other side's position must always be a prime factor in any decision to go to litigative war. For a plaintiff to win, in theory, at least, he must have a good case to win. By the same token, a resisting defendant must have a good position.

### *Cost*

Cost is one of the most apparent factors. It can be high to both sides.

### *Collectibility*

Another factor in bringing suit in civil cases is whether the defendant has the ability to pay the judgment that is handed down against him. Is it collectible? If it is not, the defendant is considered "judgment proof." Winning a case against a person who cannot pay is wasted effort. For this reason, lawyers in accident cases customarily bring suit only against defendants who are insured for legal liability for injury to others.

### *Lack of Proof*

Can you prove your case?

Whether you are suing or being sued, the availability and strength of proof is critical to winning. If you are suing, you are weakened if you do not have convincing proof, especially if the decision turns on one person's word against another's. Conversely, if you are being sued, the weakness of the plaintiff's proof helps you, because, to win, the plaintiff must prove his case.

Proof means written contracts, receipts, notes, letters, and other documents. It means photographs and objects such as weapons, product samples, and police records. It means witnesses, both friendly and hostile. The reliability and availability of witnesses must always be regarded skeptically. People are afraid of courts and unwilling to be caught in the middle. The missing witness, the recanting or nervous or terrified witness, the equivocal witness who suffers over his precise memory or who qualifies his story hopelessly are all common to litigation. More than one litigant has had his heart broken by a supposedly faithful witness.

### Skeletons in the Closet

Yet another factor in bringing or resisting suit is whether there are any skeletons in your own closet that may be brought out in the course of a fight. If you have evaded tax payments or done illegal deeds, you may be vulnerable to pressure. Litigants with records of past indiscretion are often deterred from going to court. But do not count on it. Claims of "having something" on someone else usually prove less forceful than originally imagined.

## Grinding Down

Parties with greater assets and lesser personal involvement have obvious advantages in litigation over concerned individuals who are neither lawyers nor wealthy. Large corporations and governments know this and use it by putting on litigative pressure. They play on their adversaries' lesser sophistication and greater needs for money. This process of wearing out the other side through endless and costly moves is known as "grinding down." The method is commonly used by parties who perceive their adversaries as weak. Many lawyers by habit toss every motion and every discovery device in the book into a contested case to make it more difficult for the opposition. Such lawyers may unwittingly grind down their own clients by harassing opposing parties financially stronger and more willing to do battle.

Threats to sue large corporations or, particularly, the government normally fall on deaf ears. When I was the county attorney of Nassau County, New York, I continually heard threats of lawsuit that were meant to be intimidating. Few realized that the county's litigation staff was there precisely to go to court, itching for litigation experience and to get out of the office for the day. Indeed, more cases meant that more staff could be justified come budget time. Government legal staffs can often be indifferent to the taxpayers' or the government's burden of the legal cost, unwilling to go out on a limb, inflexible about decisions arrived at by committee, excessively concerned about political considerations, and afraid to appear to be exhibiting undue favoritism to a private interest.

In short, unless you have plenty of money, *never* try to grind down the government.

# THE SETTLEMENT GAME

The discussion of settlement of disputes is really relevant to every section of this book, whether a person is acting alone or through a lawyer, at any time.

In every area of human contact there are differences to be reconciled. There is art in resolving conflicts by mutually acceptable compromise, whether the process takes place at a clothing store, in an auto showroom, at a collective-bargaining table, at a rent arbitration hearing, at a protest demonstration, or in a courthouse. The principles of settlement are the same regardless of how formally the agreement is reached.

The cardinal principle of compromise is that you must give to get. Do not expect to get everything you want in the name of compromise; the other side calls that "losing."

## *Tactics*
### *Do Not Fear Initiating Settlement*
When confronted with litigation, always think "settlement." Do not be afraid to open settlement discussions. Some lawyers take initial overtures as signs of weakness, but most lawyers do not and are relieved at overtures. Settlement of an actual or threatened lawsuit is typically started by the defending lawyer. He remarks how weak your case seems, but expresses a willingness to pay its nuisance value, which is usually the cost of fighting the case or some lesser sum, to allow you to save face. There is no need to stand on ceremony. If the opposing defense is too stiff-necked or wants to seem tough or indifferent, do not hesitate to offer overtures of your own.

Late settlements often occur because of a lawyer's schedule, availability, or the low intensity of his involvement. Settlement activity is something you can monitor; be in constant touch with your lawyer.

Look for the fine balance between unnecessarily compounding your legal bills by taking up too much of your lawyer's time, on the one hand, and being both an informed participant and an effective prod, on the other. If your lawyer is not willing to talk to you, get another one.

Delay in settlement is often the result of the parties feeling each other out; posturing is part of the process. Another reason for delay, especially in accident cases, is the need to clarify injuries and to allow actual bad effects to become manifest. Conversely, insurers often seek to allow the passage of time to heal minor wounds and to minimize the injuries claimed sustained. Some insurance companies will string along a claimant, not only to weaken his resolve but also to earn more interest on his money while the case inches through the creaky judicial system.

There is an obvious advantage in early settlement before the legal bills on both sides start to mount. In the early phases, money otherwise earmarked for the lawyers may be used to end the case. Moreover, the more a party invests in a case through fees, the more expensive settlement becomes.

### Do Not Start with Your Best Offer

It is always wise to open settlement talks with an inflated claim if you are suing, and a deflated offer if you are being sued. Build in some trading material. Remember that settlement means compromise: you must give up something in order to achieve your objective. For example, if you are willing to pay $3,000, offer $1,000. If you seek $5,000, ask for $10,000 and be ready to settle for $4,250.

Never start out with your best offer.

### Do Not Consider an Opening Offer to Be a Best Offer

This is the flip side of not opening with your best offer: never regard your adversary's opening offer as his best offer. Do not be stampeded by a claim that a certain sum is on the table now and if it is not accepted now it will be lower or gone later. If the other side says at the beginning, "I am not bargaining. I will pay you $15,000, no more, no less. And if you do not take it now, I will retract that offer and never settle with you," the chances are great he is dissembling. Test him. Previously made offers can almost always be resurrected, particularly with insurance companies.

Naturally, circumstances and people vary, but common wisdom tells us that there is always more flexibility than originally indicated. The art in negotiating is to gauge when the other side has reached its maximum in concession.

"Hanging tough" in negotiation—insisting that the other side take it or leave it—is largely reserved for those who are in a plainly dominant position and can afford to ignore the adversary's side. Lawyers try to avoid ultimatums; the shoe may be on the other foot someday.

### No Number Is without an Effect

Beware of throwing numbers around. If you say in a settlement discussion, "I might pay from $1,000 to $1,500," you are understood as willing to pay at least $1,500, and probably more. The $1,500 cancels the $1,000. Never use a number to illustrate a point unless you can live with that number. If you want $40,000 in an accident recovery, never say it takes $25,000 a year alone for you to live, plus all your medical expenses and without taking into account any compensation for pain and suffering. You will have signaled a $25,000 figure as the number you will accept.

Apparently casual references to numbers between experienced negotiators are bidding conventions and are taken as trial balloons to feel the way toward consensus. No mentioned number is without an effect. In settlement discussions, never mention a number if you are not prepared to accept it later.

### Do Not Bid against Yourself

It is generally not a good idea to improve an offer you have made until your adversary has made a counteroffer to your original offer. You will be bidding against yourself, and intimating that you are becoming anxious. Of course, if your first bid proved to be unreasonably low, you may want to get back in the game by making a second and higher offer. On the other side, there is danger in asking for unreasonably high sums in settlement, since your perceived irrationality may kill any further discussion.

### Never Try to Squeeze Out the Last Dollar

Parties who draw their lines too strictly and let settlement get away over a few dollars are short-sighted. Small differences in money or conduct can and should be bridged with patience and good humor. Never try to squeeze out the last dollar.

A famous Rothschild tale centers around one of the fabled Barons, who, when asked the secret of his trading success, replied, "I always sold too soon."

### Keep in Touch

Communication is the key: make the extra phone call, pay one more visit, write one more letter. Sometimes, throwing in a new negotiator (perhaps a fresh lawyer or a friend, preferably an older person or one who seems to be very wise) can help. It is worth a try.

Skillful negotiators have the knack of activating stalled settlement discussions by opening up new avenues of approach. Innovation is frequently the key to success in negotiations. Do not let a favorable settlement fall apart over small differences. Keep in touch.

### Never Underestimate the Appeal of Money

Cases may involve outright monetary claims or can involve the right to work for a period, to occupy a home or an office, to use a car, to have a service rendered, or many other things that really have money equivalents. The hard reality is that most disputed claims—with obvious exceptions—can be settled by awards of money. Even the most emotionally knotted problems can be solved with surprising ease by offering money as compensation. To make payment easier to handle, there are an infinite number of ways to stretch out money payments over periods of time, with high or low interest rates, depending on who is doing the inducing.

## Tripping over Your Own Ego

Sensible settlements are not always reached, even when they are available. Many people are not capable of settling their claims, either because they are too emotionally involved or because they cannot bring themselves to make up their minds and decide their own destiny. They would rather have a judge do it. Others are inveterate gamblers.

When it comes to disputation, many people are bound by deep-seated needs for self-assertion. Such people will have great difficulty in reaching settlement. They cannot control their egos long enough to reach rational compromise. They are so busy telling their own story that they will not hear the opposing argument. They fritter away every opportunity to adjust their disputes and, failing in early settlement, become more bitter and more determined to continue to total victory. They wind up either taking their claims through the full legal process, at great expense, or abandoning it altogether.

### Lawyer as a Link

When everyone's positions and thoughts are out in the open, and there is communication, the best economic interests of the parties can be served. Often, however, effective communication is absent.

Lawyers are useful in untying knots by serving as go-betweens, although if the parties could summon enough maturity themselves to communicate with one another, the process would be a great deal easier. Bear in mind that your lawyer is not betraying you by fraternizing with the enemy. He is keeping the lines of communication open. Your lawyer should do that. It can help you.

Some people love a harsh and abrasive lawyer, who fights the other side, client and lawyer alike, incessantly. They equate nastiness with toughness. More often, however, it is the calm, articulate lawyer who gets the best results. The lawyers should be the link, keeping open all lines of communication, and this, too, is easier if they can talk to one another.

### Listening

Talking is not everything.

Try listening. Just because you are listening does not mean that you are agreeing to anything.

Remember, it is difficult to learn while you are talking. If you listen carefully, you may hear something useful.

The key to resolution of disputes is to understand the other side thoroughly, and to suggest responsive compromise proposals that offer hope. Get out the whole story, so you can figure ways of approach.

### Divorce Cases

The divorce courts are an unusually emotional battleground; divorce cases more than others squeeze the ego. Too often the parties act out their hostilities and frustrations, when in reality, by the divorce-trial stage, the only real argument is about money.

There seems to be a necessity for many couples to become blood-
ied in legal combat before reason sets in and the kind of compromise
that is in their best interests becomes possible. The early heat that
characterizes much matrimonial litigation ignores the fact that the judge
is cold to the personal rages of the parties, that he may look at their
plight in a way quite different from either or both of them. The reality that it is best to give ground dawns on many only with the ex-
haustion of extended battle.

It is a mistake for one spouse to assume that he or she is strong
and the other weak simply because the relationship has always made
it seem that way. A supportive lawyer may change all that. Moreover, the timid mouse, once cornered, may exhibit surprisingly assertive behavior.

Revenge, as opposed to vindication, is a poor reason to press a
lawsuit. Rarely can heated emotion be sustained through extended and
costly legal proceedings. Even the winner suffers anxiety, wastes time,
and pays out money in costs.

### Swallow Your Pride

Since it is almost always in your best interest to settle a case, put up
with your irritation at the other side. Perhaps the other side obtains
undeserved concessions, which bother you. Do not look in the other
one's pocket; look in your own.

Make it a goal to accomplish the settlement. Swallow your pride
and help yourself. Consider the expense and risk of trial, and see
whether your own best interest does not call for compromise, however galling.

Avoid confrontation, vicious comments, a rehash of irrelevant events
long past, and battles of the ego. It is not necessary to rise to dispute
or debate every point.

Do not respond to urges to score points or to carry on like a winner. Allow the other side his dignity.

## Be Frank with Your Lawyer

Talk frankly to your lawyer about money when a settlement is on the
table.

You and your lawyer may have different interests in settling or going
all the way in court. Your lawyer, who has the work burden, may be

well satisfied with a $7,500 recovery in settlement, out of which he receives $2,500, or one-third. The economics of law-office operations call for the maximum settlement of cases, not gambling time and expense in court. You, however, may want to gamble for $15,000. The $2,500 fee difference at that level is not persuasive to the lawyer, but to you the greater recovery is more attractive. You do not care about his law-office economics.

Conversely, you may have money needs and want an early recovery by settlement well before trial. The lawyer, who is a courtroom professional, wants to take the litigation risk because he does not have an immediate need and is wealthy enough to gamble for big stakes. If the fee is contingent (a percentage of the recovery), the lawyer is financing the case. His position is understandable, too.

Discuss your settlement thoughts frankly with your lawyer. Elicit to the best you can his own thoughts. Form an idea of how much of the settlement relates to the merits of the case, and how much to the immediacy of the money. Insist on full explanation. If you are not satisfied, say so. In the end, the settlement decision is yours.

# Chapter *Eleven*

# *Conducting Yourself in Court*

The trial of a case in open court is the end game of law. That is where the state prosecutes those people it would call "criminals," and that is the official place to resolve private disputes by legal means.

How you present yourself in court bears significantly on what happens to you there.

## COURTROOMS: SERIOUS PLACES

Courthouses can look formidable. The farther you go into them, up broad marble stairways, through wide corridors, the greater becomes your sense of foreboding. As you walk into the formal room where you will have your day in court, your stomach is bound to tighten. Most trial lawyers and all judges are used to the seriousness of the place; you are not. But do not despair; your reaction is normal.

In front of you, directly opposite your entry door, rises an enclosed wood-paneled desk platform, where the judge will sit in a high-backed black or brown leather chair. You will see the American flag and the state flag, and, on the rear wall, some official insignia and perhaps a motto. A witness stand— a chair—is close to one side of the judge, with clerical space on the other side. A court reporter waits in front with a Stenotype tripod planted on a glossy floor, or perhaps one conservatively carpeted.

Off to one side, normally nearest the witness stand and at a right angle to the judge, is another raised wood-paneled enclosure, with twelve to fourteen seats—the jury box. Facing the judge are long tables, for the parties and their lawyers. As either plaintiff or defendant, you are a "party" to the case. Throughout your case, you will sit at one of these tables, known universally as "counsel tables," except when you move to the witness stand to testify, if you do.

Behind you, toward the rear of the courtroom, a railing about three feet high separates you from rows of seats. In older courthouses, hard wooden benches serve; in newer ones, the seats are like those of a movie theater. These are for the audience: spectators, your family, prospective witnesses, and others who are waiting their turn in that courtroom. People from other courtrooms kill time there. Courthouse buffs, usually retired people who find drama in court proceedings, are commonly present. There are usually no reporters unless a celebrity is expected or a newsworthy public issue is involved. Important as your case may be to you, few others are interested except out of impersonal curiosity. The court personnel know you; they have seen you many times before, with a different name, or face, or body, or so they think.

# IMPORTANCE OF PERSONAL IMPRESSIONS YOU MAKE

The impressions you give the judge and the jury are important to you in attaining credibility and sympathy, both of which you will need.

Cases are decided on the facts. The judge and the jury have no way to learn these facts except from the testimony given. They get your version of your side of the case from you and your witnesses. You must be credible, so judge and jury will believe you and will accept your version of what happened as what really happened. The courtroom reality is that the facts of the case, which are relied upon for decision, are not necessarily what actually happened; they are what the judge and the jury believe happened. The words of people against people, sometimes corroborated by circumstances or proof, weigh heavily in legal decision. Your story must be believed if you are to put the law on your side.

Think of the signs that cause you to believe people in your daily life; that will give you an idea of the way credibility is generated in court. People tend to believe "good" persons, solid-seeming citizens, well mannered, dignified, forthright, respectful, and neatly dressed. Those who are flamboyant, the clowns, the wiseacres, the nervous and the shifty, the overemotional, the bad actors, and those who seem unconventional are less readily believed. To be sure, the town drunk may be telling the truth, and the banker in a three-piece suit may be lying his white-thatched head off, but a jury will be more inclined to believe the banker. To most people, things are usually what they seem to be; improbable circumstances are difficult to establish.

Sympathy is desirable because it makes the judge and the jury want to believe you and because it makes them willing to stretch a point in your behalf. Sympathy is the key to mercy and compassion, which may be more important to you than the letter of the law. Indeed, your lawyer may seek to avoid the merits of your case, if they are weak, and concentrate on factors that will arouse sympathy. You want the jury to empathize, to identify with you; you want them to think, There but for the grace of God go I.

By your appearance, your demeanor in court, and your conduct on the witness stand, you can bolster your credibility. You can improve your chances of success in court. You can help put the law on your side.

### Dress Code

A trial is not a funeral, although it may end sadly, but it is no disco either. Dress conservatively. Judges and jurors who tend to dress casually will not so easily be put off by conservative attire, but those who dress conservatively are not so likely to tolerate more casual attire. Play the dress odds. Dress for the middle line. When in doubt, err on the side of conservatism. This is a good rule for every legal occasion.

Dress is more important in a jury trial than at an appearance before a judge alone.

For men, a solid-color, pin-stripe, or conservatively checked suit is appropriate, although a dark blazer or some other kind of quiet sports jacket will also do. The safest colors are black, brown, blue, and gray.

Shirts should be white or a subdued blue, gray, or tan, preferably in a soft solid color. Shoes should be plain and shined; all clothes should be clean and well pressed.

For women, the range of acceptable color and costume is greater. Fresh-looking dresses, suits (but not with pants), skirts, blouses, and sweaters that are not flashy go best in court, as do simple hair styles. Dress your age, neither older nor younger. Play it straight. A woman who is seen as telling a lie in the way she dresses may be less than credible in other ways.

Women should try not to look wealthy. Minimize the appearance of jewelry, furs, and clothes that look expensive.

Some lawyers like to play games, particularly with the way their women clients dress, suggesting the costume of the little girl lost, the castoff plain and aging wife, the solid businessman, the needy elderly person, or the innocent youth. If you are uncomfortable with your lawyer's dress suggestions, do not be reticent. Question your lawyer carefully before presenting yourself as someone you are not. Talk it over fully, but, in the end, listen to him. If you do not have confidence in his suggestions, get rid of him.

These thoughts bring to mind the story of a judge sternly addressing the defendant before passing sentence.

> **Judge:** Look at you! You are a disgrace. Your clothes are filthy, your hair is a mess. You're dirty. I can even smell you up here on the bench. What do you have to say for yourself? . . . Well?
>
> **Answer:** If it please, your honor, I'm not the defendant. I'm his lawyer.

## Personal Demeanor in Court

Most of your time in court as a party to a suit will be at the counsel table, although you will probably spend some time on the witness stand, too.

### Do Not Argue with Your Lawyer in the Courtroom

Always be seen as having a good relationship with your lawyer. If you want to argue with him, ask or wait for a recess and do it out of the courtroom. Do not pull at your lawyer's limbs or clothing to get his attention while he is addressing a witness, the judge, or, worst of all, the jury.

Bear in mind that communication is not restricted to oral and written language. There are body signals as well. Do not be put in the position of saying one thing, either directly or through your lawyer, and telling a different story through your body language.

Take notes during the trial to help you follow the proceedings, to appear to be involved, and to have something to do with your hands. You can write notes to your lawyer and hand them to him, but be careful not to write too many. Don't hand your lawyer a note when he is standing apart from you and you have to rise or walk to make the delivery. Let your lawyer be your lawyer.

### Be Alert, Attentive, Unfazed

While court is in session, do not stare vacantly at the ceiling or the walls, yawn conspicuously, smirk, drum your fingers on the table, doodle compulsively, or fidget. Make an effort to keep your hands away from your face. If you must mop your brow or dry your palms, do it as unobtrusively as you can. If there is a water pitcher in front of you, drink only sparingly. You will probably be nervous, but try not to show it. Juries react poorly to displays of nervousness, relating them to fear, guilt, and lying.

Appear attentive; sit up straight and maintain your dignity. Avoid constant looking at your watch or the clock on the wall. Look at the judge, the jury, the lawyers, or the witness.

Never chew gum or tobacco. Smoking will not be a problem, because it is not permitted in court.

Be the soul of quiet confidence. When the opposition scores its points, as it must sometime, keep calm, even when some development causes the jury or the judge to turn and look pointedly at you. Under ordinary circumstances, a poker face is best; smile or weep if a proper occasion for it arises, but do not force it as a ploy. The same applies to theatrical demonstrations of outrage or exasperation. You are probably not that good an actor.

Do not, however, suppress genuine emotion or depth of feeling. I recall a case I presided over as a trial judge, in which the custody of an eleven-year-old boy was at issue. His mother took the witness stand with a flourish and testified coolly and with great self-possession. She was a beautiful, well-dressed woman, with a flair doubtless heightened by dramatic training. She was controlled in her performance, but it seemed to me just that. I, as judge, interrupted her cool testimony to advise her lawyer, out loud, in the open court, while she listened from the witness stand, that I thought he might want to instruct his client on the gravity of the occasion, that she must be apprised of the possibility of losing custody of her son. The lawyer and the woman obliged during a recess and returned shortly. This time, I heard a concerned mother expressing her feelings for her son. For the first time in the trial, she seemed to be a caring person. When she had finished testifying, she withdrew with quiet dignity, and I felt that she had made a good case for custody of her son, although earlier I had seen her as a most unlikely custodial candidate.

### Look at the Jury

You should not hesitate to look at the members of the jury or to smile in their presence. In criminal cases particularly, however, avoid overt laughter. Your case is no joke, and you do not want to be seen as taking it lightly. By the time the jury deliberates on its verdict, the laughter is over, and residual impressions of it may affect unfavorably the now totally serious jury.

Neither avert your eyes from nor try to stare down jurors. You do not want to alienate them by seeming shameful, furtive, or defiant. Do not talk to the jurors during your trial. Talking discreetly to the judge is all right during recess, particularly if he invites it, but it is not to be encouraged. You do not want to appear to be currying favor or offering proof indirectly.

If you should suddenly find yourself face to face with a juror in the corridor, in the elevator, or on the street, give a courteous greeting and make a polite departure. Never discuss your case with a juror, and tell your lawyer if you see anyone else doing it.

### When Court Is Not in Session

Bear in mind that you are always on view in the courtroom, and possibly even in the corridors, whether court is in session or in recess. Take pains to maintain your image of a decent, upstanding person who deserves to win.

If the judge or the jury has decided against you, carry your dignity with you, whether to the street or back to your jail cell. The jury may have spoken, but the judge may not have. Your lawyer or that of the other side may have special motions to make concerning the civil judgment or the criminal verdict. The judge may have to decide whether to set aside a civil verdict. You may have to face sentencing or the fixing of bail. Let the judge carry the best possible mental image of you as a person into any of his posttrial deliberations.

In places where, following criminal conviction by a jury, a second hearing by that same jury is held to determine punishment, you will want to be doubly careful.

## On the Witness Stand

The most important part of your appearance in court as a party to a suit will usually be on the witness stand. There your personal demeanor is critical; there you have your chance to tell your story. There is where your credibility will be measured, and there is the prime place for you to generate sympathy. Make the most of it.

Although you are a party to the case, you will be treated like other witnesses. However, as a party, you must expect a more skeptical reception in court, because of your obvious interest in the outcome of the case. Your self-interest hangs plainly on the line as you talk.

Observe the rules given for personal demeanor in the courtroom generally on the witness stand, too, but with some added refinements. Try to look directly at the jury as you talk, to the degree you feel comfortable. While you are answering important questions particularly, look at the jury and not to the questioning lawyer. Jurors like you to talk to them. It makes you seem frank, forthright, and confident.

Do not be afraid to correct any error you may have made. Ask the judge, "Your honor, may I correct the last thing I said?"

If, while you are testifying as a witness, the lawyers start to wrangle over objections and begin strenuous arguments between themselves or with the judge, keep out of it. It is beyond your sphere. Good witnesses speak only when spoken to.

Some courtrooms have witness-stand microphones to amply testimony. If faced with a microphone, do not hunch down to speak into it. Sit up straight and talk forward, with clear enunciation. If there is no microphone, it is doubly important to keep your voice up. Mumbling, low, or otherwise indistinct answers not only fail to communicate your message, but also give the impression that you are not being forthright.

You will probably be nervous as you begin to be questioned. This is natural, and you will probably get over the worst of it as the examination wears on. A good way to prepare for the ordeal of your trial, if you have the time, is to go to the court for an earlier trial on the same general subject as yours, preferably before the same judge, to familiarize yourself with the ground. Study the actors and the procedure carefully.

# ANSWERING QUESTIONS AS A WITNESS

The questioning of a witness is known as an "examination." A lawyer questioning his own client, or another witness for his client, is said to be conducting "direct examination." Questioning the opposing party or witnesses is called "cross-examination." Subsequent questioning may be "redirect" or "recross" examination. Theoretically, the scope of questioning after direct testimony is limited to the line of questioning immediately preceding it.

## Direct Examination
### Objections

Lawyers often raise objections to questions put by their adversaries. In direct (or redirect) examination, leading questions are not permitted, although they may be asked in cross-examination. An objectionable leading question on direct examination is one that suggests its own answer, such as "You left your home that day at 3:00 P.M., did you not?" In direct (or redirect) examination, that information may be properly elicited in the following manner:

*Q.* Were you at home at all that day?
*A.* Yes
*Q.* Please tell me how many times, if any, you left your home that day.
*A.* Once.

*Q.*   At what time was that?
*A.*   3:00 P.M.

"Leading" your own witness is a principal objection. Another common objection is to "hearsay" testimony. This means that the witness is not testifying out of his own personal knowledge. The witness is saying what he heard, not what he actually observed. For instance:

*Q.*      At what time was that?
*A.*      My wife told me it was 3:00 P.M.
*Lawyer:*  Objection—hearsay.
*Court:*   Sustained.

Or the objection may be to the form of the question; for instance, two questions crammed into one:

*Q.*      Did you find out from your wife the time when you came home and what was that time?
*Lawyer:*  Objection as to form of question.
*Court:*   Sustained.

Leading and hearsay are only two kinds of objections. Even the most casual student of legal theater knows the objecting words: "irrelevant," "incompetent," and "immaterial." The classic trio, usually uttered as a litany after a question or an answer, is really three separate objections. "Irrelevant" means that the question or answer does not tend to prove anything that bears on the case. "Incompetent" means that the question is inadmissible under the rules of evidence.

"Immaterial" is close to "irrelevant," and means that the answer is of no consequence.

### Preparation of Witnesses in Advance
To minimize objections and to improve the usefulness of your testimony, most lawyers will discuss with you, in advance, the nature of the testimony that you should present. You will then be able to present it without distracting problems of leading or hearsay.

Never deny on cross-examination that you discussed your testimony with your attorney, if you in fact did discuss any aspect of it with him. The judge and the jury will assume that you did. Do not let any sneering inferences of the cross-examiner upset you, because if you qualify your answer, another line of tricks awaits. Answer forthrightly.

It is a good and ethical legal practice for your lawyer to go over your trial testimony in advance. It is standard trial preparation. Your lawyer can tell you the questions he will ask, and you can tell him your answers. You can discuss together the form of the answer, but it is wrong for your lawyer to give you the gist of the answer. There is a fine line between preparing, which is good, and coaching, which is not. Coaching can be the subject of a valid objection to the court and the coached testimony may be stricken, or, at the judge's instigation, coaching may be grounds for disciplinary action against the offending lawyer.

## Cross-Examination: Danger. Approach with Care

Do not be confused about the lawyers. Your lawyer is for you; the other lawyer, for all the friendliness and solicitude he may exhibit, is the enemy.

You will, of course, be familiar with your own lawyer. If he is competent, you will have gone over the questions to be asked and the answers you will give. Direct testimony, in a sense, is the play after the rehearsal, although you must be constantly attentive for any departures from the "script" by your lawyer.

Cross-examination, made by the lawyer for the other side, is something else again. It is to be hoped that your own lawyer will have prepared you in advance for that, too. If your lawyer is capable, he will have rehearsed you by playing the role of the other lawyer. But do not assume that even such a rehearsal will have prepared you fully. In the real cross-examination, you are under siege.

Listen carefully to each question, and take your time in deciding on your answer. Answer each question slowly and deliberately. An advantage of slow answering is that it gives your lawyer a chance to formulate his objections and make them before you answer. Once your answer has been given, even if an objection by your lawyer is sustained, some damage has been done to you. The jury has heard it.

### Be Stingy with Your Words

If a "yes" or "no" answer will suffice, give it. Be as stingy as possible with your words. *Do not volunteer anything;* answer only the specific question in front of you.

Do not be afraid to ask the cross-examiner to repeat or clarify his question, but only if you really need to. If the jury has understood the questions right along, too many of these requests may damage your credibility.

If you must refer to a document, say so. *Never guess.* If you do not know the answer, say so. If the cross-examiner's question involves a more complex answer, give it. But do not panic before the cross-examiner's insistent demands for a "yes or no." It is your answer. If you cannot answer the question in the form put, say that to the judge.

### Do Not Fence with the Cross-Examiner

The cardinal sin of a witness being cross-examined is an attempt to outsmart the questioning lawyer. Do not match wits with him, do not say anything you think might embarrass him, do not fence verbally with him. You are playing his game on his turf. He is the professional, and you are, at best, a talented amateur. Just answer his questions if you can, and answer them briefly. Do not be belligerent or apologetic.

### Do Not Be Evasive

Avoid overcautious or evasive answers. They do not protect you in the eyes of God, the judge, the jury, or the cross-examiner who is trying to trip you up. "I think," "I'm not altogether sure, but . . ." "Mind you, I was far away," and "It was dark" are grist for the cross-examiner's mill. You may then hear: "Oh, you are not sure?" or "Do you think or do you know?" or "Could you really see?"

### Use of Pretrial-Examination Testimony to Upset You

You are not the only side with devices. The opposing lawyer has plenty. Two of the most widely used will serve to illustrate.

There is a procedure, known as "pretrial examination," at which you testify privately, usually in a law office. The opposing lawyer asks you questions in the presence of your own lawyer. It is a form of minitrial, meant to elicit information, to avoid surprise testimony, and to help the opposing lawyer prepare his case. A court reporter takes down everything that is said and produces a typewritten transcript, which you sign and acknowledge under oath to be true. If the transcript is not accurate, you can correct it.

At the actual trial, the other lawyer can read the transcript, which is also called a "deposition," to the jury. He can use it to "impeach your credibility"—legalese for "make you look like a liar." A classic impeachment ploy on cross-examination goes like this:

Q. Mr. Sweeney, at what time did you come home?

A. 3:00 P.M.

Q. Mr. Sweeney, I show you a transcript of an examination before trial conducted in my office on January 28, 1983. Is that your signature [showing it to the witness]?

A. Yes.

Q. Did you read the transcript before you signed it?

A. Yes.

Q. Are all your answers truthful?

A. Yes.

Q. I refer to page 12, line 5, where it says, "Question: At what time did you come home?" Answer: "5:00 P.M." Is that what you said?

A. If that is what it says there, yes.

Q. Did you say "5:00 P.M.?"

A. Yes.

Q. You just testified on the witness stand that you came home at 3:00 P.M. Which is correct, 3:00 P.M. or 5:00 P.M.? When were you lying, then or now?

Your Lawyer: Objection. Argumentative and assumes a conclusion not in evidence.

Court: Sustained. [The judge then says to the jury, "Please disregard that question."]

Q. I ask you again, at what time did you come home?

A. At 3:00 P.M.

Q. But you said 5:00 P.M. in your deposition. Which answer do you now say is correct?

A. 3:00 P.M.

Q.   Is your memory of that day better now, today, than it was two years ago when you testified in your deposition?

A.   No.

Q.   Are you telling the truth now?

A.   Yes.

Q.   If, as you testified, your memory was better as to the event when you testified two years ago that you came home at 5:00 P.M., why do you now testify differently?

A.   I was mistaken then.

Q,   Is it not more likely that your mistake is in today's testimony?

If the questions involved are important to your case, you can sustain a mortal wound by departing from your deposition testimony. If any contradiction is not a direct one, or the point is unimportant, the wound is not likely to be serious, but such deviations never help you.

Before you testify as a witness at a trial always read any pretrial deposition you may have given.

### The Heads-I-Win, Tails-You-Lose Caper

Other tricks used in cross-examination are simply that, are recognized by juries as such, and cause only flesh wounds if they do any harm at all. A favorite routine in negligence cases, such as a claim for damages on account of injuries sustained when tripping on a crack in the sidewalk, usually follows one of these two scenarios:

### Scenario 1

Q.   Were you walking on Surf Avenue?

A.   Yes.

Q.   As you were walking, were your eyes following the sidewalk carefully for cracks?

A.   Yes.

Q.   If you were watching the sidewalk carefully, then how did you happen to catch your foot in the crack in the sidewalk?

or

### Scenario 2

Q.   As you were walking, were your eyes following the sidewalk carefully for cracks?

*A.* No.

*Q.* What were you doing with your eyes?

*A.* I was looking straight ahead, as I always do.

*Q.* You were not looking down at the ground in front of you?

*A.* No.

*Q.* The crack was right in front of you all the time, was it not?

*A.* Yes.

*Q.* If you had been looking down you would have seen it? would you not?

The cross-examiner nicks you either way in this game, and his hope is that you will become flustered and say something foolish. The trap is not limited to cracks in the sidewalk; it can be baited with flaws in carpeting, with escalators, with differences in the height of steps, with automobile speedometer readings, or with countless other everyday items. The key is not to lose your head. The best answer always reflects the conduct of the average person in the situation; people do not normally go about their daily affairs anticipating accidents or being reckless.

### Follow Your Own Lawyer's Lead

It is a mistake to go into the law business for yourself during a trial. Your lawyer is your professional; do as he tells you.

While the other lawyer is cross-examining you, if your lawyer raises an objection, close your mouth, in the middle of a word if necessary. If on direct testimony your lawyer breaks into your testimony, stop talking and listen. When it comes to trial conduct, you rarely know better than your lawyer.

Many trial lawyers develop signals to their clients to let them known when to stop talking, overdoing, or volunteering. Be alert to these signals.

## *PRO SE.* BE A CREDIBLE AND APPEALING REPRESENTATIVE—FOR YOURSELF

Earlier, it was said that *pro se* court appearance (a person acting in court as his own lawyer) are best limited to such nonjury trial courts as traffic, family, and small claims, where an appearance without a lawyer is anticipated as a matter of judicial design and social policy. *Pro se* representation is definitely *not* recommended in regular civil trial courts of record or in courts that try criminal cases for felonies or misdemeanors, particularly when there are jury trials.

## Personal Conduct

If you do find yourself going to court on a *pro se* adventure, representing yourself, get there on time. Usually calendars are posted in the corridors that tell which courtroom to attend. There is always a central court clerk's office to give out information.

Speak to the judge in your best-modulated voice. Do not be snide; avoid jokes. Do not use profanity. Do not try to act the way you think a lawyer should act. Be yourself. Be polite to the judge; call him "Judge" or "Your Honor." Listen closely to what the judge says for hints as to your conduct—whether to press on with an argument, drop it, talk settlement, or whatever. The judge is no social companion; he is a powerful force with which you must contend if you want to win.

## Be Direct; Do Not Ramble

In all likelihood you will have the opportunity to make an opening statement. Take it. The person making the claim speaks first. Avoid a long rambling story. Mention your most important points at the beginning; alert the judge to the substance of your case. Most judges will give you the opportunity to present relevant proof at some later point.

If the complaint is about buying a damaged garment in a store at 2:00 P.M., do not begin with the fact that you woke up that morning with a bad sinus attack. Start with the fact that on Thursday, May 12, at 2:00 P.M., you bought the dress. Tell the essential elements of your story, including details of your injuries; how, for instance, you were injured by that hidden pin, or how, exactly, you were locked up by a salesperson in that dark closet with no air circulating. Make all damage seem as important as you can without overdoing it; a two-aspirin headache, after all, is just that.

Do not try to anticipate your opponent's defense. Concentrate on putting your own story in its best simple light. There will be plenty of back and forth later to fill in background. Remember, judges are busy people, anxious to get to the core of the controversy. Even before you start, they are weary of self-serving personal accusations.

If you state a fact, such as that you met the person at noon on H Street, leave it there. Do not volunteer a reason for being so positive, such as "I remember it was noon because I heard a ringing in my ear and realized it was the noon whistle." Wait to be challenged on why you remember.

## Making Proof; Be Prepared

After you and your adversary have told the judge what the case is about, he probably will ask for witnesses. Question all witnesses politely and in even tones. If, after you have pursued different directions, you suspect that your adversary is not telling the truth on the witness stand, your best bet is to remind him that he is under oath and to ask whether he would like to change his story. A facial grimace or two does not hurt, but name-calling routines get you nowhere.

Prior preparation for a court appearance is crucial to winning the case. Lay persons, typically, have not met with witnesses or even found them. Few know where to get evidence or how to organize and present it. They cannot and do not prepare adequate legal memoranda for the court. Amateur papers can hurt more than they help. Lay self-advocates usually feel they can simply present themselves physically and rely on the court to believe what they say. Do not make that mistake.

Have your proof with you. It may be letters, receipts, sales slips, contracts, photographs, tapes, or the objects involved in the case, such as a torn garment, a defective radio, or a weapon.

If there are to be witnesses, frame your questions in advance—write them down. Organize your items of proof in the order in which you want to present them. Put documents and items that you are not concealing for surprise tactical purposes within reach on the desk or table assigned to you. Know the full content of any paper you use for proof; having something used against you in a document you produced yourself can be especially destructive. If, for instance, you are claiming damages for a rented car that turned out to be defective, you must be aware that a side letter you produce, apart from the rental contract, to show the specifications of the car's equipment also says down deep in its next-to-last paragraph that you inspected the car and agreed to rent it "as is." Measure the gain of your item of proof against its harm.

Preparation for court appearances is not unlike preparation for meetings, speeches, or interviews. Have your opening sentence memorized. It will help you break the ice of the opening tension easily and gracefully. Getting started is hardest of all.

### Do Not Turn on the Judge

I have never ceased to be amazed at the ease with which *pro se* parties will, in open court, explicitly attack a judge as biased, unfair, incompetent, or worse. This can be destructive; psychiatrists would probably characterize such conduct as litigative suicide. A judge is neither your parent nor your spouse. Your petulance can only backfire. Within that black robe is a person who may take offense. The judge has heard others like you before and will hear more later. Judge-baiting is a tricky proposition for masters of the fringe bar; for uninitiated lay persons, it is hopeless.

## SPECIAL PROBLEMS IN CRIMINAL TRIALS

The same rules of personal conduct as discussed earlier apply to both civil and criminal trials. The judge and the jury watch you carefully and look for any clues as to how they should decide.

### Burden of Proof

Criminal trials differ from civil trials in important ways. In a criminal trial, the accused must be proven guilty "beyond a reasonable doubt." In civil trials, the plaintiff need only show that he is more likely than not entitled to win—he needs only a "preponderance of the evidence" on his side.

Absolutely no proof burden falls on a criminal-case defendant. He does not need to introduce evidence, call witnesses, or even examine the prosecutor's witnesses. A criminal defendant need do nothing. The law cloaks him with a presumption of innocence that remains until such time as the prosecutor establishes guilt beyond that reasonable doubt.

The criminal defendant does not have to prove his innocence. For him to prevail, the jury need only return a verdict of "not guilty." "Not guilty" is not synonymous with a finding of innocence; it merely means that the prosecution has failed to meet its burden of proving the defendant guilty beyond a reasonable doubt.

### Should Defendant Take the Stand?

A criminal defendant need not take the witness stand unless he chooses to do so. The prosecution cannot compel him to testify as a witness, as it can in a civil case. Under our constitutional law, a person cannot be forced to testify against himself. This is the famous Fifth Amendment privilege against self-incrimination. If a defendant relies on this privilege, the jury will never get to hear his story personally told by him or be in a position to judge his personal credibility. In effect, a mute defendant says, "I am innocent, Prosecutor; now prove me guilty if you can."

Whether a criminal defendant should testify is one of the ticklish and important questions of defense strategy, since it requires a prediction of the force that the prosecution's case standing by itself will exert. It also involves recognition of the fact that the prosecution often cannot make its case by means of its evidence alone, but needs some testimony from the defendant as well.

Some risk to a defendant is involved in choosing not to take the witness stand. Although admonished by the judge that the defendant has no obligation to do so, juries are naturally inclined to want to hear the defendant's side of the story, and instinctively believe that an innocent person would not sit idly by while the prosecutor parades evidence of his guilt before them. The inclination is to believe that in failing to take the stand the defendant has something to hide and must therefore be guilty. The risk of testifying or not testifying must be weighed carefully. Important factors in the weighing process are how effectively the defendant is able to communicate under the pressure of examination and cross-examination, how persuasive he is, and how favorable an impression he will make on the jury.

The general rule is that a criminal defendant who is obviously guilty should not take the witness stand unless there are mitigating circumstances of great appeal—such as the thin little wife who killed her big brutal husband. Similarly, if it is believed by lawyer and client that the prosecution has failed to make a case, classic wisdom dictates that the defendant should not take the witness stand. Although many criminal lawyers disagree, it is my belief that a public official or a person accused of white-collar crime *should* testify unless his testimony is quite likely to be destructive. I consider it too dangerous for pillars of the community to stake their chances entirely on the government's cases. The refusal of such persons to testify is more prejudicial to a jury than that of defendants accused of street crimes.

## Family and Friends in Court

Although they are helpful in all litigation, it is particularly important that the family and friends, and even the employer, of a criminal defendant be present in court during a criminal trial.

A showing of concern and support by them can only invoke sympathy from the jury, which can sometimes make all the difference in the world.

# Chapter Twelve

# The Strategies: A Summation

The law is a lively process that leaves open many ways for you to fortify your legal position. There are things to do and know and habits to acquire that can help you get the most out of your legal rights, which is what I mean by "Put the Law on Your Side." What follows is a summation—a traditional lawyer's activity—of the actions and strategies that get beneficial results in the kinds of legal transactions and circumstances that can confront most people.

## THE LAW IS FLEXIBLE

### Knowledge

Knowledge of the rules of law is a relative thing. I have been a law student, lawyer, law teacher, and a judge over a span of four decades, and I learn something new with every case and problem I approach. No one knows enough, so it is a bit much to expect the average person to become an instant legal expert when his occasion arises. But the average person can have a core of understanding. If you do not comprehend fully all your constitutional rights as one accused of a crime, for instance, at least you know you have rights—most important, to remain silent, not to incriminate yourself. Even if you are not expert in the Uniform Commercial Code, you know the item you sell or buy must be reasonably suited to the purpose for which it is sold. You have some foundation of judgment on which to proceed.

## Law Is More Than Rules; It Is a Process

You should never lose sight of the plain reality that rules of law are only that—rules—and that law is a massive process, in a dynamic society, with constant interaction between people and the rules as they see or feel them to be. People contribute in many different ways to the circumstances on which they may ultimately be judged, and judges make their rulings, not on the situations that really happened, but on the situations they believe happened. The facts of a law case are never objective reality; they are only what the court thinks they are.

## Significance of Personal Behavior

Sometimes the most obvious points can escape you. If you try to take advantage of another, if you are greedy, if you seek something you know in your heart of hearts is not meant for you, you are courting trouble. People react badly to you and strike back. You lose credibility. Your chances of success dwindle in negotiation or in court. If you associate with criminals and evil people, you increase your chances of being caught up in crime or misfortune. A strong code of personal ethics does help shield you from the slings and arrows of outraged legal fortune.

Personal demeanor is significant in nipping the buds of dispute, in avoiding arrest on minor charges, and in establishing credibility. The best ways to act in matters of disputation are to keep cool, to be conciliatory, and not to be overtly hostile.

A guiding rule of legal conduct is that it is better to settle than to sue.

# PREPARATION AND PROOF

Basic to all legal endeavor is preparation. This is the recurring lesson in every branch of law. Whether you go to court, a hearing, a meeting, or a "one-on-one" discussion, you should prepare yourself in advance. You should gather the facts you intend to put forth, and rehearse their presentation in your mind. You should organize the questions you may want to ask. Fix in your mind the way you wish to establish your points.

As you anticipate tax audits by saving the bills, canceled checks, and bank records supporting your deductions, you can use similar records to prove to a complaining creditor that, in fact, you paid his bill. Saving letters, memoranda, contracts, receipts, notes, claim checks, and other documentation and communications may later help you in, say, a breach-of-contract action by or against you. Your medical bills can help establish your charges in a personal-injury claim. If you organize and keep your documents securely, they become a bank of information on which to draw for proof and for corroboration—of what *you* say.

## GENERAL STRATEGIES

### *Possession*

Possession is a great advantage in legal strategy. Keep possession of any disputed object or fund just as long as you can.

### *Press Your Advantages*

Take any legitimate advantage available to you. In your contracts with builders or servicers, make provision for holding back money until you are satisfied with their performance. They are easier to deal with while they are unpaid.

Try to make time and circumstances work for you. For example, if you are a salesman with a monthly commission account, try to get a clause in your contract that presumes all your sales statements are correct and final unless the employer objects in writing within thirty days, instead of leaving the regularity of your account open to challenge for the length of the statute of limitations. You are in a better legal position with a conclusive statement than you would be if you remained exposed to challenge by the employer years later when you had a falling-out. In this way, you use your good work results to fortify your legal position a month at a time. Your employer is unlikely to challenge a good salesman for minor discrepancies of a month, but later on, in different economic and personal settings, he may seek to challenge a lot of old transactions. Cut him off early.

A secured creditor is in a stronger position to collect his debt than an unsecured one.

### Letters
You should not send lengthy recriminatory letters to adversaries, real, potential, or fancied. Nor should you quake at a stern letter from an opposing lawyer. The mere charge of breaching a contract is not legally harmful; it takes a court to declare a contract breached.

### Short Shots
Be assertive. Stand up for your rights.
- Do not let yourself be rushed into hasty decisions.
- Read your papers carefully.
- Never blame yourself out loud or in writing.
- Never surrender original documents on which your rights are based.

# YOUR LAWYER

In your important brushes with the law, you need a lawyer. You must satisfy yourself with his competency, compatibility, and cost. There are certain branches of the law in which you need specialized lawyers. These include: admiralty, bankruptcy, criminal, immigration, labor, negligence, patent and copyright, pension, tax, and trial. For sophisticated transactions, involving large funds, there are lawyers who specialize in corporations, estates and trusts, and real estate.

# BRANCHES OF THE LAW

### Personal-Injury Claims
Personal-injury claims are the most usual lawsuits brought by average people.

If you are the injured party in an accident, get an experienced neglience lawyer immediately. Delay prejudices your case.

If you are in an accident, inform your liability insurer promptly, in writing, of the details. Turn over any claim letters and court papers directed to you to your insurer as soon as you get them. If you are not insured, get to your lawyer fast.

Carry adequate general liability insurance, particularly insurance against liability in automobile accidents.

Never sign a release from any personal-injury claim you may have without consulting your lawyer.

When suing for personal injury, make a claim against all parties who conceivably caused your injury.

If you are injured in a work-related accident, examine whether you have a claim against builders, suppliers, or servicemen, who will not be shielded—by virtue of workers' compensation laws—from paying you damages for pain and suffering.

Never admit fault at the scene of an accident.

Get the names of witnesses at an accident scene, if you can.

Consult a doctor immediately after any apparent injury in an accident.

Do not discuss your accident with strangers.

If you wish to make a claim against a government, be alert to short time periods under the law for giving notice of your claim and for bringing suit.

If your pet animal has bit someone or shows itself to be dangerous, get rid of it or keep it under close control.

Evaluate your claim for personal injury with your lawyer. It is wiser to settle for its realistic value than to litigate. Do not be misled by big awards other people get. Your case stands on its own.

## Matrimonial Actions

Should you be so unfortunate as to become involved in a matrimonial dispute—divorce, annulment, or separation—be on your guard. Do not be lulled by the family nature of the dispute or the old relationships. You are in a genuine legal confrontation. You can get badly hurt financially and emotionally. If you are paying, do not be too generous. If you are seeking payment, do not be too reasonable. You are dealing with binding legal obligations, running to and from you. Generosity and reasonableness can be afforded voluntarily in the long aftermath.

Look for a tough experienced lawyer. Do not seek a gentle person to minimize the unpleasantness. Look for the lawyer who will get you results, preferably a good settlement without litigation, and one who will litigate hard if need be. If you are a man in the divorce courts, consider hiring a woman lawyer.

When in matrimonial disputation, do not move out of the family residence without a prior written agreement or a court order.

Remember that contested matrimonial actions are mostly about money. If you are the wife, do not panic over your husband's claims to custody of your children. Mothers are preferred by judges for child custody. If your husband indicates a willingness to trade custody for money, he is not really interested in custody and most likely will not wind up with it.

Judges have absolute discretion over child-custody awards. Do your best to impress the judge.

Alimony and child support are not the only economic elements of matrimonial actions. Depending on the state, spouses should be alert to their rights in the other's real estate and in community property. In New York, be aware of the doctrine of "equitable distribution," which allows a court to divide family wealth (capital) between the spouses.

Get tax advice, whether you are husband or wife, before agreeing to the allocation of payments between alimony and child support, whether in court decrees or in marital agreements.

When you enter into a favorable marital agreement, seek to have that agreement survive any court decree. Where husbands are good earners, wives should seek, in marital agreements, in addition to alimony, child support, and custody, life insurance for continuation of payment in the event of the husband's death, and an escalation of the alimony if the husband's income increases. Marital agreements should cover explicitly every simple benefit or duty anticipated.

Do not discuss your matrimonial disputes with your friends.

If you have any concern that your spouse will be troublesome and will drain your joint bank accounts or safe-deposit boxes during the dispute, get there first.

During disputes, change your will, your pension beneficiaries, your insurance policies, your bank signatures, and your charge cards and accounts. Safeguard your valuable things.

Palimony is not alimony. If you expect something from the person with whom you live and to whom you are not married, get it in writing.

If your husband is constantly delinquent in alimony or child-support payments, seek to have the payments made directly to the court. The court will forward the money to you.


## Criminal Law

Should you run afoul of the criminal law, you are in *real* trouble.
• Know your rights, and stand on them.
• Do not confess to wrongdoing until after you talk to your lawyer and after you decide (if you do) to plead guilty in court.
• In facing arrest, be calm, respectful, and dignified with the police. Perhaps this can forestall your arrest.
• Never flee or physically resist arrest in any way.
• If arrested, be sure you establish exactly who you are. Give the police your true pedigree.
• When in police custody, make no statement whatsoever about your arrest or its preceding events without your lawyer being present. You do not want to incriminate yourself.
• Use the telephone privilege given to you by the police to get a lawyer to your side. Tell exactly where you are located.

If you are a prosecution target, do not testify before a grand jury unless you get immunity from prosecution. Under no circumstances go before a grand jury for any reason without first talking to a lawyer.

Do not make a plea bargain unless you are carefully informed of its consequences. If you do plea-bargain, make sure that all assurances given to you about sentencing and other consequences of your plea are written into the court record.

Whenever possible, have your family and employer present at any bail hearing.


## Real Estate Law

The laws affecting leases and purchases and sale of homes and apartments—real estate law—are important and impact on almost everyone. Knowledge and right conduct pays off here very directly, in terms of both money and living satisfactorily.

Read your lease carefully.

From the standpoint of both the landlord and the tenant, leases should spell out everything the parties expect of each other. All rights and benefits should be written in the leases; no concessions or privileges should be left oral.

Whenever any conduct, whether subletting, assigning the lease, or any other tenant action, is subject to the landlord's consent, the lease should specify that such consent shall not be unreasonably withheld.

Tenants should always seek options to renew their leases.

Report all complaints you may have to your landlord in writing and promptly. Keep copies.

Pay your rent by check, identifying on its back your apartment designation, and the period for which the rent is paid.

Listen to real estate brokers, but never rely solely on their assurances or inducements, whether in leasing, buying, or selling.

When buying a home or apartment, remember that the broker represents the seller. Even though a prospective buyer contacts the broker originally, the seller pays the broker. Never forget that a successful broker's first loyalty is to his commission.

If you are the seller, have an agreement with your broker that his commission is to be paid only if the sale closes. No circumstances should justify the payment of a commission unless the sale is in fact concluded.

Exclusive listing agreements with brokers should be for a specified period of time.

Neither the seller nor the buyer should sign a binder agreement for a real estate contract, nor should either of them sign an offer or acceptance, without first talking to their lawyers.

Read your real estate contracts with care.

Before buying a home or apartment, be sure you have the place physically inspected by an expert.

As a buyer, if you need a mortgage to consummate your purchase, be sure the contract has an explicit condition allowing you to give up the contract if you cannot get the mortgage you want.

Always try to get a provision in your mortgage that enables you to prepay it at any time without penalty.

A contract for purchase and sale of real estate should specify just what goes with the sale. Nothing important should be left to oral understanding.

It is dangerous to leave a seller in possession of real estate after the title closing. Take possession of your purchased real estate immediately on title closing.

Put your homeowner's insurance in place at or before the closing. Take out title insurance when you buy a home or apartment.

## Laws for Employee and Employer

Employment rights involve unions, social legislation, contracts, and common law.

If you are a union member, report to your union representative promptly if you are fired, sexually harassed, subject to unsafe or unfair working conditions, or if the employer is withholding any of your wages.

If you are not a union member, appropriate federal or state agencies may help you. For unsafe working conditions relating to chemical infiltration, radiation, and technological hazards, go to the U.S. Department of Labor. For physical safety conditions and fire regulations, go to your state labor agency. For civil-rights discrimination and sexual harassment go to the EEOC.

If you are an employee without an employment contract, you generally can be fired at will. But if there is something particularly abusive about your firing, such as forfeiture of important pension or severance benefits about to become due, consult a lawyer.

If you are an employee, your wages can be seized by creditors under the legal proceeding known as "garnishment." There are limits as to how much can be taken. Check these.

Employment contracts should be read and should specify every single employment assurance. There should be no reliance on oral assurances. Besides financial inducements, try to get assurances of the kind of work you will be doing, your status, and the places where you can be obliged to work.

Employment contracts favor employees. Employers try to avoid them unless they need to get a promise from the employee that he will hold the confidentiality of business secrets or refrain from competition after the expiration of a contract. Employees should resist these restrictions to the maximum extent of their bargaining ability.

As an employer, seek to have all inventive, artistic, research-and-development personnel assign to you in writing all products developed on your time or at your facilities.

As an employee, seek to have a written agreement protecting your rights in any inventions or artistic or literary creativity.

When you require a release from legal liabilities, you should also obtain releases in favor of all your employees, directors, agents, and affiliated corporations.

### Contract Law

"Contract" and "agreement" are synonymous words. Generally, agreements may be written or oral, but there are certain types of agreements that must be in writing. Irrespective of legality, it is better to have your agreements in writing. This effects a written record for the parties as to what they intended, and most people will live up to it. Writings minimize the questions of what was agreed upon. They help you to prove your case. Give credence to the legal quip that "an oral agreement is not worth the paper it is written upon."

Read your contract. Never sign anything that you do not understand.

Contracts for the sale or leasing of interests in real estate must be in writing.

Contracts that cannot, according to their own terms, be fulfilled within one year of execution or in the promisor's lifetime must be in writing.

Agreements to pay the debts of another must be in writing.

Contracts to make a will, that promise something upon marriage, that transfer copyrights and patents, or deal with the sale of goods worth $500 or more (unless the buyer accepts delivery or pays partially when the sale agreement is reached) must be in writing.

All releases from liability should be in writing.

Contracts with minors and incompetents, subject to a few exceptions, are unenforceable. In dealing with someone in either category, secure the guaranty of a responsible adult to guard against disaffirmation of that contract by the minor or the legal guardian of the incompetent.

If it is important that your contract be performed exactly on time, provide expressly for the time deadline and specify the magic words "time is of the essence."

When a contract is broken, usually only money damages are payable.

If you wish to be assured that the seller will go through with the actual contract as agreed, be sure to write into your agreement that the contractual subject is unique, and that the contract may be "specifically enforced" (carried out). Sales of real estate, art, and antiques are typically ordered to be specifically enforced even without such express provision, because they are deemed unique by nature. But, specify it anyway.

All payments of significant sums should be by check and their purpose described by endorsement on the back of the check.

If someone breaches a contract with you, do not delay in asserting your rights. Six years is usually the maximum period in which suit can be brought, but this is subject to many exceptions.

All bills of sale should specify in sufficient detail so you can readily identify the nature and and description of any important thing you are buying.

In making purchases, do not rely on oral warranties or assurances. Get them in writing.

If you buy something "as is," you take the full risk of the condition of the purchased item.

If you must carry your valuables around with you when you travel or go out, insure them adequately with your own insurer and do not rely on recovering from hotels, restaurants, or the proprietors of other such places.

Do not sign any document in blank.

Always obtain for yourself copies of all signed documents of transactions to which you are a party or in which you have an interest.

Get a written receipt for everything you hand over to a tradesman, repairman, serviceman, or anyone else who handles anything important to you.

To protect copyrighted material, put a notice of copyright on a copy and deposit it, with an application for its registration, in the Copyright Office in Washington, D.C.


## Laws of Money and Investing

Much of the law involves money. When handling yours, be mindful of possible legal complications. There are many.

In important transactions, pay by check drawn on a financial institution that returns your checks to you with a monthly statement. If you must pay cash, get a receipt.

Review your bank statement monthly. Call forgeries promptly to the bank's attention.

In writing checks, fill up all the spaces. Do not leave room for addition of numbers or payees.

Do not sign blank checks.

Do not leave your checks, signed or unsigned, around for idle hands to reach.

Deposit all checks promptly. Checks get stale after a month, and banks may refuse to honor them. Do not wait.

Do not endorse a check until you are ready to deliver or deposit it.

In getting a bank loan, do not agree to pay any legal or collection fees in the event you default unless the bank will limit your liability to "reasonable" costs.

Guaranteeing other people's loans leads to trouble. There is truth in the old saying that "a guarantor is a fool with a fountain pen."

If a loan is usurious, its principal is forefeited by the lender. Do not be that kind of lender.

Whenever you are paying interest in advance, get a disclosure from the payee as to the true interest rate you are paying.

In making investments, risk and return are always functions of each other. Beware of the deal that is "too good."

Do not allow a stockbroker to exercise his own discretion in investing your funds unless you know and trust him well.

Investigate your investments carefully before you make them. There is no protection against investments that simply do not pan out.

Before investing in publicly traded securities, study the information about the issuing corporation in their reports filed at SEC regional offices.

Be especially wary of "hot" new issues of stock. Read the prospectuses and do not invest if you do not understand them. Do you have the sizzle, but not the steak?

Remember that a corporation's prospectus registered with the SEC does not mean that the government approves the merits of the solicited investment. It simply means the SEC feels, based on what was told to it, that the disclosure is apparently complete.

When investing in private companies, it is important to limit by contract the sums of money that insiders can withdraw from them.

If you are a minority investor in a closely held company, it is important to have a way to sell your stock for a plausible price. Since this is doubtful if insiders are effectively the only buyers, you should have an investment agreement that gives you the right to sell your stock back to the corporation at some formula price, or the right to compel liquidation of the corporation. Do not get locked in!

If you want to buy stock in a private corporation, and want to be able later to sell it in a public market, get a contractual stipulation that you have the right to compel the corporation to register your stock with the SEC for a public offering after a certain period of time.

Keep careful records for your tax returns.

Unless your affairs are very simple, use an accountant or a tax return preparer to do your tax returns.

Be alert to the tax timing of offsetting capital gains and losses.

Never fail to file your tax return. The statute of limitations against assessment of taxes does not begin to run until the filing.

Always disclose all your income on your tax return, even if only a schedule claiming that it is not taxable. Protect yourself from tax fraud charges.

If you cannot pay your debts, either personal or business, and need relief, be open with your creditors. Seek their cooperation.

Some of your properties are exempt from any creditor seizure. Find out what they are in your state.

Under state law, you can make settlements with your creditors, but these usually depend upon voluntary cooperation of the creditors and much patience from you.

Federal bankruptcy is a drastic, last-ditch measure, but if your creditors will not be cooperative and you want to stay in business, you must consider that route. It stops your creditors from enforcing their debts until your status is resolved.

The principal federal bankruptcy alternatives are: Chapter 7, paying your debts from the liquidation of your assets; Chapter 13, paying your debts under a plan that takes the funds from your continuing income; Chapter 11, providing for reorganization of the business. Choose carefully.

## Laws of Wills, Estates, and Trusts

Death and taxes are said to be inevitabilities. They certainly come together in the field of estates and trusts.

You are required to have your will signed in the presence of at least two witnesses who are disinterested parties.

You can change your will by adding amending codicils. You can revoke it by tearing it up or by executing a new will explicitly revoking the prior one.

If you do not leave a will, your property will be distributed according to your state's law of intestate succession. If you do not make a will, you are effectively deciding to bequeath your properties the way the state decides.

If you want to specify the guardianship of your children, name your executor, make specific bequests of property to designated people, or provide for trusts, it is necessary to make a will.

Use a lawyer to draft your will.

Sign only one copy of your will.

Never sign a will without first reading and understanding every single word of it.

Do not leave any will lying around, whether signed or unsigned.

Safeguard your will by depositing it with your lawyer, your bank, or a court. Do not use your safe-deposit box.

Much trouble arises with estates as a result of improper selection of executors and trustees. Avoid people who will have conflicts with your estate, such as your business partner or your business partner's lawyer. Be wary of naming your children cofiduciaries if they do not get along.

Name not only your fiduciaries, but also their successors. If you cannot decide on successors, authorize your existing fiduciaries to designate their own successors.

If you are a fiduciary, never mingle trust assets with your own.

As a fiduciary, go by the book. Do not be a "nice guy." Do not expose yourself to legal liability by improvident accommodations to the beneficiaries.

If you wish to have a trust, and you do not want to give trust principal to your children when they are too young, do not wait until they are too old. Thirty-five is a good target age.

In tax planning, consider your tax bracket, so you do not sacrifice any intentions for taxes that may not be saved anyway.

Satisfy yourself that you are, in your estate plan, doing primarily what you want with your assets, serving the best interests of your family, and saving tax money only incidentally.

## SETTLE RATHER THAN SUE

It is better to settle than sue. Litigation is filled with unpleasantries and inherent riskiness.

Settlement is an art.

No number used in a settlement discussion is without an effect.

Do not fear introducing settlement discussions.

Never start with your best offer.

Do not consider the other side's opening offer as his best offer.

Do not bid against yourself.

Do not insist on the top dollar.

Keep in constant communication with your negotiating partner.

Never underestimate the power of money in settling disputes. Look for equivalent alternatives.

Do not trip over your own ego. Listen to the other side.

Rely on your lawyer to be your communication link.


## THE COURTHOUSE

If you have to go to court, you will find that courtrooms are serious places. Know what to expect and how to act.

Before appearing in court, attend a trial involving someone else, preferably before the same judge, to familiarize youself with court procedure.

In court, have a lawyer. Do not appear *pro se* in courts of record.

Go over your own testimony with your lawyer in advance of trial.

Before testifying in any trial, reread any discovery depositions you may have given.

In dressing yourself for court, when in doubt, err on the conservative side.

Do not argue with your own lawyer in the courtroom.

Try to be at all times alert, attentive, and unfazed. Do not be afraid to look at the jury. Do not seem furtive.

Follow your lawyer's lead in court. If you are on the wintess stand and he starts talking, you stop talking.

When you are a witness, speak up. Face the jury.

When you are a witness, never volunteer information and never

guess. Simply answer the questions put to you directly and suc-
cinctly.

Do not overqualify what you say with excessive words of caution
in the belief you are thereby being more precise.

When you are being cross-examined as a witness, never fence with
the cross-examiner. Be stingy with your words.

If you are a defendant in a criminal trial, you do not have to testify. The government has to prove you guilty. Make the decision with
your lawyer on whether you should testify.

It is particularly important in criminal trials to have your family
and friends present in court.

## THE MESSAGE

The message should be clear to you now. There is a premium in the
law for looking out for yourself. The law is not an automatic process;
it is a product of what is fed into it, and you do part of the feeding.
Your own personality, demeanor, inclinations, and the ways you deal
with others affect your credibility and the probabilities of your succeeding in the courthouse and in every other place short of it.

Two millennia ago, the Hebrew sage Hillel declared:

If I am not for me, who is for me?
And if I am for myself only, what am I?
And if not now, when?

Hillel said it all.

# *Index*